WORKING TOGETHER FOR CHILDREN,
YOUNG PEOPLE AND THEIR FAMILIES

SERIES EDITOR: PROFESSOR OLIVE STEVENSON

Patterns of Adoption
Nature, Nurture and Psychosocial Development

David Howe

University of East Anglia, Norwich

Blackwell
Science

© 1998 by
Blackwell Science Ltd
Editorial Offices:
Osney Mead, Oxford OX2 0EL
25 John Street, London WC1N 2BL
23 Ainslie Place, Edinburgh EH3 6AJ
350 Main Street, Malden
 MA 02148 5018, USA
54 University Street, Carlton
 Victoria 3053, Australia

Other Editorial Offices:

Blackwell Wissenschafts-Verlag GmbH
Kurfürstendamm 57
10707 Berlin, Germany

Blackwell Science KK
MG Kodenmacho Building
7–10 Kodenmacho Nihombashi
Chuo-ku, Tokyo 104, Japan

First published 1998

Set in 10/12 pt Sabon
by DP Photosetting, Aylesbury, Bucks
Printed and bound in Great Britain by
Hartnolls Ltd, Bodmin, Cornwall

The Blackwell Science logo is a trade mark
of Blackwell Science Ltd, registered at the
United Kingdom Trade Marks Registry

DISTRIBUTORS

Marston Book Services Ltd
PO Box 269
Abingdon
Oxon OX14 4YN
(*Orders:* Tel: 01235 465500
       Fax: 01235 465555)

USA
 Blackwell Science, Inc.
 Commerce Place
 350 Main Street
 Malden, MA 02148 5018
 (*Orders:* Tel: 800 759 6102
           617 388 8250
      Fax: 617 388 8255)

Canada
 Copp Clark Professional
 200 Adelaide Street West, 3rd Floor
 Toronto, Ontario M5H 1W7
 (*Orders:* Tel: 416 597-1616
           800 815-9417
      Fax: 416 597-1617)

Australia
 Blackwell Science Pty Ltd
 54 University Street
 Carlton, Victoria 3053
 (*Orders:* Tel: 03 9347 0300
      Fax: 03 9347 5001)

A catalogue record for this title
is available from the British Library

ISBN 0-632-04149-8

Library of Congress
Cataloging-in-Publication Data
Howe, David, 1946–
 Patterns of adoption: nature, nurture,
 and psychosocial development/David
 Howe.
  p. cm. – (Working together with
 children, young people, and their
 families)
  Includes bibliographical references
 and indexes.
  ISBN 0-632-04149-8
  1. Adoption –Psychological
 aspects. 2. Adopted children.
 3. Child development. 4. Nature and
 nurture. I. Title.
 II. Series.
 HV875.H69 1997
 362.73′4–dc21
                    97-21647
                         CIP

Contents

Foreword
by Professor Olive Stevenson

As David Howe points out: 'Although this is a book ostensibly about adoption and the way children develop when cared for by parents to whom they are not biologically related, it can also be read as an exploration of what factors affect all children and their development' (page 2). More widely still, it can be taken as an illustration of a more general debate of profound significance to us all, about the interaction of nature and nurture, of genetic and environmental influences; matters of particular interest at the present time. The author shows that this requires complex and subtle analysis, drawing on the substantial amount of good research now available, especially with regard to the outcomes for adopted children of different ages. Adoption workers have also acquired practice wisdom about the placement of children. Yet adoption remains – perhaps forever – a concept packed with emotional dynamite, going to the heart of some of our longings and fears, conscious and unconscious. It is extraordinarily difficult to conduct and utilise research with a fair degree of objectivity, to face squarely findings which do not fit our personal and professional agendas. Then there is the political dimension; tugging at the heart strings as it does, adoption is regrettably used as a pawn in a bigger political game. On the one hand, adoption has been used, albeit deviously, to demonstrate the superiority of middle class upbringing or as a mechanism for ensuring childless people's rights to have children. On the other hand, it is seen by some as an institutionalised device used to deflect attention from the environmental and social deprivation affecting poor parents. Thus, the powerful feelings roused by the very idea of adoption are fuelled by political forces.

These factors make David Howe's book all the more important to anyone with a serious interest in child welfare who wants to use their minds in the services of their feelings. He offers a vigorous and scholarly account of present evidence. He highlights, carefully and systematically, the factors which have to be taken into account when assessing the impact of adoption upon children. (There is much more research yet to be done about the impact on birth and adoptive parents.) Howe also offers a fresh way of understanding children's responses to their experiences of adoption; much of this is also useful more generally in making sense of children's behaviour patterns.

As Howe points out, we have less research evidence on the consequences and implications of 'open adoption' than on some other matters. In my view, the increasing number of older children placed for adoption, plus the painful lessons from futile attempts to provide children 'in care' with a 'fresh start', which denied their origins, substantially increase the pressure for genuinely open adoption as the norm rather than the exception. But this will necessitate sensitive research and practice. As with many aspects of adoption, there are inherent reasons which cannot be resolved by legislation or theoretical dogmatism, only by highly individualised practice informed by the best available knowledge of the time.

I hope David Howe's book will become a standard text for professionals in the field of child welfare. It raises fundamental issues which go beyond the specialised area of adoption practice and offers fresh ways of understanding children's reactions to their experiences.

Olive Stevenson
Professor Emeritus of Social Work Studies
University of Nottingham

Preface

In 1986, Phyllida Sawbridge, the founding Director of the Post-Adoption Centre in London, invited me to carry out an evaluative study of the work being developed by this new, pioneering agency. Although I had worked in the field of adoption as a practitioner, the research provided me with a welcome opportunity to renew my interest in an aspect of child care and family social work that touches on universal themes of identity and belonging, love and relationships, loss and affection. During the course of the study not only did I have opportunities to talk with the Centre's experienced and expert counsellors but I also met a number of adopters, adopted people and women who had given up a child for adoption. It soon became apparent that when listening to people's stories about their experiences as parents and children, deeper notes about human development and behaviour could also be heard.

When academics feel curious or anxious, they turn to books and journals. I soon discovered that an enormous literature existed on the subject of adoption – its theory, practice and outcome. My interest quickly settled on research that looked at adopted children's social and psychological development, not so much as a topic in isolation but as a subject that opened a window on children's development in general. Babies born to one set of parents and raised by another tell us a lot about the relative influences of genes and the environment. The placement of older children helps us to understand the impact of early life experiences on personality and behaviour and the potential healing power of new relationships in later childhood. Writers on these matters include behavioural geneticists, developmental psychologists, sociologists, social workers, and child policy specialists. But although there is some traffic of ideas between these disciplines, it is not as great as one might expect given the common interest in adoption.

In writing *Patterns of Adoption* I had three aims: to bring together the wide range of research on adopted children and their psychosocial development, to seek patterns and themes within the major findings, and to frame the results within the organising power of a wider developmental theory. As someone who enjoys conceptual order and tidiness, I was keen to make some provisional sense of the complex, often scattered field of adoption research. Creating order and generating frameworks is, of course, intellectually satisfying, but my real hope is that the book provides some useful knowledge, guidance and understanding for the many adoptive parents raising adopted children, particularly older-placed children; adoption workers involved in making placements and supporting families; and fellow researchers and trainers concerned to present this particular human experience in a clear and compassionate light.

DH
Norwich

Acknowledgement

Throughout 1992, 1993 and 1994, I had the opportunity to interview many adopters about their experiences of raising adopted children. Their insights and observations stimulated my interest in adopted children's development in particular and all children's growth and behaviour in general. The case examples given in Chapters 10 to 14 are taken from these interviews. I am extremely grateful for the parents' time, interest and cooperation.

Chapter 1

Nature and Nurture

It is in our close relationships with others that we learn to become socially competent. The process begins in childhood and continues throughout life. In the West, our first long-term relationships form within the body of small, 'nuclear families'. This setting is fine for most children raised by one or both of their biological parents, but what of children who, for one reason or another, cannot be looked after by their mothers or fathers? Who meets their needs? Tizard (1977: p. 2) observes that 'couples without children, and children without parents, are likely to have unsatisfied needs for giving and receiving affection, and for maintaining enduring relationships.' In such situations, adoption appears to be a neat solution that solves the emotional needs of both parties in one social event.

However, these particular arrangements of helping people meet their emotional needs are not universal. Some cultures, for example, have evolved more communal patterns to bring people into close, encompassing relationships. This is reflected in the way the needs of young children are met, including those who are not looked after directly by their parents. Benet (1976) discusses a variety of adoption practices that do not involve the legal placement of a child with biologically unrelated parents. 'Kinship fostering' sees children and their upbringing being the responsibility of the extended family or whole community. She cites examples from Africa, Polynesia and the Caribbean where children are raised collectively. In this way, they are integrated into the life of the whole community. Biological parents can continue to have contact with their children but they are not totally or continuously responsible for their day-to-day care. Raising children is a shared activity.

All of this is in contrast to traditional twentieth century adoption practices in Europe and America in which relationships between children and their biological parents have to be ruptured and closed before they can 'belong' to a new set of parents. In these situations, biological or 'birth' parents of children placed for adoption are those who could not, would not or should not look after their children. They have been generally required to surrender all legal (and in effect, emotional) claims on the adopted child so that they can be transferred to a new set of parents. Modern adoption practices began to emerge towards the end of the nineteenth and the beginning of the twentieth century. The first Adoption Act in the UK, for example, was passed in 1926.

Although this is a book ostensibly about adoption and the way children develop when cared for by parents to whom they are not biologically related, it can also be read as an exploration of the factors which affect all children and their development. Heading along this road, we meet people who argue fiercely about the power of genes to influence human development, and come across others who believe that experience plays a major role in the formation of behaviour and personality. The nature–nurture debate takes us to the heart of issues concerning our psychological growth and development.

It has often been remarked that adoption is like a 'natural experiment', in which children with biological inheritances from one set of parents are raised by parents to whom they have no genetic relationship. The adopted child's situation therefore presents researchers with a golden opportunity to ask a number of sharp questions, the answers to which have the capacity to throw much light on the parts that biology and the environment might be playing in the make-up and development of human beings. People want to know whether the adopted child's achievements and characteristics are the result of her genes or her upbringing. The child's separation from her biological parents represents a socially contrived split between nature and nurture. Hence the great interest in adopted children by all behavioural scientists concerned with children's development, whether adopted or not.

Nature, nurture and their interplay

Those who believe that much of our character and behaviour is in our biological *nature* are suggesting that the way we turn out as particular human beings is essentially laid down in whatever genetic blueprint we are given. They suggest that there is an unfolding of the inherent properties of the individual as he or she develops. Our make-up is inherited. The rules for our physical and psychological progress are contained in our *genes*. The environment and experience do not play a significant part in the final outcome, but merely act as triggers for the appearance of certain traits and skills, capacities and talents. 'Under predeterminism the development of the child could be viewed as akin to the growth of a plant – a little sunshine and a little water was all the environmental contribution that was necessary to promote what was inherent in the organism' (Wachs, 1992: p. 2).

In contrast, other theories emphasise the part that *experience* plays in shaping our development. The way we are raised and *nurtured* determines which developmental pathway we take in life. The child's relationship with the world is entirely empirical, which is to say completely based on his or her direct dealings with and responses to things that actually happen in the world. Rather than those who credit nature and biology as the locus of human development, those who favour nurture argue that the organising principles that inform our development exist outside our biology and depend on our experience. It is the quality of our environment (what people and things do) that affects our make-up, formation and progress.

Locke (1690) saw the human mind as a *tabula rasa* upon which experience, via the senses, would write the content. The growth of knowledge and understanding comes from our experience in the world. His work marked the beginning of those social and psychological sciences that saw the environment, particularly the social environment, as having a major impact on our development. The way we turn out as psychosocial beings depends on our history of environmental experiences – were we rejected by our mothers, were we rewarded by teachers at school for performing well, were we stimulated to talk and reflect on our feelings?

Much current wisdom recognises that both nature and nurture are likely to be involved in human growth and development. The interaction between genes and experience is believed to be both subtle and complex. Indeed, in the hands of many investigators, the picture is no longer a simple matter of adding together a bit of nature and a dash of nurture, or the environment merely acting as a trigger to release some genetic potential. The two act on each other in an altogether more elaborate and intriguing way. The individual's personality, character and dispositions form as heredity and the social environment interact. For example, it is increasingly believed that many of our genes affect the type of environment in which our development takes place. 'At first sight,' write Rutter & Rutter (1993: p. 19), 'the notion that genes could "cause" the environment seems both troubling and implausible. Of course the environment is not itself caused by genes. Nevertheless, it is quite likely that genes do truly play a substantial role in determining the particular environments to which people are exposed.'

Plomin *et al.* (1977) usefully distinguish between three types of gene-environment correlation: passive, re-active and active. In *passive* correlations, biological parents pass on certain genes to their children as well as create particular kinds of environment. Parents and child therefore share both hereditary and environments. Parents with high measures of intelligence will not only affect the intellectual abilities of their children, they may well generate intellectually rich and stimulating environments. The bright child passively finds himself or herself in an environment that matches his or her talents and abilities. Similar passive correlations might exist between musical children and musical parents, shy children and shy parents.

Reactive correlations occur when children with a particular trait *evoke* reactions from the environment to match their trait. Even though a musical child might not have musical parents, they recognise her need and interest and create musical opportunities for her. A cheerful child might elicit warm and friendly reactions, while more irritable and miserable children produce short, snapping responses from others (Rutter & Rutter, 1993: p. 20). Parents are likely to read more to a child who enjoys being read to. Caspi *et al.* (1990: p. 32) believe that interaction styles established early in life often persist into adulthood because they repeatedly provoke other people to respond in ways which confirm and reinforce the original pattern. In effect, other people are reacting to characteristics in the child that support and help develop those particular characteristics. Some unexpected benefits arise from such responses. 'DeVries reports that among the Masai of East Africa, infants with difficult temperaments were more likely to survive a serious drought than were temperamentally easy infants. In part this is because, within this culture, infants who were fussy and irritable were more likely to be preferred and fed by caregivers, based on the fact that these infants were viewed as fitting the cultural preference for a "warrior", (Wachs, 1992: p. 110)

Active correlations witness children deliberately selecting or creating environments that suit their inherited predispositions. These have been called niche picking and niche building by Scarr & McCartney (1983). Those good at sport will find friends and places to practise and develop their athletic skills. The musical child might insist that her non-musical parents buy her a flute or she might identify a sympathetic teacher at school who is able to give her access to instruments. Children, therefore, seek out and bring about environments that give them the opportunity to develop a particular innate talent, skill or predisposition. Individuals make their own environments and to this extent, control their own experiences. It is speculated that, as children grow older, the part that reactive and active correlations play increase while passive correlations decrease. Older children become more able to modify, select, create and influence their environments (Plomin, 1994: p. 151). For example, whereas children cannot choose their parents, they can pick their peers. They can also influence as well as be influenced by friends.

In short, what is being appreciated is that genetic factors contribute to experience itself. 'That is,' continues Plomin (1994: p. xv), 'genetics plays a role in the active selection, modification, and even creation of environments.' Increasing attention is therefore being paid to how such things as innate temperaments affect other people and how other people might affect temperament. Boys in divorced families, for example, tend to be at greater risk of showing problem behaviours than boys of non-divorced families. But not all boys of divorced parents become problem children. What allows some boys to cope well with the 'environmental' stresses of divorcing parents? Early answers suggest that all kinds of factors might mediate the effect of a stressful environment on a child's development including whether or not they are temperamentally sociable and cheerful in their dealings with others, how much outside emotional support is available, and the quality of the relationship with the non-custodial parent (for example, Hetherington, 1989).

Or looked at another way, we can see that, in the case of identical twins (who inherit an identical set of genes), they tend to be much more alike than either non-identical twins or siblings. But if the twins are separated and reared apart by different parents, although they still show many strong similarities in terms of personality, temperament and behaviour, they are less alike than identical twins reared together, though still more alike than siblings reared together (for example, see Bronfenbrenner, 1986). This suggests that, although genes still play a big part in determining our development, the quality and character of our environment also plays its part in influencing the way we turn out. Plomin (1994: p. 28) observes that 'twin and adoption studies usually find more than half of the variance in behavioral development cannot be accounted for by genetic factors'.

The complexities of development have meant that adoption has held a great fascination for those keen to understand the many factors that might be influencing growth and behaviour. Children who are adopted provide researchers with the opportunity to unravel some of the knotted strands of genes and the environment. 'Adoption study research,' observes Wachs (1992: p. 96), 'nicely illustrates the operation of passive-gene environment covariance. The logic underlying adoption studies is that in adopted families caregivers only pass along environments to their children, whereas for nonadopted children their parents pass along genes, environment, and the covariance between genes and environment.' We would therefore expect children living with their biological families to show more similarities with their parents and biological siblings than adopted children show with their adoptive parents and biologically unrelated siblings. In very broad terms, the predicted pattern of stronger developmental correlations occurring in non-adoptive compared to adoptive families holds out (for example, Plomin & Bergeman, 1991), but much of the fascination is in the detail and in the exceptions as well as the rules.

Nature, nurture and adopted children: the structure of the book

In an attempt to steer a path through the great amount of adoption research, the book is organised along a number of broad lines. The central line

(1) presents the main research findings;
(2) introduces attachment and relationship-based theories to organise the findings;

(3)   develops a model of different patterns of adopted children's
        behaviour and development; and
(4)   briefly considers the practice implications using an attachment/
        developmental perspective.

The organisation of the research findings in the first half of the book
is designed to examine the relative influences of nature and nurture on
children's development. In fact, adoption studies allow us to take a
double look at this issue:

(1)   *Children adopted as babies* provide a reasonably straightforward
        opportunity to investigate the interplay between heredity and the
        social environment. Baby-adopted children *experience* an almost
        complete and continuous exposure to family members with whom
        they have no biological relation. *Their progress provides answers
        to questions about the parts that genes and environment play in
        development.*
(2)   *Children placed at older ages* present a more complex picture.
        They arrive in their adoptive home with an established environ-
        mental and relationship history. This pre-placement phase is often
        one of adverse parental care and poor development. These
        children experience a discontinuous history of care and close
        relationships. The major break takes place as they move out of the
        poor quality care environment generated by their biological par-
        ents into the good quality care environment created by their
        adoptive parents. Scientifically speaking, whereas baby adoptions
        represent a manipulation of the interplay between genes and
        environment, late-placed children illustrate what happens when
        the environment alone is manipulated. *Late-placed adopted
        children therefore provide researchers with a chance to examine
        the extent to which experiences of poor environments early in life
        adversely affect later development, and whether or not subsequent
        removal to a good quality caring environment is able to bring
        about developmental recovery.*

For each of these two major types of adoption, the research is presented
in three stages: (1) descriptions of the behavioural and developmental
characteristics of adopted children – known as '*adoption outcome*'
studies, (2) the *pre-placement factors* thought to influence adopted
children's long-term development, and (3) the *post-placement factors*
thought to influence adopted children's long-term development.
Combining the two types of adoption, the results of the outcome
studies, and the various pre- and post-placement factors associated
with different outcomes, we can present the findings of adoption
research in the following order:

Children adopted as babies:

Late-placed children:

Overview:

Once the research has been presented in Chapters 2 to 8, the next task is to try and make sense of the findings. Imposing order on empirical observations is the business of theory. Chapter 9 suggests that attachment and relationship-based theories are strong contenders when it comes to offering an explanation of the main results. The theories can also be used to identify five patterns of adoption as well as explain various patterns of practice. Thus, underpinned by an attachment/relationship perspective, the seven chapters of the second half of the book are defined:

The ability to understand the patterns of development presented by adopted children helps us to think much more sensitively about the needs of children in general and the needs of adopted children in particular. Child welfare specialists working with children who have been disadvantaged or disturbed, neglected or abused need the kind of knowledge generated by researchers to help them advise parents and treat children, plan support and provide resources, and make decisions about whether to remove a child or not from her parents. Adoption research also provides parents with information and understanding about children who have been transferred from one family to another. This knowledge is particularly important in the case of children adopted at older ages, often after a history of neglect and upset. Adoption research is carried out by an unusual array of behavioural scientists, who approach the subject as a natural experiment in human development, and child welfare specialists who are concerned to ensure the best quality environment for children in need of substitute care. Together, the two approaches help us to understand the needs of adopted children in particular and the nature of all children's psycho-social development in general.

Chapter 2

Outcome Studies of Children Adopted as Babies

Heredity and environment

The interest shown in children adopted as babies has come mainly from two groups of investigators. There are those who have seen adoption as a highly successful piece of child care policy and practice. Children who, for whatever reason, have been unable to be looked after by their biological parents have been placed with biologically unrelated parents. Child welfare specialists have therefore been interested in the general development of children raised and reared by adoptive parents as a measure of policy success.

There is a second group who have also taken a keen look at adopted children and their families. Adoption is tantamount to a natural experiment in which babies related genetically to one set of parents are raised by another set of carers with whom they have no biological links. To psychologists, behavioural geneticists and social scientists in general, to observe the growth and development of the adopted child provides a unique opportunity to explore the complex interplay between biology and environment, nature and nurture. Is an adopted boy's personality the result of his upbringing or was he born that way? What have been the greatest influences on an adopted girl's educational achievements? Close examination of adopted children, their backgrounds and upbringing throw much light on these intriguing questions.

Our review of the research literature of children adopted as babies will be handled in four stages:

(1) First, we shall consider studies which have followed the progress of adopted children from placement as a baby to young adulthood. These are conventionally known as 'outcome studies' and they have been mainly pursued by child welfare researchers and policy specialists. They tell us a good deal about the broad pattern of adopted children's development. In particular, these studies are good at comparing the developmental outcome of children adopted as babies, non-adopted children raised by biological parents of a similar socio-economic status to that of the adopters,

and non-adopted children raised by biological parents of a similar socio-economic status to that of the adopted children's biological parents.

(2)   A growing body of research is being produced by scientists who are interested in the part that genes and experience play in children's bio-psychosocial development. It turns out that these 'behavioural geneticists' find the progress of adopted children a particularly fruitful area of enquiry. By comparing the behaviours and traits of adopted children, their biological parents, and their adoptive parents, these scientists attempt to tease out the relative impact of genetic inheritance (provided by the biological parents) and environmental experiences (provided by the adopters) on a child's development. However, their main interest is in the part that children's genes play in their psychosocial progress and we shall turn to their work for particular insights into the biology of social development. In short, children's *genetic inheritances* are what they bring to the adoption and so might be described as *pre-placement factors* that possibly have a bearing on development and outcome.

(3)   Both 'outcome researchers' and 'behavioural geneticists' have also taken a long look at the adopters and their families. The behaviour of adoptive mothers, fathers and siblings and the relationships that an adopted child has with all these people constitute a major aspect of that child's *post-placement social environment*. We might describe these elements of the social environment as the *post-placement factors* that possibly have a bearing on development and outcome.

(4)   In practice, most researchers recognise that there is probably a great deal of interplay between genes and the environment. A more complex, dynamic picture is emerging in which the way genetic predispositions express themselves can often be influenced by a child's social experiences. However, what remains particularly distinctive and scientifically important about children adopted as babies is that because their pre-placement social experience is very short, essentially what we have is one set of genes, with their potential influence on behaviour and development, located in an environment of other people who possess a completely different set of genes. In the case of children reared by their biological parents, it is very difficult to separate out the relative impact of nature and nurture. Cheerfulness may be a temperament inherited or the product of living with parents who are sociable and optimistic. If the cheerful child is biologically related to sociable parents, it is not so easy to know whether the temperamental trait is inborn or acquired. Children adopted as

babies therefore provide scientists with the opportunity to separate the parts that biology and experience might be playing in social and emotional development.

Evaluating baby adoptions

The basic question for those working in the field of child welfare policy and practice is whether adoption is a successful form of substitute parenting, both for the child and the parents (Hoopes *et al.*, 1970). Policy makers and practitioners need to know how adopted children fare compared to children generally and to children with similar socio-economic beginnings to themselves but who remained with their biological parents. Are adopted children at risk of greater psychological disturbance? Educationally, do they outperform children who remain in families disadvantaged by social and economic hardship?

Over the years, but particularly during the 1960s and 1970s, there has been a steady number of studies that have looked at the outcome of adopted children placed as babies. Conventionally, for the purposes of adoption studies, most researchers define a baby as a child under six months of age. In practice most babies are placed with their new families within the first two or three months. Seglow *et al.* (1972: p. 53), looking at children born in 1958, found that 90% of the children who were eventually adopted were no longer with their biological mothers by the time they had reached three months of age (see Thoborn and Sellick, 1996 for a useful review of outcome studies in adoption and fostering).

In broad terms, most investigators have reported similar findings for adopted children's physical, intellectual and psychosocial development. However, problems arise when comparisons are made between studies. Some investigations have looked at children's progress during their first few years of life prior to adolescence. Others have taken a longer time frame, measuring progress during adolescence and beyond. And yet other studies observed children at all ages and at all stages of their adoption without always making it clear whether their conclusions were age specific or not.

Some of the more potent research designs are those that prospectively follow adopted boys and girls through childhood. The technique involves approaching a given cohort of baby adopted children and their parents and contacting them at various stages during childhood. This allows the researchers to examine possible links between past measures, made contemporaneously, and current observations. Research of this kind has produced rich and detailed information. The continued vigour and strength of such studies depends on retaining as many children and parents of the original cohort as possible who are willing to take part in the longitudinal study. Inevitably, it is rarely possible to keep 100% of the original sample involved as the study years roll by. Some children are 'lost' to the study through emigration, death, addresses being unknown, and simple refusals by parents or child to take part. It is not always easy to interpret the effect of losing some 'respondents' on the overall picture. Most researchers try to ensure that they take into account whether or not the missing people were atypical in some way, but there always remains the nagging doubt that those children and families who refused to participate at later stages of the study might differ in some important way. One such worry is that parents of adopted children proving particularly difficult might decide against remaining part of the study population. The effect of their departure from the cohort is to produce a more positive final 'outcome.'

Social and economic status of adoptive families

It is not surprising that on average parents who adopt babies are found to enjoy a good standard of living. Historically, the majority have come from the middle or skilled working classes. So when comparisons are made between adoptive families and other families, the adoptive families tend to emerge as the most socially and economically advantaged.

For example, Hoopes *et al.* (1970: p. 41) point out that 80% of their 100 white, American adopted children were placed with families in Classes I, II and III. The authors report that in the general population only 31.8% are classified in these upper and middle groups leaving 68.2% placed in the lower classes of IV and V. A similar picture is reported in the UK by Seglow *et al.* (1972: p. 85). These researchers note that in their cohort, twice as many adopted children were in Social Class I compared to children in the general population. Indeed, with the passage of time most adoptive families continued to improve their material conditions (Lambert & Streather, 1980: p. 129). In New Zealand, Fergusson *et al.* (1995) compared 32 adolescent adopted children with other non-adopted adolescent children. They observed that: 'In general, children placed in adoptive families emerged as having the most advantaged mix of childhood, family and related circumstances whereas children in single parent families had the least advantaged mix' (Fergusson *et al.*, 1995: p. 606).

All of this is in marked contrast to the lot of adopted children's biological parents. Researchers repeatedly confirm that 'birth mothers' at the time of their baby's adoption are younger than the adoptive parents, younger than other single women who choose to keep their babies, more likely to be living in poor material conditions, and in possession of fewer educational qualifications and achievements. Seglow *et al.* (1972: p. 43) report that 71% of the birth mothers in their study were unmarried. A further 18% were married women whose husbands were not the fathers of the adopted children. Only 11% were born to parents who were married to each other.

Political observers of baby adoptions point out that the practice has represented a movement of children from poor but fertile single women to affluent but infertile married couples. The sharpness of these observations is increased in the case of overseas adoptions which see a steeper gradient of material difference between birth parents and adopters.

Outcome studies of children adopted as babies

The skewed distribution of baby-adopted children towards more advantaged homes has been emphasised to note the very positive social and economic context in which most adopted children find themselves. Social scientists know that in broad terms, children of more socio-economically advantaged families perform better educationally, physically and psychosocially. Therefore, the performance of children born to single, lower class biological parents adopted as babies by socially advantaged parents might tell us whether genetic inheritance or environment is playing the bigger part in determining developmental outcome. If adopted children do as well as other middle class children, then environment and upbringing might appear to be winning. On the other hand, if adopted children perform less well than their socio-economic peers, then biology and genes might be thought to be more influential than environment and experience.

'Outcome' research in the case of children adopted as babies generally compares their development with one or more of the following three groups of children:

(1) The general population of children.
(2) Children born to, raised by or restored to parents from a similar socio-economic background to the adopted children's biological parents. Many of these families are headed by lone or single parents.
(3) Children born to and raised by parents from a similar socio-economic background to the children's adoptive parents.

Clearly, the thinking behind using different comparison groups is to see whether or not adoption favours children who might otherwise have been brought up in socially and materially disadvantaged families.

We shall consider adoption research that looks at the developmental outcomes of children adopted as babies under the following five headings:

(1) Physical development.
(2) Cognitive competence.
(3) Social and emotional development.

(4)   Mental health clinic studies of adopted children.
(5)   Parental satisfaction.

Physical development

Although birth mothers of adopted babies tend to be rather poor at looking after themselves during their pregnancy, this appears not to have any major adverse long-term outcomes as far as their adopted child's physical development is concerned. Of course, there are exceptions. Mothers who drink heavy amounts of alcohol during their pregnancy may have a child who suffers foetal alcohol syndrome. Some adopted children are born with AIDS.

Babies with low birth weights are also at increased risk of experiencing learning difficulties and minor physical disadvantages such as a tendency to be 'clumsy' (Seglow *et al.*, 1972: p. 50). In their study of all 17,000 children born in the UK during one week of March in 1958, Seglow *et al.* (1972) compared adopted children, children who remained 'illegitimate', and children who were born 'legitimate'. The birth mothers of the adopted children were younger, likely to be single and in most cases the baby was their first-born child. A large number of the mothers smoked during their pregnancy. If they attended ante-natal clinics, they did so later and less frequently than their older, married counterparts. All these factors increase the risk of delivering low birth weight babies. Indeed, 'almost twice as many of the adopted babies fell into the low or very low birth weight category (2000 g and under) as compared with the legitimate group' (Seglow *et al.*, 1972: p. 51).

However, in spite of these poor ante-natal and birth histories, the researchers found the subsequent physical development of the adopted children to be very good. At age seven, there was no increase in the number of physical disabilities compared to other children in the cohort. An exception was reported for adopted boys (but not girls) who were found to be less physically co-ordinated and restless as judged by their class teachers than seven year-old non-adopted boys. On the other hand, more seven year old adopted children were tall for their age compared to children in the total study population.

These physical achievements continue through until adulthood. By the age of 16 years, the adopted children were 'taller, brighter and heavier than children in disadvantaged working class homes' (Bagley, 1993: p. 39). Plomin (1994: p. 44) says that for height, hereditary accounts for 90% of the difference between individuals. This suggests that if adopted children are taller than children who remain in adversity, then high nutritional environments are allowing adopted children to reach their full height potential while this is not the case for disadvantaged children.

The main message, therefore, is that early physical disadvantages can be overcome by subsequent good quality physical care. Physical deficits are retrievable. Given the high material, social and health standards provided by most adoptive homes, children adopted as babies should expect to reach their full physical potential. 'It looks as if the anticipated ill-effects of poor birth circumstances,' write Seglow *et al.* (1972: p. 61), 'have been largely negated by the age of seven as a result of beneficial influences in the adopted children's home.'

Cognitive competence

The evidence is equally strong that children adopted as babies achieve their full cognitive potential (Plomin & DeFries, 1985). If a home provides certain physical and social opportunities during the first few years of a child's life, he or she will become cognitively competent. According to Wachs (1992: p. 34) aspects of home life that are positively related to good cognitive performance are

(1)   availability of stimuli,
(2)   variety of stimuli,
(3)   organisation and regularity of home routines,
(4)   low levels of noise, overcrowding and 'home traffic patterns',
(5)   parental interest and involvement,
(6)   high levels of tactual and kinesthetic stimulation,
(7)   parental awareness and responsiveness,
(8)   verbal stimulation, and
(9)   physical opportunities to explore and investigate.

As children grow older, their cognitive development is facilitated further if parents are able to offer help and guidance in joint teaching, participatory learning and shared problem-solving play and activity. One critical aspect of parent–child involvement is the *pacing* of the interaction. 'Optimal development occurs when the adult does not pressure the child to learn, leave the child to deal with tasks that are too difficult for the child to handle, or take the task from the child. Rather optimal development occurs when adults adjust their level of interaction to the child's own level of competence' (Wachs, 1992: p. 35). Given the rigour of the assessment and approval procedures that prospective adopters have to negotiate, it is not surprising that most adopters provide high quality learning environments.

An early study by Skeels & Harms (1948; Skodak & Skeels, 1949) found that adopted children placed before the age of six months whose biological parents were of low socio-economic status nevertheless achieved cognitive levels of ability which equalled or even exceeded the mean of the general population. This success appeared to be maintained into adolescence and into adulthood (Skeels, 1965). Hoopes *et al.* (1970: p. 42) found that 100 adopted children in the age range 10 to 15 years had a mean IQ of 112.2 compared to a mean IQ of 117.2 for a group of socio-economically matched controls. Remembering that the national norm is 100.0, the adopted children were performing well above the general average. These results are confirmed by Fergusson *et al.* (1995: p. 613) who measured 32 adopted children, 842 children born to two parent families and 60 children born to single parent families. Their longitudinal study examined the children at various ages. At aged 12, the adopted children achieved an intellectual performance measure higher 'than would be expected given their biological parentage but lower scores than would be expected on the basis of the social background and characteristics of their adoptive parents.'

Comparing adopted, legitimate and illegitimate children, Seglow *et al.* (1972: p. 141) found that by the age of seven 'the adopted did markedly better than the other cohort children in respect of general knowledge and oral ability.' The illegitimate children who remained with their biological mothers, the majority of whom continued to live in the most disadvantaged homes, performed least well. For example, the average reading age of the adopted children was 12 months higher than that of the illegitimate children. Seven year-olds in families in which there were three or more siblings tended to have lower reading ages. But again, because adoptive families on the whole were smaller, the advantages ran their way and against those born illegitimate who remained with their biological mothers in families that tended to be larger. A similar picture emerged for mathematical abilities with the 145 adopted children matching the mean for the total cohort of around 17,000 children. In contrast, the illegitimate children were around five months behind in their 'arithmetic' ability (Seglow *et al.*, 1972: p. 70). In broad terms, the educational strengths of the adopted children continued to be maintained through to 11 years of age (Lambert & Streather, 1980). In reading, the adopted children were outperforming the mean ability of the whole cohort, adding further testimony to the value of socially and materially advantaged homes.

In mathematics the 11 year-old adopted children were slightly behind the average of the legitimate born children but still a long way ahead of the illegitimate children still living with their biological mothers (Lambert & Streather, 1980: p. 104). Very similar results were found by Bohman and his colleagues in Sweden (Bohman & Sigvardsson 1990: p. 103) who measured IQs of their three subject groups at the age of 18 years: 'In all four IQ subtests there was no difference between adopted boys ... and their controls. In contrast, boys who had grown up with their biological mothers or in foster homes scored significantly lower in most [intelligence and psychological tests] compared to their controls ... They were also more likely to be exempted from military service for social or psychological reasons than the adoptees...'

Maughan & Pickles (1990) continued to follow the UK National Child Development Study cohort through until the age of 23. Their findings add yet more evidence that adopted families help children reach high educational standards:

'Adoptees had achieved well both educationally and vocationally; over 80% had some formal qualifications by aged 23, by comparison with just over 75% of the legitimate group. The illegitimate young people, and especially the women, had fared much less well; just over 30% of the men and over half of the women had no formal educational or vocational qualifications at all by this stage.'

(Maughan & Pickles, 1990: p. 49)

Social and emotional development

Whereas outcomes for children adopted as babies in terms of their physical and cognitive development hardly differ from those achieved by children born and raised in similarly advantaged middle and working class homes, the same cannot be said for their psychosocial adjustment. It is not that adopted babies are destined to become seriously maladjusted. Rather, they appear to be at a slightly higher risk of experiencing some problems in their social and emotional development compared to other middle class children. These minor adjustment difficulties appear most pronounced during the school years (for exceptions, see Norvell & Guy, 1977; Elonen & Schwartz, 1969).

In an early study by Nemovicher (1959), 30 boys adopted before the age of six months were compared with a group of matched controls. Teachers and clinical psychologists found that the adopted boys differed significantly from the controls displaying higher levels of tenseness, hostility and dependency. Witmer *et al.* (1963) reported that although there was no significant difference in intelligence and school achievement between 484 adopted children and 484 controls, some of the adopted children were rated by teachers as less popular and more aggressive than their classmates. There is a hint here that although on average adopted children have more adjustment problems, it may be that these difficulties are concentrated in some children and may be entirely absent in others, notwithstanding that numerically there are more problem adopted children than problem controls. We shall return to this observation later in this section.

In a study of 105 adult people, Raynor (1980: p. 65) rated 70% as well-adjusted and 25% as marginally adjusted. She classified 5% as poorly adjusted. These people 'were ... clearly unhappy and depressed.' In a non-representative sample of 122 baby-adopted people, Howe (1997) identified a majority (76%) who had a trouble-free adolescence who went on to enjoy stable, well-adjusted young adulthoods. However, a minority of people in this group of baby-adopted adults (24%) had exhibited at least one problem behaviour (stealing, aggression, lying) or had attended a mental health clinic. In the most extreme cases, the problem behaviour was severe resulting in exclusion from school, court appearances and in three instances imprisonment.

Hoopes *et al.*'s (1970) study of 100 adopted children and 100 matched controls (in terms of age, sex and social class), measured children whose ages ranged between 10 and 15 years. This group therefore spans pre-adolescent and adolescent children. Teachers were asked to rate the children's overall level of social adjustment in the classroom. 78% of the adopted children and 87% of the control children were rated in the top two (of five) adjustment categories. However, whereas 46% of the controls were placed in the very top group of 'very happy – excellent adjustment' a more modest 24% of the adopted children were given this top rating. This may appear a small difference, a case of splitting hairs. But remembering that the control children were matched for age, sex and most particularly social class, this statistically significant under-representation of adopted children in the top adjustment group is not without interest.

More pronounced findings were described by Lindholm & Touliatos (1980). Their study used teacher ratings and reported higher levels of conduct disturbance among adopted elementary children. Along with many other studies, the investigators found that adopted boys showed more social disturbance in the classroom than adopted girls and that this difference was greater than that shown between non-adopted boys and non-adopted girls.

The National Child Development Study was used by Seglow *et al.* (1972) to compare the 182 adopted children (most of whom were placed in their first six months of life) with non-adopted 'illegitimate' and 'illegitimate' children at age seven. In terms of behaviour and adjustment at school, the researchers found that in general the degree of maladjustment increased from high to low socio-economic families. The children born illegitimate who remained with their biological mothers showed the highest levels of 'maladjustment'. Overall, in terms of social adjustment, adopted children did as well as all other children in the cohort. However, adopted boys did show higher rates of 'maladjusted' behaviour than both adopted girls and the overall cohort of boys in the study. But even this finding can be refined. Against the normal trend, adopted boys in middle class homes showed higher incidence of 'maladjusted' behaviour than both non-adopted boys from middle class homes and adopted boys from working class homes (Seglow *et al.*, 1972: p. 76):

'Further examination showed that in the case of "hostility to children" the difference was entirely due to adopted boys showing a markedly higher degree of such hostility than all the boys in the cohort; whereas there was no difference at all between adopted girls and those in the cohort. However, with regard to 'anxiety for acceptance by children', there is the same marked difference between adopted and cohort boys, but there is also a difference between adopted girls and all cohort girls; though not so marked, it is in the same direction, a higher proportion of adopted girls show-ing such anxiety.'

(Seglow *et al.*, 1972: p. 80)

Lambert & Streather (1980) followed the National cohort, including the adopted children through to age 11. The authors remind us that most adopted children were being raised in materially and socially very favourable families, even by middle class standards. Taking these factors into account allowed the study to conclude that 'adopted children's social adjustment was poorer than that of legitimate children, and showed signs of having deteriorated relative to that of other children since the age of 7' (Lambert & Streather, 1980: p. 133).

When children adopted as babies are followed through into adoles-cence and early adulthood, there appears to be an improvement in social adjustment and behaviour. Many studies conclude that there are few major differences at these ages between baby adopted children and non-adopted children raised in families of a similar social standing. The higher rates of nervous and behavioural disturbances in 11 year-old adopted boys compared to classroom controls shown by Bohman (1970; Bohman & Sigvardsson, 1990) had all but disappeared by the time the adopted boys had reached the age of 15. Children from adverse backgrounds who remain with their biological families continue to show the highest rates of disturbed behaviour and poor social adjustment. True, fewer adopted children appear in the 'very well adjusted' categories compared to control groups, but in spite of a slight excess of mild emotional and behavioural problems, adopted children do not show an excess of marked disturbance.

Bagley (1993), using the National Child Development Study data, compared adopted children with children *permanently separated* from their biological mothers (because of death, separation, long-term hospitalisation, divorce, surrender to foster or institutional care) by the age of seven years and all other children in the cohort. Using a battery of outcome measures, at the age of 16 years the adopted children compared favourably with the non-adopted, non-separated children. Only on a small number of items did adopted children show relatively high rates of disturbance: an inability to settle (20% of adopted children; 20% separated non-adopted children; 10% of non-separated children); inclination to tell lies (21%; 21%; 13%); and unpopular in class according to teachers (24%; 23%; 16%). At age 16 years, the non-adopted, separated children scored highest on most problem adjustment measures. In terms of children's own reported behaviours, adopted children were the most likely to feel that their parents were 'very anxious' for them to do well at school (32%; 14%; 23%). Bagley (1993: p. 95) concludes that adoption '... appears to be dramatically successful in terms of developmental outcomes by mid-adolescence.'

Adult-adopted people continue the general pattern of being relatively well-adjusted, though an element of insecurity and anxiety can still affect many. As part of a mental health survey, Bagley (1993) studied a random sample of an adult population in Calgary, Canada. The sampling produced 679 people. He identified two subgroups: 23 adult adopted people, and 24 adoptive parents (but not of the adoptees). The research found that adopters had better adjustment levels than others of similar age, sex and social class. This may be seen as a vindication of the selection and preparation procedures used by adoption workers. The adopted people did not show an excess of individuals with poor mental health. But their mental health scores did appear to concentrate in the middle ranges. 'Thus the adoptees have fewer individuals with very good mental health than the controls; but they also have some- what fewer individuals with very poor mental health ... The adoptees in this random sample do ... show an excess of individuals with mild mental health problems...' (Bagley, 1993: p. 117).

Maughan & Pickles (1990) picked up the National Child Develop- ment Study cohort when the children were aged 16 and again when they were aged 23 years. The response rates in the 16-year analyses were considerably down from the original numbers (for example, by age seven, 182 of the surviving illegitimate children had been adopted but only 82 of them were available for analysis at age 16). As well as missing and difficult to trace cases which were particularly high for the illegitimate group, there was a 20% refusal rate by adoptive families and 7% by the 'legitimate' sample. These low return rates need to be borne in mind as the researchers report that 'at age 16 again showed illegitimate adolescents having the highest rates of difficulty overall, and the adopted group falling between the legitimate and illegitimate' (Maughan & Pickles, 1990: p. 45). On more specific problem beha- viour measures, the adopted children did experience some particular difficulties. Although the adopted children did not differ from the legitimate group on either restless or antisocial items, they did record 'the highest scores on items reflecting unhappy, anxious behaviour, and, like the illegitimate group, were rated as showing significantly greater problems in their relationship with peers' (1990: p. 47)

By the time the cohort had reached age 23, the illegitimate group continued to show the highest rates of social disturbance and difficulty. The adopted and legitimate children were found to be functioning at a broadly similar and high level. For example, over 30% of illegitimate women had become pregnant as teenagers compared to only around 10% of both adopted and legitimate women. Indeed, overall, adopted women were generally functioning as well as legitimate women. However, adopted men were not finding their transition to adulthood quite so smooth. Their rates of job instability was higher than that for the total cohort. They also experienced a higher chance of suffering a breakdown in an intimate relationship, although group differences were small and not significant (Maughan & Pickles, 1990: p. 57).

More recent studies have given a slightly less rosy picture of the adopted adolescent. For example, Fergusson *et al.* (1995) contrast their findings with the earlier and more optimistic adolescent adoption outcome study of Maughan & Pickles (1990). The researchers describe the results of a 16-year longitudinal study of 1265 children. Of the total cohort, 1123 (88.8%) entered biological two-parent families, 98 (7.7%) entered single parent families, and 44 (3.5%) were adopted. The children of adoptive parents enjoyed the highest social and economic standards, followed by the biological two parent families. The single parent families experienced the greatest social and material disadvantages. There were no significant differences between the three groups of children in terms of depression, anxiety and the mood disorders ('internalising symptoms'). The 'illegitimate' children experienced higher rates of low self-esteem. However, there were significant differences between the three family groups for 'externalising problem behaviours'. The rates of conduct/oppositional disorders, self-reported offending, and daily cigarette smoking were highest for adolescent children of single parents and lowest for two-parent families, with adopted children falling in between. Non-adopted adolescents of two parent families showed the lowest rates of 'externalising problem behaviours'.

Although the overall rates of social and emotional difficulties are higher for adopted children than matched controls, the majority fall well within the normal range for social and emotional adjustment. However, a minority of baby-adopted children do show high levels of psychological difficulty, particularly during adolescence. Their numbers are higher than might be expected given the socio-economic status of their families.

Rates of socio-emotional difficulties do tend to fall with age and by early adulthood adopted children compare with non-adopted children from matched controls. Slightly higher levels of anxiety are reported in social relationships, but overall the research suggests that around 80% of adopted people grow into normally adjusted adults. Nevertheless, more adopted people present at clinics with personality disorders and substance abuse problems than might be expected from their socio-economic background. Adopted men continue to experience slightly higher levels of vulnerability in peer and intimate relationships than adopted women.

Mental health clinic studies of adopted children

If, as Brodzinsky (1987) believes, there is an increased psychosocial risk in being adopted, we might expect higher rates of referral to child psychiatric and mental health clinics for children adopted as babies compared to the general population of children. This, in fact, appears to be the case. Estimates vary, but referral rates seem to be around twice that of non-adopted children and adults in general (Sweeney *et al.*, 1963; Howe and Hinings 1987). The figures are even higher if adopted children are compared with non-adopted children of similar socio-economic backgrounds to the adopters. Adopters tend to be of a higher socio-economic status than the parents of other children referred to psychiatric clinics. More adopted than non-adopted children experience social adjustment problems, although we need to remind ourselves that it is still only a small minority of baby-adopted children who are referred. To put matters in further perspective, although adopted children are more likely to attend a clinic than non-adopted children from similarly advantaged social backgrounds, according to Seglow *et al.* (1972: p. 83) their rates of referral remain lower than those for non-adopted children of economically disadvantaged single parent families.

Various reasons have been put forward to explain these higher referral rates. It might be that adoptive parents are more inclined to refer their children to the mental health services. Their threshold of concern might be lower than that of parents of non-adopted children (Warren 1992). On the other hand, it might be that overall, more adopted children do exhibit problem behaviours that warrant clinical advice and intervention. The cause of these problems may involve genetic factors, early attachment problems, anxious parenting by adopters, the experience of being adopted or any combination of these and other factors. Thus, many factors are present that might interfere with the successful development of adopted children (Bohman & Sigvardsson, 1990). But whatever the causes, the conclusion is that adopted children appear at slightly greater risk of socio-emotional disturbance. Again, we need to remind ourselves that the majority of children adopted as babies are *not* referred to the mental health services. We are merely detecting an increased risk.

Adopted children in clinical populations are most likely to show aggressive and antisocial problems, learning and school-related difficulties, and low self-confidence (Brodzinsky, 1987: p. 27). Boys are more often affected than girls (Hersov, 1990: p. 499; Lipman *et al.*, 1993). Being adopted *and* having a poor school performance was a significant risk indicator for a psychiatric problem four years later (Lipman *et al.*, 1993). Compared to non-adopted clinical populations, adopted patients generally appear to show more 'externalising' than 'internalising' disorders. Zill (cited in Brodzinsky 1987: p. 29) sampled over 15,000 families of which 348 contained non-related adopted children. Adopted children were rated higher on behaviour problem index scores. They were also more likely to have been referred to a psychologist or psychiatrist at some time in comparison to non adopted children (13% compared to 5%). These studies do not always differentiate between early and late-placed adopted children making interpretation of the results difficult.

Humphrey & Ounsted (1963) examined the characteristics of all the adopted children (53 boys, 27 girls) referred to their Oxford child psychiatric clinic over an 11 year period. They calculated that the rate of referral for adopted children was twice the expected frequency of non-adopted children. The rate of referral increased with the onset of puberty. The 46 children placed before the age of six months displayed a similar range of problems to a group of matched controls, both showing high rates of 'emotional reactions' (disobedience, obstinacy, jealousy, temper tantrums and over-dependency).

In a study of 111 adopted and 1134 non-adopted children drawn from a children's mental health centre, Jerome (1993) observed that in both groups the ratio of boys to girls was approximately 3:1. The 'adopted families were significantly likely to have fewer children, a professional father and both parents at home than the non-adopted controls' (1993: p. 292). No differences were found in symptom checklists between the adopted and non-adopted groups for conduct, emotional and speech disorders. Significantly higher rates of hyper-activity and attention deficit disorders were reported for children adopted under the age of six months.

Kotsopoulos *et al.* (1993) carried out a follow up study of adopted children and a matched control (for sex, age and socio-economic background) of non-adopted children who had attended a psychiatric clinic five years earlier. At the original referral, the adopted children were referred at over twice the rate expected for children of that age and background. They were much more likely to have been assessed as having a conduct disorder than the matched controls. At the five year follow up, both adopted and control children had improved, but the biggest gains had been made by the earlier placed children. The children who had been adopted as babies (under six months) were much less likely than those adopted at older ages still to have a psychiatric diagnosis. The 'baby adopted' group also had significantly better levels of 'adaptive functioning' (Kotsopoulos *et al.*, 1993: p. 394).

Levels of satisfaction

Researchers consistently report high levels of satisfaction amongst parents of baby-adopted children. Interviewing 160 adopters whose children were young adults, Raynor (1980: p. 34) found that 85% felt very satisfied or reasonably satisfied with their overall experience. 5% viewed the experience as 'very unsatisfactory'. In each of these eight negative cases, the adopted child was a boy. Satisfaction appeared to be related to how quickly and easily the parents felt the child had settled into their home. Satisfied parents said that their baby had settled early and well. In contrast, a third of the 'unsatisfied' parents said that their child took a long time to settle. Rates of reported satisfaction, though slightly lower, were very similar when the grown-up adopted children were asked about their adoption.

Social, emotional and clinical outcomes and their possible causes

Although evidence on the outcome of baby-adopted children's psychosocial development is far from complete, a few broad patterns can be discerned:

(1)   In general, baby-adopted children appear to be at a slight developmental risk psychosocially compared to non-adopted children raised in families of similar composition and socio-economic status. In this sense, something about being adopted places children at an increased risk.

(2)   However, compared to non-adopted children raised in lone parent and/or socio-economically disadvantaged families, adopted children are at a lower risk of developing social and emotional adjustment problems. In this sense, adoption appears to offer children more protection.

(3)   For adopted children, the risks are highest in late childhood and adolescence. Few differences between adopted and non-adopted children are found before children reach around seven years of age.

(4)   Baby-adopted children show marginally higher rates of over-dependent behaviour and an anxiety to be accepted by adults. Low self-esteem and feelings of insecurity are also more likely to be present.

(5)   Rates of social adjustment and 'externalising' problem behaviours are higher for adopted children than the 'internalising' problem behaviours such as depression. Externalising problem behaviours include conduct and oppositional disorders; poor, hostile and aggressive relationships with peers and family members; acting-out; attention deficit disorders; offending; smoking and high alcohol use.

(6)   Adopted boys (like boys in general) are more at risk of poor social and emotional adjustment than girls. The ratio of boys (including adopted boys) to girls (including adopted girls) referred to child psychiatric clinics is roughly 3:1.

(7)   Although the majority of baby-adopted children fall within normal ranges of psychosocial adjustment (and in most cases therefore do not present in the clinical setting), a small minority do show sufficiently high levels of psychosocial maladjustment to warrant referral to the child mental health services. Baby-adopted children are referred to clinics at rates two to three times higher than non-adopted children from similar socio-economic back-

grounds. A small number of baby-adopted children exhibit severe 'externalising' problem behaviours during adolescence in proportions higher than might be expected for children from their adoptive parents' social and economic background.

The behaviours, developmental characteristics and personality traits of baby-adopted children generate a profile that seems sufficiently distinctive to differentiate them from their two main comparison groups, that is children raised by or restored to their socially and materially disadvantaged biological parents, and children raised by their socially and materially advantaged biological parents. The fact that overall they have distinctive developmental profiles *and* that they differ from both non-adopted children raised in adversity and non-adopted children brought up in good quality environments, suggests that there is something in the nature–nurture configuration of being adopted that has a particular impact on their psychosocial development. But whether it is to do with genes, environment or some interaction between the two is not resolved by simply cataloguing the main features of adopted children's psychosocial development.

We need to explore a little deeper to unravel some of the subtleties of human development in different social contexts. In the following two chapters we turn our attention to research that has attempted to understand the adopted child's socio-emotional progress from the point of view of genetics on the one hand and the environment on the other.

Chapter 3

Children Adopted as Babies: Genetic Influences on Development

The part that genetic inheritance might play in child development has long intrigued psychologists. How big a part, however, has varied with the scientific times. Fashions in developmental psychology have seen both genes and the environment come in and out of favour as ways of explaining behaviour and personality. As adoption represents a huge environmental change for children, it has fascinated both geneticists and environmentalists. Are adopted children more like their biological parents, in which case genes might be the major controlling element in development? Or are adopted children more like their adoptive parents, in which case the environment might be the main influencing factor on the growing child?

For much of the twentieth century, the belief was that the quality of a child's upbringing was the main factor influencing his or her psychological development. In the case of adopted children, whatever the biological background of babies, the greatest impact on their behaviour would be the qualities of the adoptive home. If adoption workers could ensure that adopters were of the highest social, emotional and material quality, the psychological prospects of the child would be very good indeed. Reflecting on this optimism, Hoopes *et al.* (1970: p. 13) wrote 'Practitioners in adoption have probably felt that placement of a child in a good environment would lift him above his genetic history.'

The relatively successful outcome of baby-adopted children seems, at first sight, to indicate that it is the positive impact of advantaged environments that is having the improving effect. And yet, in spite of this generally good news, researchers were aware that overall adopted children from disadvantaged backgrounds were performing not quite at the level of their non-adopted siblings within the adoptive home, either educationally or psychosocially. Although this performance gap might have been explained by other environmental factors (differential treatment of adopted and non-adopted children, the child's psychological experience of being adopted, etc.), it still left room for genetic influences as a way of accounting for some or all of the adopted child's personality and achievements. *Nature* refers to what is inherited. *Inheritance* denotes the genetic material transmitted from one generation to the next.

The influence of hereditary factors is most easily accepted in the case of children's physical and medical condition, though it has had a harder time convincing many people in the case of intelligence, behaviour and personality. There is, for example, a high correlation between the height of adopted children and the height of their biological parents. The same correlation is low between adopted children and their adoptive parents. Huntingdon's disease is clearly a genetically inherited condition over which the environment plays no part.

However, when it comes to behaviour and personality, the part that heredity plays is less clear cut. The scientists who have done most to develop enquiries in this field refer to their discipline as *behavioural genetics* or *quantitative genetics*. Much of their work has focused on the behaviour and development of twins and adopted children. Their investigations therefore warrant particular attention.

Behavioural genetics

Behavioural or quantitative genetics looks at particular behaviours and traits and attempts to measure how much influence genes have on their expression. It examines the extent to which the genetic differences between people accounts for the differences we see in their behaviour, temperament and personality. None of this is to deny that the environment might also be involved and may well exert its own influences. People's susceptibility to tooth decay has a high genetic component, but whether or not they actually develop serious tooth decay depends on the kind of environment in which they find themselves. If their water is fluoridated, the incidence will be low. If they live with a family which eats and drinks products with a high sugar content, levels of tooth decay will rise (Rende & Plomin, 1994: p. 26).

Matters are further complicated when it is appreciated that rarely is it one gene that determines a behaviour or a trait. Many genes acting in complex ways in varied environments produce whole spectra of behaviours. The notion, for example, that there might be a single gene responsible for crime is rejected by behavioural geneticists. Rather, they suspect that when certain genetically controlled predispositions (say, high inhibition, poor concentration, and low empathy) find themselves in particular environments (say, low parental warmth, slack moral codes, and opportunities to offend), the chance of an individual with those characteristics committing a crime increases. In contrast, an individual who is naturally shy and easily aroused, even if he finds himself in a high risk environment, is unlikely to commit crime. We shall be looking at the prevalence of crime in adopted and non-adopted people later on in this chapter.

'Human behavioural genetic research relies on family, adoption and twin designs. As in studies on non-human animals, family studies assess the extent of resemblance for genetically related individuals, although they cannot disentangle possible environmental sources of resemblance. Genetically related individuals adopted apart provide evidence of the degree to which familial resemblance is due to hereditary resemblance. This is like a natural experiment in which family members share heredity but not environment. The flip side of the adoption design tests the influence of nature by studying the resemblance of genetically unrelated individuals living together in adoptive families.'

(Rende & Plomin, 1994: p. 30)

In this way, behavioural genetic methods can assess the magnitude of the genetic effect. So, if identical twins are reared apart in different family environments and yet the majority of pairings measured the same on a given behavioural characteristic, this would suggest that the amount of genetic influence is high and that the environment is having little effect. On the other hand if the same population of reared-apart twins shows wide variation between pairs on a particular behaviour, this indicates that their environment is having the bigger impact and that heredity is playing little or no part.

It will be apparent from what has been said so far that behavioural genetics is capable of assessing the part that the environment plays in influencing behaviour every bit as much as it is able to measure the impact of hereditary. 'Genetic influence is often substantial but rarely accounts for more than half of the variance of behavioural dimensions and orders,' write Rende & Plomin (1994: p. 27). 'A decade ago, the important message from behavioural genetics was that, contrary to the environmentalism that dominated behavioural thinking, genetic influence was indeed an important source of variability among individuals. Now, however, the rush of the behavioural sciences away from environmentalism may be going too far, to a view that all behaviour is biologically determined' (Rende & Plomin, 1994: p. 27). Attention is increasingly being paid to the interaction between genes and their environment. Indeed, ironically it is genetic research that is providing us with important insights about how the environment also influences behaviour.

Behavioural genetics, therefore, has the potential to unravel the dynamic relationship between genes and experience as they shape behaviour, development and personality. This is important when it comes to understanding the relationship between adopted children, their parents and family life. Children clearly affect parents every bit as parents affect children. Outcomes for a temperamentally difficult child may differ depending on whether he finds himself living with an extrovert or introvert family. An adopted daughter who is musical and temperamentally shy may fare differently with parents who are quiet compared to parents who are sporty and boisterous.

If we are to understand the complexities of children's development, complexities that are particularly marked in the case of adopted children, we also need to remind ourselves of the various gene-environment correlations identified by Plomin *et al.* (1977) discussed in the first chapter. In *passive* correlations, biological parents pass on certain genes to their children as well as create particular kinds of environment. Parents and child share both heredity and environments. The child passively finds himself or herself in an environment that matches his or her temperament, talents or abilities, an experience which is likely to amplify these qualities. *Reactive* correlations occur when children with a particular trait *evoke* reactions from the environment to match their trait. A warm, sociable child may induce cheery responses in those who care for her. *Active* correlations occur when children deliberately select or create environments that suit their genetic predispositions. A boy who likes excitement and risk-taking may join a local gang or take up rock-climbing depending on his local social environment.

Passive correlations seem to be stronger during infancy and young childhood. But by adolescence, passive correlations diminish and active correlations increase (Scarr *et al.*, 1981; Plomin, 1994: p. 163). This is not surprising when it is realised that as children grow older, they are increasingly able to select their own environments. These environments (friends, places, activities) are more and more likely to match the children's temperament and personality. To this extent, as we move into adulthood, we can select, modify and create our own environments, our own experience. Genes increase their influence as we grow older.

Behavioural geneticists take a particular interest in children who have been adopted as babies. Essentially, these children have genes from one set of parents that find themselves in a social environment generated by another. The younger the babies are at the age of placement, the more complete is the transfer. The family environment created by their biological parents has had little time to exert much influence on the behaviour and personality of the children. Therefore, if the social environment is found to be having an effect on children and their development it will be the environment created by their adoptive family. Adopters and their adopted children help the scientists sort out the relative impacts of passive, reactive and active gene–environment correlations:

'If a gene–environment association were found for a measure of the family environment in nonadoptive families, this gene–environment association could represent passive as well as reactive or active [gene–environment] correlation. However, if the association also emerged in adoptive families, it could not be due to passive [gene–environment] correlation because adopted children do not inherit genes passively correlated with environments from their adoptive parents. Such an association in adoptive families must be attributed to reactive and active [gene–environment] correlation. Adoptive parents might respond to characteristics of their adopted children associated with this gene (reactive [gene–environment] correlation). Gene-associated characteristics of the adopted children may also underlie their attempts to use their parents to get what they want (active [gene–environment] correlation).'

(Plomin, 1994: p. 165–66)

Heredity and adopted children's development

The work of scientists in the field of behaviour genetics is helping to unravel the relative effects of heredity and upbringing on the developmental pathways taken by adopted children. Studies of adopted children and their behaviour have been particularly interested in (1) intelligence, (2) personality traits, and (3) psychopathology, including crime and psychiatric problems, and the extent to which each of them is being influenced by either heredity (biological parents) or environment (adoptive family). We shall consider these developments and behaviours under the following four headings:

(1) Intelligence, education and occupation.
(2) Temperament, personality and behaviour.
(3) Psychiatric disorders.
(4) Conduct disorders and criminal behaviour.

The choice of behaviours by scientists is often that which also concerns policy makers and practitioners: education, mental health and antisocial behaviour. To this extent, the knowledge produced about adopted children's development appears a little imbalanced, concentrating mainly on the disturbed and the deviant. More 'normal' behaviours receive less attention. Thus, a digest of behavioural genetic research that might interest adoption workers needs to be read with this distortion in mind. By association, one can have the feeling that because these scientists write a lot about schizophrenia or crime using adoption as one of their 'natural experiments', then adoptions themselves are beset with these behaviours. This, of course, is not the case. Nevertheless, the research does help to disentangle the possible effects of inheritance and environment, adding to our understanding of the growth and development of adopted children, albeit in those areas of human behaviour that are often seen as disturbed or difficult.

Intelligence, education and occupation

Intelligence

It is generally well recognised by psychologists that genes, experience and their interaction affect people's cognitive development and their

IQ. There appears to be a strong correlation between the IQ of individuals and their biological parents. It has also been demonstrated that heritability increases with age (see Bouchard *et al.*, 1990: p. 224). But equally important is the quality of the individual's environment. For example, the language abilities of children raised in very large families are not so good as those brought up in smaller households (cited in Rutter & Rutter, 1993: p. 223). Although children need to be in a stimulating language environment, talk that is noisy, confused and undirected is less effective than communication that is responsive, reciprocal and engages the child personally and individually.

In more general terms, a child's cognitive development is helped if she is stimulated, there is a variety of stimuli, other people respond sensitively and with interest, and learning takes place in an organised, structured and guided way. Learning is inhibited in homes that are noisy, unstructured, restrictive, and in which parental involvement is low. When several environmental 'risk' factors occur together, correlations between 'poor' environments and reduced IQ scores increase: the more risk factors, the lower the score. A study by Sameroff *et al.* (1993) showed that the poorest IQ scores could be predicted by the combined presence of low level of mother's education, maternal mental illness, poor standard of living, and large family size.

We can attempt to separate the relative effects of genes and environment in adoptions where we know the IQ scores of children, both their biological and adoptive parents, and their non-adopted siblings. Identical twins raised together show very high IQ correlations. When raised apart, identical twins have slightly lower IQ correlations but the rates are still higher than for siblings raised together. This suggests that inheritance is playing a large part in cognitive ability, although environment is having some influence.

The study of adopted children makes the picture clearer. Adopted children whose adoptive parents enjoy a higher socio-economic status than their biological parents typically score 10–20 IQ points higher than their biological parents. However, these same children on average tend to score lower IQ levels than their adoptive parents. Adopted children show higher IQ correlations with their biological parents than with their adoptive parents (Skodak & Skeels, 1949; Capron & Duyme, 1989; Cardon *et al.*, 1992; Loehlin *et al.*, 1989; Dumaret, 1985). So, if a child's biological parents had a high IQ the chances are that the child will also have a high IQ. Similarly, work by Willerman (1979) revealed that 15% of adopted children of biological parents with low IQs had scores at or below 95 compared to 0% of adopted children from high IQ biological parents.

The conclusion is that in the case of intelligence, genetic inheritance plays the major part in a child's cognitive performance, but the environment can certainly modify the score, either up or down. In the case of most baby adoptions, the tendency is for children to move from lower

IQ parents to higher IQ parents. The effect is for the children to find themselves in homes which help them realise more of their cognitive potential. Children adopted by parents with a higher IQ than their biological parents gain at least ten or more points over siblings who remain with biological families.

Education and occupation

Although by no means a cast-iron relationship, the number of children adopted as babies pursuing similar educational paths and occupational careers to one or other of their biological parents is higher than might be expected by mere chance. Teasdale (1979) looked at the occupational status of 2467 pairs of adopted-away adopted sons and their biological fathers. He found a modest, but noteworthy positive correlation (0.2) between biological fathers and sons. Identical twins reared apart and who have never met tend to have surprisingly similar jobs (Moloney *et al.* cited in Westen, 1996: p. 110). In his discussion of these findings, Plomin (1994: p. 100) suggests that heritability appears to be playing a definite part in people's achievements at school, occupational and socio-economic status. On an anecdotal level, Howe (1996a) gives several examples in which adopters note wryly that an adult adopted son or daughter is busily pursuing, often unwittingly, a career similar to that of their biological mother or father.

> 'It seemed uncanny to some adoptive mothers and fathers that their children should choose careers and occupations that were the same as those of their birth parents. Several daughters of nurses went into nursing; a son whose birth father was a journalist became a writer; a daughter who was very good at horse-riding discovered that her birth mother was a point-to-point champion.'
>
> (Howe, 1996a: p. 137)

Of course, no one is saying that there is a gene for nursing or journalism. Rather, certain temperamental characteristics and innate talents might combine to make some jobs more appealing than others. It must also be remembered that even if heritability is as high as 50% in matters of education and occupation, environmental experiences are still accounting for the remaining 50%. Nevertheless, genes and inheritance appear to play a surprisingly significant part in people's social achievements, including their choice of job and economic status.

Personality and temperament

Some of our temperamental style and personality make-up also appear to be influenced by our genetic inheritance. Again, this is not to say that the environment is not having a major impact, but it is in the interplay between biology and experience that governs much of our behaviour. A small proportion of any population inherits a propensity to be obese. But many adults become overweight because they overeat, not because of their genes. Conversely, some people who genetically might expect to be obese take strong measures to control their diet and keep their weight down. The outcome of our responses to the environment is therefore a product of our genetic predisposition and the nature of our response.

Looked at another way, different temperaments will respond differently to the same environment. For example, children who cope best with adverse, high stress social environments are those who have high levels of sociability, cognitive competence and good self-esteem (Hetherington, 1989; Masten 1989 cited in Wachs 1992: p. 110). It is speculated that these children might be better at getting whatever few positive emotional resources the family might have, and their characteristics might also help them avoid too much parental criticism, anger or abuse.

Personality and temperament refer to those characteristic ways in which an individual behaves and feels about situations. They can refer to the style that a person adopts when performing a behaviour – persistent, slipshod, energetic, hesitant. Or they might refer to the emotions that go with the behaviour – aggressiveness, coldness, tension, warmth (Loehlin, 1992). These behavioural features have to be reasonably persistent and durable to count as a part of person's personality and temperament.

'The essence of personality is behavioural consistency across time and place. People are said to "have" certain personality characteristics when they are observed by others or themselves to behave in predictably similar ways over variable events and situations.'

(Scarr *et al.*, 1981: p. 885)

Of course, people's personality and temperaments can and do change over time, but there are assumed to be underlying traits that are regarded as broadly characteristic of the individual. Clusters of temperaments tend to compose a personality type. Someone who is temperamentally shy might also be quiet, introverted, self-conscious and anxious, traits that make up a personality type. One of the simplest classifications recognises *emotionality, activity* and *sociability* as the three major cluster of temperamental traits (Buss & Plomin, 1984).

Psychologists have recognised five major dimensions of personality which they have dubbed 'The Big Five': extroversion, agreeableness, conscientiousness, neuroticism and openness to experience (McCrae & Costa, 1990). Traits and their opposite traits fill out each of the dimensions so that to describe someone as extrovert tends to mean that they are talkative, affectionate, outward-going and forceful, in contrast to someone who is introvert described as quiet, reserved, inward-looking and shy.

- *Extroversion* includes the following dimensions: quiet–talkative, passive–active, loner–joiner, reserved–affectionate, shy–forceful.
- *Agreeableness* includes: irritable–good natured, combatative–acquiescent, wary–trusting, cold–warm, ungiving–generous.
- *Conscientiousness* includes: lazy–hard working, negligent–conscientious, disorganised–organised, quitting–persevering, thorough–careless.
- *Neuroticism* includes: calm–worrying, comfortable–self-conscious, content–self-pitying, equable–moody.
- *Openness to experience* includes: uncreative–creative, prefer routine–prefer novelty, literal–imaginative, incurious–curious.

In adoption, researchers wonder about the extent to which adopted children's temperaments and personalities match those of either their biological or adoptive family. If they correlate with their biological parents, then to some extent personality is being genetically determined. On the other hand, positive correlations with their adoptive parents suggests that the social environment is having a significant influence. Thus, in terms of temperament and personality traits, the question is 'To what extent and in what respects do adopted children resemble either their biological parents or their adoptive parents?'

A number of major studies have been carried out in Europe and America that have looked at the behaviour and personality development of adopted children, comparing them with their biological and adoptive families (Eaves *et al.*, 1989; Scarr *et al.*, 1981; Loehlin *et al.*, 1985). The findings are subtle as well as complex, but overall it appears that many behaviours and personality factors have a hereditary component. For many temperaments, adopted children are more like their biological than their adopted parents (Plomin *et al.*, 1990). However, some traits appear to be more heritable than others. For example, sociability and openness to experience shows a large genetic influence. In contrast, traits associated with agreeableness and conscientiousness show low heritability, most influences appearing to be caused by family environmental factors. Extroversion and neuroticism are influenced by both genetic inheritance and non-shared environmental experience.

On this last trait, Loehlin (1992: p. 46) concludes that for extraversion, genes account for nearly 40% of individual variation. Sharing an environment (for example, the same family) seems to play little part in developing this trait. The remaining influence appears to come from gene–environment interaction, non-shared aspects of the environment and errors of measurement. Interestingly, with age, twins and siblings share less and less of the same social environment. They occupy a particular and unique spot in terms of the way they personally experience family life, begin to mix with different friends outside the family, have varied classroom experiences and go to different places. All of these represent the 'non-shared environment' and it is this that appears to have an increasing influence on many personality traits that have both a genetic and environmental component, including extroversion and neuroticism (Loehlin *et al.*, 1990). Shared family influences play only a small role in their development.

Loehlin *et al.* (1990) studied 229 adopted and 83 non-adopted children in their Texas Adoption Project. The children's parents were asked to rate their children in terms of their Extraversion, Socialization and Stability. The researchers returned ten years later and repeated the exercise, thus obtaining information about whether the children had moved on any of the measures and in which direction. Lying behind the study was a series of questions. Do genetically unrelated individuals reared together tend to show similar personality changes over time? Do the personality characteristics of the biological or adoptive parents have greater power in predicting the changes that occur in the adopted children? Does ten years living with adoptive parents increase or decrease the resemblance of genetically unrelated individuals? (Loehlin *et al.*, 1990: p. 227)

Two answers emerged. The shared environments created by adoptive parents appeared to have little influence on changes in the children's perceived levels of Extraversion, Socialization and Stability. The non-shared environments seemed to be having the greater impact. However, with time genetic factors also began to play a greater part:

'At the time of the first testing the adopted children were seen as somewhat more extraverted, better behaved, and more emotionally stable than the nonadopted children in these same families ... By the time of the second testing, however, there had been significant relative changes in the direction of poorer socialization and less emotional stability in the adopted children ... Given that the genetic parents of adoptive children were less well socialised and emotionally stable than those of nonadopted children, this represents a shift of children's personalities in the direction of their biological parents.'

(Loehlin *et al.*, 1990: p. 239)

'What is one to make of these two kinds of outcome? The correlational evidence suggests that most individual change is non-familial, that is, neither due to shared genes or shared environment. The relative shifts in groups means, however, suggest that some systematic change is taking place, and at least some of this change is in the direction of making children on the average more like their genetic parents. The answer, we believe, is that both perspectives are appropriate and relevant.'

(Loehlin *et al.*, 1990: p. 240–241)

In a study of 500 same-sex pairs of middle aged identical and non-identical twins, half of whom had been reared together and half adopted apart in early life, Plomin *et al.* (1992) examined the heritability of *optimism* and *pessimism*. In self-reports, the researchers found that heritability for optimism was 23% and for pessimism 28%, figures that roughly compare with other personality traits.

'Optimism and pessimism may be especially important personality traits because of their associations with mental health. Although pessimism predicts hostility and cynicism but optimism does not, both optimism and pessimism add to the prediction of depression and life satisfaction ... In other words, individuals with a genetic propensity towards low optimism and high pessimism are also at genetic risk for mental health problems.'

(Plomin *et al.*, 1992: p. 928–929)

'The evidence,' concludes Westen (1996: p. 471), 'thus points to heritability estimates in the range of 0.15 to 0.40 for most personality traits, with the balance attributable to the environment.' The intricate and myriad differences between individuals and their genes mean that even though there is a strong genetic component, even biological siblings in the same family will be reacting differently to people and events, such that people and events will be reacting differently to them. This is partly why siblings are different (Dunn & Plomin, 1990). Although a significant fraction of our personality make-up is inherited, the way we each react to other people means that, in effect, we create a unique social environment for ourselves. Some of the 'same' inherited traits will therefore be expressing themselves in a world of social responses which are different for each person. If we are to understand the details of a person's temperament and personality profile, we should have to examine their individual life history. 'Each sibling in a family ... has different experiences within that family and outside of it, and these unshared experiences can be as important in shaping personality as shared environment' (Westen, 1996: p. 472).

Maurer *et al.* (1980), using Thomas and Chess's simple three-fold classification of temperaments, found that temperament in adopted children could predict later behaviours. Three primary patterns of temperament were identified: the Difficult Child, the Slow-to-Warm-Up Child, and the Easy Child (Maurer *et al.*, 1980: p. 522):

(1) Difficult children are distinguished by irregular biologic function, predominantly intense negative reactions, slow adaptation to new situations, negative moods, high withdrawal, prone to cry as infants, and difficult to comfort.
(2) The profile of the slow-to-warm-up children include shyness, slow acceptance of new foods in infancy, mild reactions, and a pattern

of slow adaptation characterised by initial withdrawal reactions with eventual adjustment.

(3) The easy children are positive in mood, highly regular, low or mild in intensity, cope well with stress, and quite adaptable to new situations.

Examining the behaviour of 162 baby-adopted 14–17 year olds, Maurer *et al.* (1980) were able to show that children placed in the 'difficult' group at an earlier age were much more likely to show problem behaviours in adolescence than either the slow-to-warm-up and easy groups. Moreover, on one specific behaviour – accidental poisoning as a preschooler – the difficult group again proved to be more vulnerable. The authors take accidental poisoning to be the result of a more impulsive, dare-devil, overactive, noncompliant attitude. Thus, they suggest, different temperamental types can predict certain behaviours. Adopted children who are temperamentally 'difficult' will be at increased risk of showing some problem behaviours, irrespective of the characteristics of their adoptive family. More generally, Wachs (1992: p. 128) has shown that children with a 'difficult' temperament tend to more reactive to environmental stresses than those with an 'easy' temperament. It might also be the case that because of the circumstances leading to children being placed for adoption, adopted children are at increased genetic risk of having a 'difficult' temperament. Biological parents with weakened psychosocial resources may be able to cope with an 'easy' child but fail with a 'difficult' child. To this extent, there might be a slight selection bias towards relinquishing 'difficult' babies for adoption.

Perceptions of family life

An intriguing line of enquiry reveals that is not only a significant fraction of personality genetically inherited, it also influences the way children rate and perceive their social environment. Plomin (1994: p. 62–3), reviewing much of this research, observes that children's perceptions of family life are, in part, inherited. Twins and siblings placed for adoption in different families are more likely to perceive similar family characteristics in the different families than non-related children in different families. There appears to be a genetic contribution to children's perceptions of family warmth, affection and control. Of course, it may be that the children and their personalities 'create' elements of a family's social style, or that children with certain personalities cause parents to react to them in a particular way. In either case, it is the child's temperament and personality that is influencing the family and children who share some of their genes are more likely to perceive themselves to be in similar kinds of family environment.

In similar vein, Plomin (1994: p. 69) describes research that looked at the resemblance between the way parents and their children perceive family life. To a modest degree, it seems that parents and children who are biologically related perceive more characteristics of the family environment in common than do adopters and their adopted children. The findings were most pronounced for perceptions of 'warmth' (cohesion and expressiveness) as a feature of family life.

In the Colorado Adoption Project, further research along these lines involved videotaping mothers interacting with their non-adopted (biological) children and adopted children when the child was aged 1, 2 and 3 years old (Dunn & Plomin, 1986; Dunn *et al.*, 1990). At each age the mother and one of her children were videotaped for five minutes. Three types of interaction were involved. In the first, a 'structured task' (mother teaching the child to do something) was carried out. In the second, a moderately structured task was set in which the child was given a specific set of toys with which to play. The third session was unstructured in which the child was allowed to play freely. The mother–child interactions were analysed in terms of affection, control and verbal responsiveness. At all three ages, affection between mother and biological child showed higher rates of correlation than between mother and adopted child. No genetic contribution was found for verbal responsiveness or control, with the exception of control at three years. In other words, the incidence and similarity of affection factors was higher between biologically related mother–child pairs than biologically unrelated pairs, suggesting a modest genetic contribution. Completing his review of research in this area, Plomin writes that:

> '...half a dozen twin and adoption studies converge on the conclu-
> sion that genetic factors play a role in children's perceptions of
> parenting. Evidence for genetic contributions emerges for all
> dimensions of children's perceptions of parenting with the interesting
> exception of control-related dimensions. Children's perceptions of
> their siblings' behaviour toward them also shows genetic effects.
> Genetic effects are not just limited to children's perceptions of their
> family environment. Parents' perceptions of their parenting implicate
> genetic contributions...'

> (Plomin, 1994: p. 79–80)

None of this is to say that the family environment is not having an effect. It is. What is less familiar is the contribution that genetic factors play in

(1) influencing the individual's temperament, personality and per-
     ceptions,
(2) shaping personal environments, and
(3) affecting the way people react to individual temperaments and
     personalities.

Psychiatric disorders

On the face of it, it appears that some psychiatric disorders can be inherited. For example, adopted children of schizophrenic biological mothers are more likely to suffer schizophrenia than adopted children whose biological mothers have not had the illness (Heston, 1966; Kety *et al.*, 1978; Tienari *et al.*, 1990). However, although having a mother with schizophrenia is a genetic risk, adopted children again illustrate the complex interactions that occur between genes and their environment.

About 1% of the general population might expect to suffer schizophrenia. But although the rate of having schizophrenia for children who live with a schizophrenic parent is 10%, this drops to only 3% for children of schizophrenic parents if they are raised by adoptive parents (Lowing *et al.*, 1983). For example, adopted children of biological mothers with a serious mental illness raised by adopters who do not have a mental illness show a 50% drop in the expected rate of psychiatric illness themselves (Eldred *et al.*, 1976). Good adoptive parenting appears to protect genetically vulnerable children from developing mental illness.

Tienari and his colleagues further refined their basic observations about the heritability of mental illness. Whether or not an adopted child develops schizophrenia seemed to depend on the quality of parenting and family life offered by the adopters. The less favourable is the parenting environment, the more susceptible are children to poor mental health. In 'healthy-rearing families the adoptees have little serious mental illness *whether or not their biological mothers were schizophrenic*' (Tienari *et al.*, 1990: p. 273; emphasis in original). In contrast, adoptive homes in which child-rearing practices are not good produce a greater number of disturbed adopted children whether the biological mother has a psychiatric condition or not. The adopted children most at risk of developing schizophrenia are those who have a biological mother with schizophrenia and who were in adoptive families displaying poor relationship and parenting skills. Of adopted children raised in 'seriously disturbed adoptive homes', 63% of those born to mothers with schizophrenia were rated as having severe mental health problems compared to only 23% of those born to non-schizophrenic mothers (Tienari *et al.*, 1985).

But the picture, even with this refinement, remains complex. It is possible to interpret the findings another way. It may be that children who have an inherited mental health problem are difficult children to parent. It is not so much that the adopters are poor carers. Rather, their apparent problems with parenting are simply the result of having to look after a disturbed child:

'Genetically transmitted vulnerability, to be expected in only a portion of those at risk, may be a necessary precondition for schizophrenia, but a disturbing environment may also be significant in transforming the vulnerability into clinically overt schizophrenia. Being reared in a healthy family may also be a protective factor for a child at risk. Finally, there is the possibility that the genetic vulnerability of the offspring manifests itself in a way that includes dysfunction in the adoptive family ... The question of the direction of control between adoptive parents and adoptees must remain open ... This issue can be expressed as a question of whether illness in the adoptees induces dysfunction in the adoptive parents, or whether parental dysfunction contributes to pathology in the adoptees, and parental healthy functioning promotes health in the adoptees despite the genetic risk associated with illness in a biological parent.'

(Tienari *et al.*, 1990: p. 377).

Nevertheless, more general research in the field of mental health and social conduct suggests that styles of parenting and the quality of family life do appear to have a bearing on development and behaviour. Families rated as 'warm' and able to communicate and express thoughts, feelings and emotions in a clear way, seem able to protect children who might otherwise be at risk of developing schizophrenia (Leff & Vaughn, 1985). Conversely, families where there is stress and high levels of intrusion and criticism, precipitate illness in family members genetically vulnerable to developing schizophrenia. Social environments seem able to mediate genetic expression just as much as genetic predispositions can influence the way other people react.

Genetic vulnerability to depression in adopted children is less clear cut. There is less research on the topic and what there is remains inconclusive (Cadoret, 1990). Mendelwicz & Rainer (1977) studied the adopted-away children of parents who suffered mania and depression (bi-polar depression) and found strong evidence for a genetic factor. But the presence of environmental factors as correlates of depression in adopted children seems, if anything, a little stronger. Stresses in the adoptive home (a family member who has a drink or behavioural problem, adoptive parental death or divorce) appear to increase adopted children's susceptibility to depression (Cadoret *et al.*, 1985). The nature of the interplay between a possible genetic vulnerability to depression and adverse factors in the adoptive family remains unclear.

Conduct disorders and criminal behaviour

Broad sweeps of people adopted as babies regularly find that girls appear to make better psychosocial adjustments than boys (for example, Jaffee & Fanshel, 1973: p. 71; Raynor, 1980: p. 68). Antisocial and criminal behaviour, because of the social concern they cause, have generated a good deal of research. Again, adoption has proved to be an area of particular interest as it provides investigators with the opportunity to try and tease out the relative influences of biological inheritance and social environment on the causes of criminal behaviour. Antisocial conduct covers a wide range of behaviours, including truancy, persistent lying, stealing, vandalism, truculence, poor concentration at school or work, fighting, impulsiveness and in adulthood, poor parenting abilities.

We know a number of useful things about those who commit offences. Although as many as a third of males may commit offences at some time, the bulk of crime (possibly as much as 50%) is committed by only around 5% of this group. These are known as 'chronic offenders'. The majority of chronic offenders exhibit antisocial behaviour before the age of ten, but not all children who behave antisocially before ten become chronic offenders (Farrington, 1995). Antisocial behaviour that first appears in adolescence appears to be less disturbed and not last as long as delinquent behaviour that begins in pre-adolescence. Antisocial behaviour that begins young is more likely to be associated with aggression, poor peer relationships and family psychopathology (Rutter, 1996: p. 4). It is also more likely to persist into adult life.

A number of genetic, environmental and physiological risk factors have been identified for offending behaviour:

(1) There is evidence that children of criminal parents, even when reared apart from their parents, are more at risk of committing crimes than those of non-criminal parents.
(2) Environmental risks include family discord, weak family relationships, parental criminality, ineffective discipline and supervision, deviant peer groups, weak informal controls and communities in which there are opportunities for committing crimes (Rutter, 1996; Smith, 1995).
(3) Neurophysiological impairment may put some children at risk of behaving anti-socially, though the numbers are thought to be small.

Genetic researchers do not suggest that there is a gene for crime. Rather, it is argued that certain inherited temperamental and personality traits place some individuals at risk of behaving antisocially in certain environments. For example, we might wonder if a particular behavioural disposition might be realised, say, if a child's parents are hostile, rejecting or poor on supervision, but not if they are warm and establish clear behavioural boundaries.

In broad terms, the following findings hint at the different ways in which genes and the environment interact to either suppress or realise a particular behaviour (Crowe, 1974; Cloninger & Gottesman, 1987; Rutter & Rutter, 1993: p. 19):

(1) Very low rates of criminal behaviour are reported in adopted children if neither their biological parents or adoptive parents have a criminal record.
(2) Rates of criminal behaviour in adopted children increase slightly if one of their adoptive parents has committed one or more offences. This suggests a modest environmental contribution to criminality.
(3) However, rates of criminal behaviour in adopted children increase further if a biological parent has a criminal record. This suggests a modest genetic contribution to criminality.
(4) The highest rates of criminal behaviour occur in adopted children when both biological and adoptive parents have a history of offending. This suggests some form of gene–environment interaction.
(5) Adverse environmental factors put adopted children whose biological parents have committed offences more at risk of criminal behaviour than adopted children whose biological parents did not have a criminal record.

The nature of these gene–environment interactions is by no means clear, but the research does suggest that genetic effects on certain psychological predispositions associated with criminal behaviour may be more likely to be activated in adverse than non-adverse environments. In other words, children with a psychological make-up that might predispose them to commit antisocial acts will only do so if they find themselves raised in a socially adverse environment, while children who do not inherit such a predisposition will be less likely to commit offences even if raised in an adverse setting. For example, Cadoret & Cain (1980, cited in Bagley 1993) found that adopted boys in stable adoptive families did not have an excess of behaviour problems compared to controls. But adopted boys who lived in homes in which there were high levels of stress caused by divorce or psychiatric illness, were much more likely to show disordered behaviour. Rates were highest for boys whose biological parents had also exhibited antisocial behaviour.

Studies of criminality and heritability have explored two other conditions in the parents of adopted children: alcohol abuse and psychiatric illness. These cast further light on the complex interactions between genetic effects and the quality of the environment and are worth looking at in more detail.

Adopted people, crime and alcohol

The Stockholm Adoption Study investigated the effect of different genetic and environmental factors on the development of criminal behaviour in adopted children and adults (Bohman 1970; 1996). Alcohol abuse by biological parents and their adopted offspring was found to have a bearing on children's criminality. The people studied comprised 862 men and 913 women. They were born between 1930 and 1950 and placed for adoption at an early age with families of relatively good and stable social and economic standards. 'The placement agency also selected against criminality and alcohol abuse in the adoptive parents. This restricted the range of social risks, so that the environmental influence was minimized compared to the general population' (Bohman, 1996: p. 100). The aim of the study was to identify genetic and early environmental antecedents of adult criminal behaviour and alcohol abuse.

The first finding was that the presence of a criminal record for adopted people was roughly the same as that for the general population in Sweden (12.8% in adopted men; 2.9% in adopted women). Biological parents were also studied. They were two to three times more likely to have a criminal record than the general population (29.0% in men; 6.4% in women).

A similar picture emerges for alcohol abuse. The rates of abuse amongst adopted people were approximately the same as found in the general population (16.1% in men; 2.4% in women). The rates of alcohol abuse in biological parents were much higher (34% in biological fathers; 4.6% in biological mothers).

None of the adoptive parents had a criminal record and only 2.3% appeared on the register for alcohol abuse.

In his preliminary analysis, Bohman (1978) found a significant positive correlation between alcohol abuse in the biological parents and their adopted-away children. This initial finding suggests a genetic component in the risk of developing alcohol abuse. He also found a correlation for the possession of a criminal record between biological parents and their adopted children. On top of this, there was a small correlation between alcohol abuse and criminality. But what was not clear was whether a proneness to abuse alcohol or commit crimes were separate tendencies or linked in some way.

Further analysis revealed that:

• Adopted sons whose biological fathers had a criminal record but who did *not* abuse alcohol were more at risk of having a criminal record (8.9%) than adopted sons of all other non-criminal fathers (4.2%). However, the offences of both non-alcoholic criminal fathers and sons tended to be non-violent and petty. Turned around, of the 39 adopted men who had committed petty criminal offences, 21% had at least one biological parent with a record of petty crime and no alcohol abuse.

• Female crime in adopted daughters was mostly petty (property offences, shoplifting), non-violent and rarely associated with alcohol abuse. 109 of the 811 adopted women studied had at least one biological parent who had a criminal record. Of those who had a criminal biological parent, 4.9% had committed at least one offence compared to only 1.4% of adopted women whose biological parents did not have a criminal record. Of the 16 women who had committed petty criminal offences, 31% had at least one biological parent with a record of petty crime and no alcohol abuse. Although the rates of criminal behaviour in adopted women is lower than in adopted men, female criminal adoptees have a higher percentage of criminal biological parents than male criminal adoptees. 'It is reasonable to hypothesise, then, that the women who do become antisocial may have a stronger genetic predisposition toward this behaviour than the men who become antisocial.' (Brennan & Mednick, 1993: p. 21).

- Most criminality appeared to be a consequence of alcohol abuse. The offences of both alcoholic–criminal biological fathers and adopted sons tended to be more violent and frequent.

- '. . . neither the [low] social status of the adoptive parents nor that of the biological parents were sufficient to predispose their children to petty criminality, but both did increase the risk of criminality in children when the biological parents were *themselves* criminals' (Bohman, 1996: p. 105).

These results encouraged Bohman and his colleagues to believe that underpinning both criminality and alcohol abuse were more stable personality and temperamental traits. Different traits were thought to be governing the different behaviours (petty crime, violent crime, alcohol abuse). Thus, the findings were beginning to suggest that certain personality traits could be inherited but the nature of their expression would depend on the type of environment in which they found themselves. Particular personality factors in certain environments could lead to alcohol abuse, petty crime or violent offending.

'. . . our studies indicated that the transmission of these behaviours between generations is largely associated with personality factors, which are moderately inherited and continuously distributed in the population . . . Such differences in personality or temperament are more stable traits that are involved in the adaptation of an individual with the environment, whereas criminality or alcohol abuse represent the result of this interaction.'

(Bohman, 1996: p. 106–7)

Therefore, there is no suggestion that there is a gene for crime. Rather, individuals *can* inherit particular personality traits that, in certain socio-economic environments, can lead them to behave in an antisocial and criminal manner. Further analysis of adopted children at age 11 and 27 years revealed that traits such as 'novelty-seeking', 'harm avoidance' and 'reward dependence' could interact with certain 'risk' environments and produce increased rates of alcohol abuse, violent crimes and property offences (Cloninger & Gottesman, 1988; Sig-vardsson, Bohman & Cloninger, 1987). Adopted individuals who were rated high on 'novelty seeking' but low on harm avoidance and reward dependence were more at risk of committing aggressive and violent offences. Petty, non-violent criminals scored lower on these traits, though still higher than non-criminals. High novelty-seeking and low harm avoidance were most predictive of the early onset of alcohol abuse.

These suggestions square with the idea that boys who have a *high* threshold of arousal – that is, it takes a lot of stimulation to bring about excitement and emotional arousal – push their behaviour to extremes before they experience feelings of excitement, fear, danger and anxiety. Depending on the kind of social and physical environment in which they find themselves, possession of such high arousal threshold personality traits might lead to daring but wholesome pursuits (rock climbing; parachute jumping) or criminal and antisocial behaviour (breaking into and entering other people's houses; getting into fights).

These Swedish adoption studies nicely capture the intricacies of gene–environment interactions. The children's adoptive parents had no criminal record (environment). Rates of criminal activity amongst the biological parents was much higher than that for the general population (genes). Adopted children had rates of criminal behaviour similar to the general population. This suggests that both genes (in the form of inherited personality traits) and the environment (non-criminal adoptive parents) are interacting in some way. The result of the interaction is that adopted children produce rates of criminal behaviour greater than that of their family environment but lower than that of their biological parents (also see Fergusson *et al.*, 1995: p. 609). To this extent, adoptive families who have been selected on high social class and family stability appear to offer protection against the risk of behaving criminally.

Adopted people, crime and psychiatric illness

Studies of the Danish Adoption Cohort have also examined the role of genetics in criminal behaviour. Although the reasoning is similar in terms of gene–environment interactions, the ingredients used to explore rates of criminality in adopted children are different. In particular, much interest has been taken in the heritability of some forms of mental illness.

The study looked at 14 427 non-familial adoptions occurring between 1924 and 1947. Information was available on the adopted children, their biological parents and the adopters. The basic hypothesis was that (all things being equal) children of criminal biological parents will have higher rates of criminal behaviour than the biological children of non-criminal parents.

The following rates of one or more criminal convictions were found (Mednick *et al.*, 1987; Brennan *et al.*, 1996):

Adopted boys: 16.6% (n = 6129)
Adopted girls: 2.8% (n = 7065)
Adoptive fathers   6.2% (n = 13 918)
Adoptive mothers   1.9% (n = 14 267)
Biological fathers   28.7% (n = 10 604)
Biological mothers   8.9% (n = 12 300)

It can be seen that biological fathers were nearly five times more likely to have been convicted than adoptive fathers. Analysis reveals that there is a significant relationship between the number of convictions of the biological parents and their adopted-away sons. The more criminal convictions held by biological parents the more likely it was that their adopted son had committed an offence. For example, 16% of the adopted sons of biological parents with one conviction had a criminal record. In contrast, 27% of the adopted sons of biological parents with three or more convictions had been convicted for an offence. Indeed, as a function of criminal recidivism in biological parents (1) the proportion of chronic male adoptee property offenders increases, and (2) the mean number of convictions for the chronic adoptee property offender increases (Brennan & Mednick, 1993: p, 22–3). As with non-adoptive populations, only a small number of individuals are responsible for a large proportion of crime. 'The male chronically offending adoptees who have chronically offending biological parents comprise only 1% of the male adoptees but are responsible for 30% of the convictions in the male adoptee cohort!' (Brennan *et al.*, 1996: p. 117).

These figures appear to support the hypothesis that some heritable trait or traits pass from biological parents to children that increase the risk of being convicted of a crime. Further support is provided by similar rates of criminal behaviour found in siblings who have been adopted by different families but who share a biological parent with a criminal record.

The researchers then noted that earlier research by Heston (1966) had found that not only was there a significant increase in rates of schizophrenia in the adopted children of schizophrenic biological mothers, but also that the levels of antisocial behaviour, including violence, appeared at higher rates in the adopted children of these women. Moffitt (1987), working on the Danish Adoption Cohort, observed that if a biological parent had both a criminal record and an admission to a psychiatric hospital, the chances of their adopted sons exhibiting violent behaviour increased. The analysis also found that the risk of conviction among 5182 adopted men was 15% (Moffitt, 1987). If the adoptees' biological parents had never been admitted to a psychiatric hospital, 14.5% were found to have a criminal record.

However, if at least one biological parent had been admitted to hospital with a mental illness, the criminal conviction rate of adopted men rose to a statistically significant 19.25%.

Biological parents who suffered a personality disorder or abused drugs or alcohol contributed most strongly to their adopted-away sons' risk of being criminally convicted. However, Moffitt is keen to add the reminder that even though there is a definite increased risk of offending in the children of criminal and mentally ill parents, the 'clear majority' of these offspring, in fact, do not commit serious or frequent crimes. The correlations also held in the opposite direction – a three-fold increase was found in the rate of schizophrenia for adopted children of biological fathers convicted of violent offences (Brennan *et al.*, 1996: p. 120).

The authors searched for possible confounding factors that might be involved in the relationship. One possibility was that violent men were more likely to marry women with increased rates of mental illness, but a modest association between violent fathers and schizophrenic children persists even when all cases of a violent father marrying a mentally ill mother were removed. However, if the mentally ill mothers are retained, the rates of schizophrenia rise to the highest levels in adopted children whose biological fathers are violent and biological mothers have been in hospital with a mental illness.

It seems that in these cases, adopted children and their biological fathers share a heritable trait that increases risk of violence in the fathers and increases risk of schizophrenia in the children. The researchers could not identify what specific characteristic might be inherited. They could only speculate that it might involve an inherited deficit in information processing that somehow contributed both to the illness of schizophrenia and the likelihood of being criminally violent.

In his response to both Bohman's and Mednick's adoption studies, Plomin (also see Cloninger & Gottesman, 1987: p. 105) highlights the various interactions that can take place between genes and environment in the case of criminal behaviour in adopted children:

'...for adoptees without a genetic propensity (that is, adoptees whose biological parents had no criminal record), the rate of criminality was 3% if their adoptive parents had no criminal record and 7% if their adoptive parents had a criminal record. This suggests some environmental effect in that the rate of criminality doubled in adoptees if their adoptive parents had a criminal record. In contrast, for adoptees with a genetic propensity (that is, adoptees whose biological parents had criminal records), the rate of criminality was 12% if their adoptive parents had no criminal records and an amazing rate of 40% is their adoptive parents had a criminal record. The greater average rate of criminality in adoptees with a genetic propensity suggests a genetic effect. However, the most striking aspect of these results is the evidence they provide for genotype–environment interaction ... they suggest that the environment has the biggest effect on those who already have a predilection towards criminal behaviour.'

(Plomin, 1996: p. 132)

Adoption: interactions between individuals' inherited predispositions and the social environment of their adoptive family

Adoption as an 'experiment of nature' allows scientists to explore the relative impact of inheritance and environment on human behaviour and development. Depending on how similar adopted children are either to their biological or to their adoptive parents on a given characteristic, the relative impact of either nature or nurture can be estimated.

This review of the research literature on adopted children's development has recognised a subtle picture in which genes and environment interact in many and various complex ways. The strength of a particular characteristic being straightforwardly inherited varies. Genetic influences are strongest in the case of physical characteristics such as height, body shape and colouring. Cognitive ability and IQ measures also seem to carry a significant genetic component, although here the environment begins to play a more significant part. Favourable environments stimulate children to reach their intellectual potential. Given that most adoptive families provide children with greater material, interactive and educational opportunities than they might have expected if they had stayed with their disadvantaged biological families, IQs are generally above their expected levels in terms of the children's socio-economic birth backgrounds, although their scores still correlate positively with their biological parents.

In the case of personality traits, temperaments and social behaviour matters become both more difficult and interesting. Behavioural geneticists still believe that genes and inheritance play an important role but the environment mediates their expression to produce wide ranges of behaviour. And as environments can be both:

(1) *shared* – for example, children can receive similar styles of parenting, schooling, etc. which act to make individuals similar, and

(2) *non-shared* – for example, children can receive as well as generate different environmental experiences in the form of non-shared peers, different parental reactions, chance encounters, etc. final outcomes can vary considerably even between siblings raised in the same family. Non-shared environments, often selected and created by the individual and his/her inherited predispositions, are those that act to make people different.

Full siblings are much less alike than their shared 50% of genes might predict, though they are more alike than they are to their adopted siblings with whom they share no genes. The conclusion is that shared family influences, in fact, play only a very small part in individual development. At first sight, this might seem strange. On the face of it, it might appear that siblings growing up in the same family share the same environment and therefore might expect to have many characteristics in common. 'However, this represents a misunderstanding of what is meant by non-shared. The effects may stem from some general feature (such as discord or deprivation) but the effects can be non-shared if they impinge differently on different siblings because, for example, siblings vary in age or temperament or parental expectation ... Family discord represents a shared factor to the extent that all children in a family are exposed to it and experience similar effects from it. However, it is possible that siblings may also have unique responses to the discord for various reasons such as differences in age or temperament' (Rende & Plomin, 1994: p. 40).

Studies of adopted children have helped scientists appreciate how genes affect experience and experience affects genes. Even more intriguing is the realisation that genes contribute to the character and quality of an individual's experience, thereby generating an environment unique to that person – their non-shared environment. As we have seen, genetics helps people actively select, modify and create particular environments both by design and default. Even in the case of identical twins who share all of their genes, small differences in the way parents, siblings and peers react to them in effect create minor differences in their social environment. Although monozygotic twins remain much more alike than unalike, these small differences can be enough to reduce their similarity on some traits from 100% down to values of 75–80%. Such differences become even greater if identical twins are raised apart.

But – and this reminds us that genes are still doing their work, albeit in a much more interactive way than previously imagined – identical twins *raised apart by different parents* bring about similarities in their social environment! There is a high degree of correlation between reared-apart twins (but not reared apart unrelated children) and their perceptions and experiences of family life. In other words, shared inherited personality traits cause the different parents to react to each twin in a similar way, even though the two sets of parents share no genetic temperamental qualities (Plomin, 1994: p. 54). This is an example of a *reactive gene–environment correlation*. These occur when other people, whether genetically related or not, react to children on the basis of children's inherited predispositions and proclivities. In a real sense, in the case of both reactive and active gene-environment correlations, *genes bring about their own environment*. In turn, the environment generated by that genetic predisposition then affects that individual's development.

Thus, most psychological variance between individuals comes about through different experiences of the environment. But because to a large extent, individuals are selecting and creating their environments to suit their predispositions, experience is also being guided by the individual's inherited genetic proclivities. Bouchard *et al.* (1990: p. 227, emphasis added) quote and agree with Martin *et al.* (1996) who see 'humans as exploring organisms whose innate abilities and predispositions help them select what is relevant and adaptive from the range of opportunities and stimuli presented in the environment. *The effects of mobility and learning, therefore, augment rather than eradicate the effects of the genotype on behavior.*'

Adoption: risk and protection factors

We might conclude, therefore, from this examination of gene–environment correlations and interactions that adoption is acting as a major protection factor for many children. Comparisons between children from disadvantaged material and psychosocial backgrounds, some of whom were adopted by more advantaged families and some of whom remained with their biological parents, reveal the developmental and behavioural benefits accruing to the adopted children. Adopted children achieve higher IQ scores, lower rates of criminal behaviour and fewer psychiatric hospital admissions than their non-adopted controlled counterparts. Whatever genetic risk factors adopted children bring with them, the interactional qualities generated by their more advantaged adoptive families act as a developmental protection factor. Rates of antisocial behaviour are much lower than expected, though still higher than for non-adopted children raised in families of similar socio-economic standing to that of the adoptive homes.

It is not adoption itself that is acting as a preventative measure. Indeed, as we shall see in later chapters, the knowledge of being adopted may in fact be a psychosocial risk factor. Rather, for children from severely depriving and damaging family backgrounds, it is the psychosocial environment provided by adopters and with which adopted children interact, that appears to be protective (Rutter, 1995a: p. 26). It might also be the case that the coherent and positive 'internal working models' that children are able to build in secure, responsive and consistent social environments allow them to develop a stronger sense of self-control, self-confidence and basic trust. This improves social competence and helps children deal with future environmental stressors (Wachs, 1992: p. 122). Self-esteem and secure attachments are recognised resilience factors that help children cope with adversity. Adoption, therefore, can also act as a psychosocial protection factor by improving children's resilience.

Chapter 4

Children Adopted as Babies: Environmental Influences on Development

Once babies are placed with their adoptive parents, passive gene–environment correlations no longer play a part. There are no genetic links between parent and child. Therefore, the social environment initially created by the adoptive parents can be regarded as independent, having an influence on the child that is free of any inherited transmissions. To the extent that adopted children assume characteristics that are more like their adopters than their biological parents, then it is reasonable to assume that those traits have been influenced by experience. In the previous chapter, we regarded genes as a pre-placement input – things that the child brought with him or her. But it soon becomes apparent that children's inherited characteristics continue to play a part in what happens after they are placed. Genes interact with the environment; children and their traits influence and are influenced by parents, family and peers. So the previous chapter, although ostensibly about genes, was equally about the impact of the environment on cognitive and personality development.

More traditionally, studies of post-placement influences on adoption outcomes have examined the relationship between the characteristics of adopters and the behaviour, feelings and attitudes of their adopted children. Whereas behavioural genetics has been driven by a scientific interest in human development, research that has looked at success and failure in adoptions has been more inspired by the need to develop good policy and practice in the field of child placement. These studies have attempted to identify what factors appear to contribute to successful adoptions.

In the case of baby adoptions, what adoptive parents are like, the kinds of family life they create and how they handle the implications of being adopted, all add to the quality and character of the post-placement environment. So, although the adoptive parents' qualities and behaviours are the product of their own inheritance and experience, the immediate concern is to identify the characteristics that lead to successful placement outcomes. This produces a very different kind of research conducted by investigators whose backgrounds and interests are in social work, social policy and the applied social sciences. The aim is not to unravel the subtleties of gene–environment interactions but to understand and improve adoption practice.

The research has focused on two main areas: (1) the characteristics of the adopters and their families, and (2) the way the experience of being an adoptive parent and child is handled by the adopters. Clearly, these two elements are linked. The meaning given to adoption and the way parents help their children deal with it will be affected by the parents' own experiences and personality. In contrast to behavioural genetics, less attention has been paid to the qualities of the child as they might affect the outcome. It is the characteristics of adoptive parents that have received most attention. The baby-adopted child is seen as the passive recipient and end product of appropriate and inappropriate parenting practices. This is understandable given that adoption-workers can select who adopts but have little choice in who is available for adoption.

Environmental influences on baby-adopted children's development

Research that has examined how adopted children develop and perform in terms of the character and behaviour of adopters and adoptive family life is described under the following five headings:

(1) Socio-economic status of the adopters.
(2) Physical characteristics of the adopters.
(3) Adopters as parents.
(4) Composition of the adoptive family.
(5) Coping with the meaning of adoption.

Socio-economic status of the adopters

At the time of placement most adopters are able to provide their children with good material standards. For most children, adoption represents a marked shift up the socio-economic scale from their family of origin. Of course, material standards *between* adopters do differ. However, findings about whether or not these differences affect adopted children's psychosocial development remain inconclusive and difficult to interpret.

The children of fathers in higher socio-economic occupations have higher social adjustment levels than those of manual jobs according to Raynor (1980: p. 72). However, other studies report the opposite association to be the case (for example, Kornitzer 1968; Jaffee & Fanshel, 1970). In their study of 100 white adopted children, Hoopes *et al.* (1970) found that the social class of the adopters had a bearing on some outcome measures. Adopted children from the higher socio-economic status families appeared better adjusted to school life. They also achieved stronger academic successes. However, socio-economic status 'was not ... related to the scores on the California Tests of Mental Maturity or Personality. So, it is possible that this relationship holds only for adjustment in school, where upper middle-class family styles are more congenial for the child's adjustment in school...' (Hoopes *et al.*, 1970: p. 53).

McWhinnie (1967: pp. 203–7) found no relationship between the 'financial circumstances' of adoptive families and the adjustment levels of adopted children. Well-adjusted and poorly-adjusted children were equally likely to be living with parents with or without financial worries. Although not commenting on the adopted children's social adjustment, Raynor (1980: p. 56) did report that levels of satisfaction were higher amongst the adopted children of professional and managerial fathers than those of semi-skilled manual workers.

Overall, little or no significant associations appear to exist between adopters' socio-economic status and the social adjustment levels of their baby-adopted children. Raynor accepts this possibility and concludes that rather than class, such factors as the quality of parenting are probably more important.

Physical characteristics of the adopters

The age and health of adopters have been examined in a number of studies. The mean age of adoptive mothers at the time of the adopted child's birth is considerably higher than that of birth mothers. For example, in Fergusson's (1995) New Zealand studies, the mean maternal age of adopters was 30 years and for birth mothers it was 19 years. The worry is that older parents are more likely to suffer ill health and that this will affect their ability to care for their children. Seglow *et al.* (1972: p. 98) found that a third of adoptive mothers were in poor health when their adopted children were aged seven years. The researchers estimated that at least one in ten adoptive mothers had experienced a mental health problem. Comparisons with the general population were felt to be difficult, but it seemed 'that among the mothers there was a high incidence of poor health, whereas the fathers' health, considering their age, seemed fairly good' (Seglow *et al.*, 1972: pp. 98–99). It was also found that rates of poor health were significantly higher amongst adoptive mothers who were infertile.

However, the evidence seems to suggest that the age of the adoptive mother at the time of placement is not a good predictor of adopted children's future levels of social adjustment. Seglow *et al.* (1972: p. 95) felt that the age of the adopters was not a significant factor in terms of adopted children's progress, at least up until the age of eight or nine years. Similar conclusions were reached by Hoopes *et al.* (1970: p. 50) who said 'that the data from their study do not support the contention that the older age of adoptive parents leads to poorer adjustment in the children.'

In a further analysis of her data, McWhinnie (1967: p. 39) did find that although age of adoptive parents at the time of placement did not appear particularly significant, length of marriage did. Couples of the same age but married longer produced a higher proportion of successful placements. McWhinnie believed the success was higher for adopted couples who had more time to adjust to their infertility.

From the viewpoint of adopted children, Raynor (1980: p. 55), when talking to adult-adopted people, found that their level of satisfaction dropped with the mother's increasing age. 'Nine out of ten with a mother under 30 at the time of placement were satisfied with the adoption, but this was true of only two in every three whose mothers were 40 or above' (1980: p. 55). The children who felt less happy having relatively old parents said that they were conscious of the age difference, their parents inability to be physically active, and being out of touch with 'modern trends.'

Adopters as parents

One of the most regular and widespread findings that adoption researchers report is that the quality and style of parenting that adopters employ has a profound affect on the outcome. Within this perspective we can include ways of handling children, feelings about adoption, issues around infertility, and the relationship between parents. Indeed, Seglow *et al.* (1972: p. 31) believe that the 'age, income and social class of the adopters are far less important.'

Much more critical, according to Jacka (1973), is that adopters have 'the right attitude' to children. Warmth and acceptance, and a sensible attitude to infertility, illegitimacy and birth parents are positively associated with the adopted child's sound development (McWhinnie, 1967; Tizard, 1977; Lambert & Streather, 1980). Berry (1992), reviewing a 1968 study by Ripple, notes that poorer adjustment was observed in children whose adoptive parents were not judged high on warmth or feeling positive about the child. She goes on to say:

'...serious child behavior problems were more likely when, at placement, parents had been angry about their childlessness ... Also predictive of later difficulties were a non-positive initial reaction to the child, a negative reaction to the former foster parents, or the absence of the adoptive father on placement day. About half of the children with later behavior problems had early placement difficulties, compared to 12% of well-adjusted children.'

(Berry, 1992 p. 530)

However, the interpretation of these findings may not be always as obvious as they appear at first sight. Maurer *et al.* (1980) remind us that temperamentally difficult children can cause poor parenting every bit as poor parenting can lead to difficult children. A third variation recognises that some parents describe their children as difficult when objectively this appears not to be the case.

The effect of adopters' parenting and the quality of family life on the developmental pathways taken by adopted children will be considered under the following three headings: infertility, adopters' marriage, and parenting attitudes and skills.

Infertility

The loss of the ability to produce a child of one's own requires a period of grief and mourning. Failure to resolve and adjust to feelings of the loss can interfere with the ability of adopters to parent effectively and appropriately. It may also mean that they are less able to help their child cope with their feelings of loss that are part and parcel of being adopted. Brinich (1990) also observes that in the aftermath of failed infertility treatment, parents who learn of their infertility and decide to adopt are then subjected to a further round of investigations before they can be approved as adopters. Feelings of inadequacy, anger, resentment and guilt over yet another intrusive experience are quite normal. Often these feelings can interfere with the adopters' ability to settle in with their newly placed baby. The strong feelings associated with the adoption process can become suppressed, though they surface if the hopes and expectations of being a parent are upset. Babies who cry and demand a great deal and children who soon begin to assert their independence and own needs can easily trigger unresolved feelings. All of these can put a strain on the marriage as well as the couple's ability to parent. The adopted child becomes an expression of the parents' sense of failure. Feelings of anger and hostility are then projected onto the child.

Brebner *et al.* (1985) report that the diagnosis of infertility was a traumatic event in the lives of the 20 couples whom they interviewed. The psychological task at the heart of the infertile couple's adjustment is to mourn the loss and revise their own self-identity. The study showed that in 'the immediate post-placement period there were dynamic forces from the blow of infertility still at work in some of the adoptive parents which could lead to future problems in their relationship with their adopted child' (Brebner *et al.*, 1985: p. 11). Two inappropriate reasons for adopting were found amongst some of the couples: the hope that adoption would cure infertility, and the wish to please a marriage partner.

The ability of adoptive mothers and fathers to discuss and accept infertility was measured by Hoopes *et al.* (1970: pp. 55–56). The

surprising result was that whether or not adoptive mothers had
adjusted to their loss did not appear to have a bearing on the adopted
child's later functioning. In contrast, the ability of adoptive fathers to
discuss and accept their infertility did appear to have a marked affect on
the adopted children's levels of adjustment. The study went on to
recognise that failure to discuss and accept infertility leads to certain
kinds of problems in the father–child relationship. The more poorly
adjusted fathers were more critical of their adopted children. In turn,
children of critical fathers showed poorer levels of personal adjustment,
social adjustment and academic performances at school.

> 'In this sample ... it was clear that when the father's feelings about
> providing blood continuity in the family were unresolved he was
> later critical of the adopted child, and this in turn affected the child
> adversely. It may be that the mother, through early feeding and
> caring for the infant, establishes a kind of link which the father is not
> able to do.'

(Hoopes *et al.*, 1970: p. 80)

Echoes of these adjustment and acceptance problems in infertile
parents might be detected in a number of earlier studies that found
more adopters, given a choice, preferred to adopt a girl rather than a
boy (Brenner, 1951, cited in Seglow *et al.*, 1972; Kirk, 1964; Jaffee &
Fanshel, 1970). Bohman (1970) also noted in his study that the reluc-
tance to adopt a boy was greater if the infertile partner was the man.
Women also tended to prefer adopting a girl if they were infertile.
Another insight into this phenomenon is offered by Seglow *et al.*
(1972). In the National Child Development Study, 22% of adopters of
eight to nine year-olds expressed doubts about the adoption.
Dissatisfaction was higher if the adopted child was a boy. In their
discussion of this issue, Lambert & Streather (1980: p. 43) wonder
whether these dissatisfactions arise as a result of parents having to
adopt boys against their preference for a girl.

Whatever the interpretation, we have a number of pieces of evidence
that when linked suggest that parental attitudes may be affected by
their feelings about being infertile, particularly in the case of adoptive
fathers. Negative parental attitudes adversely affect the quality of
relationships that parents have with their children. Poor quality parent–
child relationships lead to reduced levels of psychosocial adjustment
and problem behaviour in children.

Adopters' marriage

The quality of the relationship between parents forms a major part of
the family's emotional and social climate. It not only affects the feelings
of mothers and fathers towards each other but it can also influence the

way each of them relates to their children. Moreover, children are aware of and sensitive to what is happening between their parents. Accurately or inaccurately, they often feel that in some way they might be contributing to or responsible for their parents' relationship. Thus, in a number of rather complex ways, it matters to children how their parents are getting on.

In adoption research, the basic finding has been that the more stable and cohesive the relationship between adoptive parents, the more successful the child's outcome along most adjustment measures (Brenner, 1951 cited in Seglow *et al.*, 1972; Witmer *et al.*, 1963).

It is often speculated that adopted children who have already had to adjust to one major parental loss, are particularly vulnerable to a second. Levels of stress therefore might be expected to be particularly high for adopted children whose parents either die, desert or divorce. Seglow *et al.* (1972: p. 96) report that by the time the children had reached the age of seven, about 7% were no longer living with both their adoptive parents.

Hoopes *et al.* (1970: p. 58) showed that role compatibility in decision-making between parents was positively correlated with the child's personal and social adjustment. Parents who enjoyed a high degree of compatibility tended to have children who were better adjusted than children of less compatible parents. Similar findings extend to children's attitudes to school and even their own adoption. Parental role incompatibility was associated with children who had a somewhat more negative view of adoption:

> '... the children of parents showing relatively high degree of warmth and affection tend to be better adjusted. Thus, the child's adjustment can be seen as a dependent variable in which variation in child scores are explained in some degree by variations in parental warmth and affection.'
>
> (Hoopes *et al.*, 1970: p. 60)

That the quality of relationships between parents affects children's socio-emotional states is not surprising. McWhinnie (1967) reached similar conclusions arguing that it was essential that marriages should be stable, happy and mutually satisfying. However, she does remind us that not only might parents affect children but that children might also affect parents. She found evidence that adoption could put extra strains on a marriage. 'There was evidence too that some couples seeking to adopt a child did so because of incompatibilities in the marriage' (McWhinnie, 1967: p. 261). The quality of relationships between family members certainly has an affect on adopted children's social development, but we must not forget that children's predispositions and experiences make them active participants in the generation of these relationships. Relationships are where we learn about ourselves.

As children, if people react negatively to us (for whatever reasons), we learn to see ourselves negatively.

Quality of parenting: attitudes, skills and expectations

Whereas what goes on between parents creates an indirect emotional climate in which children grow, much of what parents say, do, think and feel is aimed directly at children. The quality of the relationship between parent and child is recognised as one of the major experiences that affects psychosocial development. In her study of 58 adopted people, McWhinnie (1967: p. 261) felt that responsive parenting produced better adjusted children. Her formula for effective child-rearing included parents offering their children emotional security and acceptance, consistent discipline, encouragement, and freedom for children to develop along their own lines. To succeed with this formula, McWhinnie felt that both parents had to be equally enthusiastic about adopting a child and that their main motive had to be one of love for children.

These recommendations turn out to have been rather prescient. Twenty five years later, Wachs (1992: p. 36), reviewing the research on effective parenting, echoes much of McWhinnie's findings on what produces a successful adoption. Parental sensitivity and responsivity promote secure attachments, high self-esteem and self-confidence and problem-solving competence. Parental control strategies also prove critical in helping children to cope with their own behaviour and emotions. What are known as 'power assertive control strategies' (anger, shouting, smacking, sarcasm, criticism) often lead to poor impulse control and less compliance. Strategies which employ reciprocity (give and take), reasoning and suggestions appear much more successful in helping children achieve impulse control, compliance and self-reliance. 'Consistently harsh parental *punishment*, *rejection* of the child, and, *inconsistent discipline* tend to predispose to antisocial, aggressive, and delinquent behaviour on the part of the child' (Wachs, 1992: p. 37, emphasis original). Bagley (1993: p. 55) also observes that the level of self-esteem in adopted children correlates with parental love and warmth; consistency of norms and rules governing behaviour; and consistent reactions to rule-breaking.

In the 5% of cases in which parents found the experience of adopting 'very unsatisfactory', Raynor (1980: p. 37) observed that the attitudes of the adopters to their child were cool or critical. One father felt from the beginning that an adopted child would never amount to much. An extremely rigid adoptive mother and a marriage breakdown was the home environment in which one rejected son was raised. 'Fathers seemed to come into conflict with adopted children, usually sons, much more often than mothers, especially in [the] matter of moulding a child to their ways' (Raynor, 1980: p. 39). Indeed, it seemed to Raynor that parents who felt that their adopted child was similar to them or their family in some way such as looks, intelligence, talents, were more inclined to view the adoption as a highly satisfactory experience. Perceived differences appeared to act as a barrier: 'he always seemed different to the rest of our family'; 'she never really belonged.'

Hoopes *et al.* (1970: pp. 61–62) found that the levels of adoptive mothers' warmth, affection and ability to demonstrate love were positively associated with adopted children's personal and social adjustment scores. Adoptive parents, particularly infertile couples, also need to feel that they are 'entitled' to their child (Jaffee & Fanshel, 1970). Research findings, therefore, hint at a number of factors in both the adopters' own experience and that of their children, that might affect their attitudes and parenting skills.

A balance between acceptance and expectation of children is not always easy to maintain. The more parents expect children to turn out one way rather than another, the greater will be the tension between children as they are and as their parents would prefer them to be. Inappropriate expectations place adopted children under stress. Lacking a shared genetic inheritance the mismatch between what adopters want and what adopted children can do can become quite pronounced. The more demanding and discrepant the expectations, the more likely it will be that the adopted child has problems of adjustment (McWhinnie, 1967: p. 217; Mandell, 1973; Seglow *et al.*, 1972).

Hoopes *et al.* (1970: p. 77) point out that their 100 adoptive parents were primarily from the middle and upper classes, 'soundly educated and economically secure.' These parents were said to value achievement and social cooperation. Ideally, the researchers believed that parents should accept children for themselves and help them develop their own talents and potentials. In most families this, indeed, seemed to be the case. But they observed that some adopters had unduly high expectations of their adopted child's intellectual and academic abilities. These children tended to show a more negative attitudes toward school, produce poorer work and had adjustment problems at school (Hoopes *et al.*, 1970: p. 57). To emphasise the point, the study notes that whereas 19% of a control group of middle class non-adopted children had IQs in the range 130–149, only 7% of the adopted children fell into this range. The opportunities for mismatched expectations were therefore high. Not being able to live up to parental expectations was felt to be a particular problem for some adopted children.

But in spite of the regular claims by researchers that the skills and sensitivities of adoptive parents appear to be extremely important factors in affecting outcomes, surprisingly few studies have investigated the relationships between parenting skills, children's adjustment levels and socio-emotional development. It may be that the findings of mainstream developmental research on effective parenting, quite reasonably, are taken to apply with equal force to adoptive parent-child relations and there is little need to treat the parenting practices of adopters as different. Certainly Raynor believed this when she concluded:

> 'Relationships in the family are ... central ... The emotional climate in the home and the young person's estimate of his status in the family while growing up were both closely linked with present adjustment. Where there had been an atmosphere of well-being and security in the home four in five children had grown up into well-adjusted adults. Only a little more than half were now doing well if they came from homes characterised by conflict, worry, insecurity or pessimism.'

(Raynor, 1980: p. 74)

In her 1992 review, Berry reached similar conclusions. She identified six parental factors at placement that contributed to a positive outcome: 'satisfaction with parental role, acceptance of adoptive role, communication on adoption, warmth toward child, role compatibility in parental decision making, and the couple's satisfaction in marriage' (Berry, 1992: p. 531).

Composition of the adoptive family

The main interest in family composition has been in family size and sibling environment. Families that have adopted babies have tended to be small, the majority having just one or two children. In the National Child Development Study, 82% of adoptive families consisted of one or two children compared to only 43% of families made up of biological 'legitimate' children (Seglow *et al.*, 1972: p. 85). This also meant that fewer adopted children lived in overcrowded conditions than either 'legitimate' or 'illegitimate' children.

There is little evidence that the relatively high number of 'only children' among those adopted increases their adjustment problems. However, Bohman (1970: p. 184) found that being male, adopted and an only child appeared to increase the risk of adjustment difficulties while of school age. 'No such association was found for the girls, for whom the tendency if anything was the opposite.' In fact, Hoopes and her colleagues (1970: p. 48) found slightly higher levels of adjustment amongst the 'only' children compared to those who had brothers and sisters.

The presence of siblings who are the biological children of the adopters has been found to be a risk factor for adopted children in some studies (for example, McWhinnie, 1967) but not in others (Bohman, 1970; Raynor, 1980). Hoopes *et al.* (1970: p. 53) did not find a significant relationship between the presence of biologically-born siblings and social adjustment levels in adopted children. What they did find, though, was that when there were 'born' siblings present, adopted children tended to hold more negative views about adoption. The authors observe:

'...that there is perhaps some resentment on the part of certain adopted children, for reasons real or imaginary, toward adoption when there are natural children in the home ... It should be reiterated, however, that the presence of natural children had no effect on the adopted child's emotional or school adjustment.'

(Hoopes *et al.*, 1970: p. 53)

As part of a study which looked at parent-reported problem behaviours in adolescent adopted children, Howe (1997) identified two groups amongst those who had been adopted as babies. There was a large group of adolescents who exhibited *no* serious problem behaviours during adolescence, either at home or school. The second group was made up of a smaller number of children who did show problem behaviours. The mean number of problem behaviours shown by this second subgroup was 2.7 out of a maximum of 10 (compared to a score of 0.0 out of 10 for the no-problem group). Of the children in the problem-group, 63.3% were referred to the mental health services at some time during their adolescence. Parents of these more problematic children often described them as 'difficult.'

The data collected revealed only one significant risk factor in baby adoptions – the presence of siblings who were the biological children of the adoptive parents. Adopted children who had non-adopted siblings were twice as likely to show at least one behaviour or psychiatric problem during adolescence compared to those children who were placed with families where there were no birth children of the adoptive parents. Twice as many problem children had at least one sibling who was the biological child of the adopters. Three times as many problem behaviour children had at least one sibling who was a biological child of the adopters born *after* the placement. The total number of adopted and birth children in the family (the size of the sibling group) was not associated with problem behaviour. In adoptive families in which there were no biological children, only 14.7% of children adopted as babies displayed either a behaviour or psychiatric problem. In families where there was at least one biological child, this figure rose significantly to 40.4%. Other studies have also found that the presence of biological children is associated with increased breakdown rates as well as behaviour problems (Trasler, 1960; Parker, 1966). In contrast, the presence of other adopted children, particularly those placed after the child joined his or her family appeared to act as a slight protection factor.

Coping with the meaning of adoption

A number of investigators have explored how children and their
adoptive parents handle what it means to be adopted and what it means
to adopt. They fall into two groups. There are those who recognise the
importance of these questions from their clinical work with adoptive
families, and there are social science researchers who are interested in
adoption as a social phenomenon. In both cases, it is recognised that
many issues surrounding people's experience of adoption involve loss
of one kind or another.

One of the first people to study how parents and children handle
adoption was Kirk, an adoptive parent himself as well as a sociologist.
He realised that people who decide to adopt, particularly childless
couples adopting babies, have to cope with a number of difficulties.
They have to approach other people to acquire a child. They are not
certain about the status of the parent in adoption. And they are unclear
about the status of their relationship with the adopted child (Kirk,
1964; 1981). To some extent, these issues may act as a handicap in
people's performance of the role of parent. Kirk points out that
adopters are faced with conflicting obligations. They are required to
integrate the child fully into their family. But they are also expected to
tell their child that they are adopted and that in some way they are
'*different*'. There is therefore a tension between integration and dif-
ferentiation that both parents and child have to try and resolve. Kirk
also calls this 'the paradox of adoption'. From the children's point of
view, they have to reflect on the fact that they are both chosen (by the
adopters) *and* given up (by the birth parents). Thus, both parents and
children have to handle a number of conflicts and tensions which can
affect parent–child interactions.

In his early formulations, Kirk (1964), in a meta-analysis of his
research studies of over 2000 adoptive families, believed that adopters
resolved the tension in one or other of two ways: by rejecting 'difference' or by acknowledging 'difference' (low versus high distinguishing
families according to Kaye, 1990).

Rejection of difference covers adopters who *deny* that there is any
difference between adopted and non-adopted children; that the fact of
being adopted is not seen as a relevant difference. The parents cope
with the role handicaps of adoptive parenthood by taking the 'sting'
out of adoption 'by simulating non-adoptive family life as closely as
possible' (Brodzinsky, 1990: p. 19). The argument is that denial and the
rejection of difference may help assuage the pain of loss and infertility
but in the long run it undermines the child's integration into the family.
This strategy may be effective while children are young, but by the time
they reach adolescence and begin to ponder on such matters as origins
and identity, problems can arise.

'It has been generally assumed that adolescence would constitute a period of increased vulnerability for adoptees, with its concerns over issues of identity. The higher rates of anxiety and emotional problems among adoptees at age 16 would be consistent with this view. Insofar as their poor ratings do reflect stresses associated with coming to terms with adoptive status, however, the findings suggest that this process may have begun considerably earlier.'

(Maughan & Pickles, 1990: p. 56)

'Telling'

It becomes difficult for adolescents who are not encouraged, allowed or supported to reflect on their adoption. Parents in these cases find it difficult to talk about adoption matters with their children and fail to empathise with their situation. It leaves no room for adopted children to express grief, anger and loss. They find it difficult to work out the nature of their relationship with their adoptive parents. All of which impairs their ability to resolve the tensions and feel more secure (Kaye, 1990). According to Triseliotis (1973), an understanding of our past helps us develop a complete sense of self. Adopted children, he argued, should be given full information about their origins and background. Lack of opportunity to examine one's identity and roots produces 'genealogical bewilderment' (Sants, 1972; Brinich, 1980). Adopted children may not feel secure enough to differ from their adoptive parents and for this difference not to be perceived as threatening. One way for adopted children to deal with this dilemma is to collude with their parents and also deny that there is any relevant difference. In more extreme cases, parents may not 'tell' their children that they are adopted or they provide background information reluctantly or in a very incomplete fashion. Both Sants (1964) and McWhinnie (1967) felt that not 'telling' results in bewilderment, confusion and poor mental health.

Adopted adults in Raynor's (1980: p. 60) study were inclined to feel more satisfied if they thought that their parents 'accepted their backgrounds'. If children believed that their parents were critical or disapproving of their birth parents, they were more likely to evaluate their adoption negatively. Interestingly, and contrary to findings reported for older placed children, Raynor found that 'of the 23 adoptees who expressed interest in contacting their birth parents nearly 40% were dissatisfied with their adoption, whereas of the much larger number who expressed no such interest only 11% were dissatisfied' (1980: p. 61). She also observed that adopted people were better adjusted if their parents had met the birth mother and felt positive about the contact. However, Raynor (1980: p. 146) concluded that the value of contact between adopters and birth parents was not entirely proven. The adopters' ability to feel 'entitled' to their child was enhanced in some cases where they had met the biological parent, but impaired in others.

Parents' ability to talk about adoption also affected how well they 'told' their child about being adopted. Although many adopted people felt that their parents were uncomfortable discussing adoption, even amongst those deemed to be well-adjusted, levels of poor adjustment increased if the adopted person reported that their parents seemed ill-at-ease talking about their adoption (Raynor, 1980: p. 77). A surprising 60% of adopters said that they had kept some information back from their child about some aspect of their background. Faint but persistent feelings of insecurity continued to affect many adopters, even when relationships with their children were good. A vague fear of 'losing' their son or daughter to the birth mother if contact was made, no matter how unlikely, lay at the back of many adopters' minds. 'In summing up it must be said that many adoptive parents and children in the study had a great deal of difficulty in talking with each other about the child's background and adoptive status' (Raynor, 1980: p. 102). Parents worried that open discussion might threaten the child's sense of belonging. If adopted adolescents felt that the problem of discussing their adoption was particularly chronic their level of social adjustment tended to worsen.

If children sense that the subject of adoption makes their parents feel anxious, they may suppress any mention of matters that clearly carry a high emotional charge. Anxiety in parents causes anxiety in children who may fear a second rejection. This refusal to face up to and deal with highly pertinent information can distort relationships and interfere with the ability of adopted children to establish a clear self-identity. Rejection of difference therefore frustrates opportunities for the adopted child to discuss a centrally important topic. In some cases, the feeling begins to emerge that to be different is somehow to be either deficient or deviant. 'Difference' receives a negative connotation. Some children handle this negativity by denying important aspects of being adopted. However, these coping strategies can affect children's self-esteem and ability to adjust to the realities of what it means to be adopted. Brinich (1990: p. 7), in his clinical experience, found that in such cases adopters accepted certain aspects of their child while rejecting others. The bits of the child they did not like were projected onto the child's biological inheritance: 'she doesn't get that from us.'

Acknowledgement of difference occurs when parents recognise that there are aspects of adoptive family life which are different to family life in which children are biologically born to the parents. Kirk (1981: pp. 46–47) believes that parents who are able to acknowledge difference can relate and communicate more openly and accurately with their adopted children. They are also able to empathise with their children.

Empathy and good communication are associated with readiness on the part of the adopters to think about and acknowledge their children's birth parents, their roots and origins (Kirk, 1964: p. 95). What at first sight might appear paradoxical – that acknowledging difference promotes integration – makes sense in terms of allowing sensitive, responsive relationships to develop between parents and children. To acknowledge difference is not to give it a negative connotation. It is simply to accept that it is present. It gives children a stronger sense of identity and of who they are.

Brodzinsky (1987) develops Kirk's classification by adding a third strategy in which some adopters not only acknowledge difference but accentuate it. He calls this adverse coping strategy *insistence of difference*. Adopted children are not seen as an integral part of family life. Children may 'see themselves as so different from their parents and siblings that they feel totally alien within the family; they may be unable to find anything within the adoptive parents with which to identify; they may feel psychologically rejected and abandoned in the midst of their own family' (Brodzinsky, 1987: p. 42). Further studies have suggested that the children of adoptive mothers who display an 'insistence of difference' pattern have lower levels of social competence and higher behavioural problems than children who experience either of the other two strategies (Brodzinsky & Reeves, 1987 cited in Brodzinsky, 1990).

In his research, Kaye (1990) also refined Kirk's original two-fold classification. Without denying that some adopters do reject difference while others acknowledge it, he found that most parents and children expressed a mixture of high and low distinguishing strategies. He felt that low distinguishing families were not necessarily 'rejection of difference' families. It seems that in some families adoption has not been a major distinguishing factor, not because denial is taking place but that 'difference' really is not looming large in the conduct of family relationships.

> 'So "openness" is certainly important. But there is no evidence that asserting "I don't feel that I myself or my relationships with my family are different in any important way because I'm (or he's or she's) adopted" has anything to do with a lack of open family communication ... For at least some adolescents, and probably for their parents as well, "denial of difference" is simply a manifestation of actually not having experienced many negative experiences, rather than of having repressed them ... Perhaps the *moderately* acknowledging, are the best adapted adoptees'
>
> (Kaye, 1990: p. 140)

McWhinnie (1967: p. 265) had reached similar conclusions over twenty years earlier: 'Although those interviewed wanted to be told of their status, they did not want frequent discussion of it at home.' But perhaps Kaye's most important observation is that the ability of adopted children to develop a strong, secure sense of self is inseparable from them having a strong sense of belonging.

Reviewing the research triggered by Kirk's original classification, Brodzinsky (1990: p. 21) concludes that perhaps while children are young, 'rejection of difference' coping patterns 'may serve the family well by supporting the primary socialization goals of building family unity, connectedness, and interpersonal trust.' But in later stages of the family life cycle when the full meaning of adoption becomes apparent to the child, rejection of difference may be a much less successful strategy. Openness, honesty and acknowledgment of difference form a more effective basis of communication.

Brodzinsky's (1987; 1990) work in this area helped him develop 'a stress and coping model of adoption adjustment'. The model adapts Erikson's (1963) work on psychosocial development.

'The basic thesis of the model is that the experience of adoption exposes parents and children to a unique set of psychosocial tasks that interact with and complicate the more universal developmental tasks of family life ... it is assumed that the degree to which adoptive parents and their children acknowledge the unique challenges in their life, and the way in which they attempt to cope with them, largely determines their pattern of adjustment.'

(Brodzinsky, 1987: p. 30)

Thus, the adopted child has the same developmental tasks as the non-adopted child plus few more in addition that are peculiar to being adopted. The successful negotiation of these extra tasks requires adopters to be responsive and empathic, accepting and flexible. Adopted children have to work out what adoption means to them and other people in order to work out who they are, both to themselves and others. If they are successful in this, self-esteem and self-confidence – both known to be major protection factors – increase.

Brodzinsky, like McWhinnie (1967) before him, believes that there is a 'psychological risk factor' in being adopted; that there are stresses associated with adoption. Of course, this does not mean that all children will run into difficulties. It simply reminds us that adoption carries extra information about oneself, the meaning of which has to be handled and interpreted. Loss is a central feature of the adoptive experience for both parents and children. Infertile parents have to adjust to the 'loss' of the child they wanted but never had. Children have to understand the 'loss' of their first parents and what this signifies and means. As children begin to understand the full implications of this original loss, it conjures up the potential loss of stability in the relationship they have with their adoptive parents. Loss, in turn, creates stress which increases people's emotional vulnerability. Some of the psychosocial difficulties that adopted children experience can therefore be seen as simply the 'manifestation of an adaptive grieving process' (Brodzinsky, 1990: p. 7).

The meaning of being adopted is not fully understood until adolescence. 'Telling' children about their adoption in early school years is fine, but cognitively children are not ready to appreciate all that is connoted by being adopted.

'Preschool age children tend to focus primarily on being adopted by their parents – that is, being incorporated into their new family. This focus parallels the nature of the story presented by most adoptive parents which emphasizes aspects of family building and minimizes aspects concerning the birth mother's surrender of the child. As children mature cognitively, however, their capacity for understanding logical reciprocity leads them to a profound insight – to be adopted, one first must be relinquished or surrendered. *Thus in the elementary school years, children view adoption not only in terms of family building, but also in terms of family loss.*'

(Brodzinsky, 1990: p. 13, emphasis original)

The impact of realising the true nature of the loss can lead to behavioural, emotional and attitudinal changes. *There seems no getting away from the fact that your biological parents, for whatever reason, either chose not to look after you or even worse, rejected you. The anxiety is that this might say as much about you and your desirability as it does about them and their lack of commitment.* Ambivalence about being adopted can therefore occur. Some children may feel angry and restless. This, believe people like Brinich and Brodzinsky, is part of the normal adaptive grieving process experienced by all people who have experienced a significant loss. This sense of loss may increase in adolescence as adopted children realise that they are disconnected genealogically. This can interfere with the normal attempts in the teenage years to establish a clear, autonomous identity for one's self.

Brodzinsky, Brinich and others use this model to account for the relatively high rates of problem behaviour seen in adopted children compared to control groups of non-adopted children. An element of insecurity may remain in many adopted people's relationships with others. There is a 'fear of abandonment' that can make adopted people 'hang on to unsuitable friendships and romantic relationships' (Cullom-Long cited in Bagley, 1993: p. 68). Some adopted children 'internalise' their feelings which appears as self-blame, withdrawal and mildly depressive behaviour. Other children 'externalise' their feelings in the form of oppositional behaviours, aggression, lying and stealing (see Chapter 2). The ability of adoptive parents to accept and understand what is happening helps children to feel secure, that their parents are committed to them and that they belong. Children who do not feel trust or experience commitment exhibit higher rates of problem behaviour.

It is at this point that Brodzinsky joins many other adoption researchers in recognising the pivotal part that adopters play in helping their children cope with and adjust to their loss. The attitude of parents to adoption, their own losses and those of their child affect the quality and content of parent–child relationships and hence the child's behaviour. According to Hoopes (1982), adopters of babies are well-motivated but they can sometimes become over-involved, over-protective and possessive. The more warm and accepting are parental attitudes, the more positive is a child's adjustment to being adopted. Adopters who fail to adjust to their own losses, who have mental health problems or who remain ambivalent about adoption create parent–child relationships in which warmth and full acceptance are incomplete or confused. Adopters' emotional availability is limited at a time when adopted adolescent children's sense of loss and level of anxiety are heightened.

Overview: the influence of the post-placement environment on adopted children's psychosocial development

We can collapse the variety of post-placement factors associated with outcomes into two major categories:

(1) *The physical and demographic characteristics of the post-place-ment environment.* These include age of adopters and their socio-economic status. On the whole, the evidence suggests that in themselves the material and demographic characteristics of the adopters and their family have little effect on adopted children's social adjustment.

(2) *The quality of the psychosocial environment.* This refers to a variety of matters including the quality of relationships between parents, between parents and their children, and between siblings. Here, the evidence suggests that the quality of parenting and family relationships do affect adopted children's social and emotional adjustment. Adoption studies of children placed as babies consistently report that the outcome is heavily influenced by the skills, attitudes and relationship style of the adopters. Parents who are able to relate to and communicate with partners and children in an open, accurate, sensitive, stable and empathic way are most likely to produce well-adjusted children:

> 'The emotional climate in the home during growing-up years had been important, as it is for all children, and it influenced

very much the adoptees' feelings about their whole experience. If they had a family where relationships were warm and harmonious and the climate of well-being and security throughout their childhood, nine in ten adoptees felt well satisfied with their adoption. But when the atmosphere had deteriorated later or the prevailing climate over the years had been characterised by conflict, worry or insecurity, only seven in ten now felt satisfied. Like most young people the adopted persons were much more often satisfied when parents had given them some freedom to follow and develop their own interests, choose their own friends and career and take some risks.'

(Raynor, 1980: p. 58)

Adoptive parents, like all parents, bring a range of skills, attitudes and aptitudes to the parenting task. Each parent's abilities are a product of his or her own temperament, experience and personality. Like any normal population of parents, some are better skilled at rearing and relating to children than others. The result is that we should expect a range of adjustment outcomes in adopted children just as we would expect in non-adopted children. Set against this, adoption agencies attempt to select, prepare and approve only those parents who appear to be well-suited to the task of raising children.

We might therefore expect that, all else being equal and assuming that the selection process does identify competent would-be parents, fewer adopted children than non-adopted children would have social and emotional adjustment problems. However, this is not the case, at least when adopted children are compared with non-adopted children raised in similar social and economic circumstances. So, either adopters are less skilled parents than non-adoptive parents; baby-adopted children vary in some way that increases the risk of a slightly poorer social adjustment; or there is some combination of the two:

(1) Being an adopter and being adopted are not emotionally neutral facts. Children as well as many of their parents have experienced a major loss. Both have extra developmental tasks to negotiate that are peculiar to adoption. In some cases, though by no means all, this can raise anxiety and increase insecurity. There is the suggestion that these psychological risks associated with being adopted can be overcome if the children's parents themselves have adjusted to their own losses. This helps them to empathise with their children. Adopters who have not adequately adjusted to their own infertility or whose parenting skills and attitudes are less positive may amplify children's anxieties and uncertainties.

(2) Children's temperament and behaviour can also affect the quality of parenting that they receive. Difficult children may weaken further the skills of those parents who either have not adjusted

well to their own losses or whose aptitude for parenting was not high in the first place. Temperamentally easier children may cope well with less skilled parents. Indeed, they may boost the confidence and abilities of parents who, for whatever reasons, begin parenting from a lower skill base.

Chapter 5

Outcome Studies of Older Children Placed for Adoption

During the 1970s a number of events conspired to encourage the placement of older children for adoption. Changes in contraceptive practices, the legal availability of abortion, a less socially hostile reaction to having children without being married and improved financial support for lone parents meant that the number of babies available for adoption dropped drastically. However, there were still far more people wanting to adopt than there were children needing to be adopted. It was at this time that researchers noted that many older children appeared to be either drifting or languishing in public care (Rowe & Lambert, 1973). Adoption practice up to this time believed that early deprivation or physical disabilities rendered children 'unfit for adoption'. But this long held wisdom came under increasing pressure. Pioneering attempts to place older children for adoption were proving successful, encouraging further innovation and experimentation in placement practice. Thus, the adoption of older children became increasingly common. In the UK, children aged one year and older at the time of placement now outnumber baby adoptions, running at around several thousand annually.

Historically, the reasons for older children being accommodated in either foster homes or residential care have varied. Some have been rejected by their parents while others had been neglected, abused or abandoned. Some parents fail to cope with the behavioural problems of their sons or daughters. Many children come from homes where there is poverty, discord and upset or a parent suffers a psychiatric illness. Children with physical disabilities or learning difficulties could also find themselves in care if their parents feel unable or unwilling to care for them. Children of a minority ethnic background were often thought to be hard to place and so would remain in care. Many children had experienced multiple moves between their families, foster homes and residential care. Others had remained 'institutionalised' in children's homes for years. If a family of children were in care as a sibling group, then previously social workers might have presumed that adoption was not an option if the children were to stay together. Collectively, these became known as 'special needs' children. By the mid-1970s determined efforts were made to place as many of these previously 'hard-to-place' children as possible. Pioneering projects in the United States, Britain and other countries showed that it was possible to locate these children with willing and able adoptive parents.

In order to facilitate the placement of 'special needs' children, new principles were developed to underpin the work. Rowe (in Fratter *et al.*, 1991: p. 11) records that prospective adopters began to be seen as colleagues and that more direct work with children was necessary to prepare them for their move into a new family. Infertile couples no longer formed the biggest pool out of which adopters were selected. People who could demonstrate that they understood the needs of children (because of their work, established parenting skills or innate empathy) were thought more likely to provide loving, competent homes for children whose needs were often unusually high.

If these children were to enjoy sound psychosocial development, they need to be in long-term, stable family relationships. The cry was soon heard that no child should be seen as 'unadoptable'. The aim of permanency planning, as it was soon to be called, was to provide children with an opportunity to form life-long relationships, whether with their biological families or new adoptive parents (Triseliotis & Russell, 1984; Thoburn, 1990). There was a good deal of optimism about the ability of adopters to cope with the particular needs and demands of older placed children, even those who had been badly disturbed by the emotional upsets and adversities suffered in their early months and years. A poor start in life no longer meant that a child could not be adopted. Indeed, the idea that given a good social environment, full developmental recovery might be expected quickly gained ground. Enthusiasm for placing older and 'special needs' children soon became the dominant mood in adoption practice.

Early trauma and developmental recovery

The placement of children who have suffered adversity and disadvantage early in life into stable, responsive families becomes something of a testing ground for two contrasting theories of children's psychosocial development. The first believes that poor quality care in an emotionally adverse environment during the first year or so of life has long-lasting negative effects on development and personality (for example, Bowlby, 1952). The second argues that full developmental recovery is possible if the disturbed child is introduced into a fresh, good quality social environment (for example Clarke & Clarke, 1976). The placement of older children was encouraged by the belief that the damage caused by early life traumas could be reversed. Our review of late-placed adopted children and their outcomes feeds directly into this debate and reveals something of the power of early and late psychosocial environments to influence children's development.

There has been some debate about when an adoption should be described as late. Placement before the child's first birthday might count as a baby-adoption. However, many analysts, basing their decision on developmental criteria, believe that adoption after the age of six months is sufficient to warrant it being categorised as a late placement. By this age, the child has begun to form selective attachments. Relationships, even when poor, are nevertheless becoming established and familiar. For example, Humphrey & Ounsted (1963: p. 606) believe that 'although infants vary widely in their rate of personal–social development, it is generally agreed that irreparable damage is less likely to occur in the first six months of life.' Although others might disagree that the damage is irreparable, it is still possible to accept that adversity which continues after the age of six months deepens the level of developmental disturbance and thus places greater demands on any therapeutic, restorative relationships that the child might subsequently enjoy.

In terms of relationships, late-placed children go through a series of attachment and loss experiences: formation (or not in the case of institutionalised children) of original attachment relationships → the breaking and loss of initial relationships with selective attachment figures → formation of new attachment relationships with a new set of parents. In the light of these experiences, the key question becomes: *Can late-placed children show developmental recovery after a history of disturbed attachment relationships and experiences of environmental adversity?*

Outcome studies of older-placed adopted children

Many of the measures used to examine 'outcomes' in baby adoptions have also been used to look at the adoption outcomes of older placed children. Outcome studies of late-placed children are reviewed under the following six headings:

(1) Disruption rates
(2) Physical development
(3) Cognitive competence
(4) Social, emotional and behavioural adjustment
(5) Psychiatric clinical studies of adopted children
(6) Rates of satisfaction

Disruption rates

The placement of older, disturbed children is recognised as a higher risk activity than the placement of babies. A number of adoptions 'break down' either before the child is legally adopted or sometime after he or she has been adopted. There is some discussion about whether the term 'disruption' should be applied only to placements that break down before the child has actually been adopted or whether it might be used to describe all breakdowns both before and after a child has been officially adopted. We shall follow the majority view that defines disruption as 'the end of the adoptive placement' at whatever point this takes place during childhood or adolescence (Berry & Barth, 1990).

Different studies report different rates (for reviews see Festinger, 1986; Barth & Berry, 1988). Disruption rates seem lower if foster children, who are subsequently adopted, are included in the study population. Analysts suggest that foster parents who decide to adopt both know their child and have had plenty of time to make their decision. The feeling is that such adoptions are less likely to disrupt because parents and child have had a chance to see if the placement will work. Studies that include foster-parent adoptions produce lower 'breakdown' rates. For example, Barth & Berry (1988) included a majority of foster-parent adoptions in their examination of older placed children adopted before the age of ten years and reported a disruption rate of 10%, most within 18 months of arrival. The figures rose to 22% and 26% for those adopted aged 12–14 years and 15–17 years respectively. Disruption rates were higher for children not adopted by their foster parents.

In a small, prospective study of boys placed after the age of five years, eight years after placement, Rushton *et al.* (1995: p. 693) reported a 19% disruption rate. The aggressive behaviour of the boys was one of the main reasons given for the breakdowns. Thoburn and Rowe (1988) found slightly higher rates over a shorter placement period. Out of 1165 older-placed children 21% disrupted within a period of 18 months and $6\frac{1}{2}$ years after placement, again with the finding that rates were lower for younger age at placement and higher for those who were older. A similar rate of 20.6% is reported by Borland *et al.* (1991). Most studies observe that rates of breakdown are highest during the first year of placement. Summarising the research on disruption rates, Borland and her colleagues write that:

'One consistent finding is that disruptions for children placed when under the age of ten are below 10%, but for those aged ten and over they vary from between 15 and 50 per cent. When increased age and increased disturbance go together the disruption rates are expected to be higher.'

(Borland *et al.*, 1991: p. 19)

Nevertheless, in spite of these high breakdown rates, many commentators are keen to put a positive spin on the figures. They emphasise that around 75% of sometimes disturbed and often very hard-to-place children typically do *not* 'disrupt.' However, a note of caution has to be added. It is worth pondering the implications of these various disruption rates when interpreting the other psychosocial 'outcome' measures being considered in this chapter. Many children whose adoptions break down will not be counted when researchers attempt to determine the rates of other behavioural outcomes in the placement of older children. To this extent, their omission gives a rosier picture of how things turn out – they often only analyse those children whose adoptions survived. On the other hand, outcome studies that take a longer timeframe may well include many children whose adoptions eventually disrupt but who are nevertheless around long enough to be counted and measured at some stage in their placement prior to their departure from the adoptive family. The survival of a child in placement does not necessarily mean that behaviourally and interpersonally all was well. There is one final twist: it is also possible to argue that even though a child's behaviour is problematic and appears grim on a variety of outcome measures, the adoption might still be regarded as a success and with satisfaction by the child, the parents and the placement agency.

Physical development

The evidence is very strong and encouraging that children who suffer severe physical, nutritional and material deprivations during early childhood enjoy more or less complete physical recovery once placed in a safe, nourishing environment. Good health is restored, height and weight potentials are reached and normal physical milestones are achieved (for example, Rathbun *et al.*, 1958, cited in Tizard, 1977: p. 13; Winnick *et al.*, 1975).

Several large scale studies involving intercountry adoptions report good physical recovery of children who arrive in their new country with a variety of health problems including malnutrition, skin diseases and physical disabilities (Gardell, 1980, and Hoksbergen *et al.*, 1987, cited in Triseliotis *et al.*, 1997: p. 188). Thompson (1986) describes the case of a severely deprived three year old Columbian boy who was adopted by an American couple. His general recovery, including his physical development and health, was good.

Cognitive competence

The ability of children initially under-stimulated and physically deprived to achieve normal levels of cognitive competence in adoptive homes is well-established (for example, see Seglow *et al.*, 1972: p. 72). Even children who have been severely malnourished prior to adoption show good intellectual developmental recovery. In their study of 138 Korean female children placed with American families at an average age of 18 months, Winnick *et al.*, (1975) found only modest differences in IQ between various groups several years after placement. Those who had been well-nourished in their first year scored an average of 112;

those moderately nourished 106; and those malnourished 102. A study of the social and intellectual development of children adopted into England from Romania is currently being carried out by a team led by Sir Michael Rutter (M.R.C., Institute of Psychiatry, University of London). This project should add considerably to our knowledge and understanding of children's cognitive and socio-emotional progress in adoptive families.

The children in Tizard's study (1977) had spent the first two to seven years of their life in a residential institution. Children were returned either to their biological parents, fostered or adopted from the age of two onwards. The majority of birth parents had worked in relatively low-skilled occupations. The average age of the mothers at the time of their child's birth was 22 years. Three were aged under 16 years. Of the children who left the institution to return to their biological home, more came from minority ethnic backgrounds or from a slightly higher socio-economic status family than those who were fostered or adopted. The adoptive mothers were on average ten years older than the birth mothers at the time of the children's birth. Whereas the birth fathers held skilled or unskilled manual jobs, adoptive fathers had professional or managerial jobs. At aged four and a half years, those children who had either returned home or been adopted at the age of two were tested. The mean IQs of the restored home children was 100 while for the adopted children it was 115. There was little difference between their verbal and non-verbal scale scores. Tizard (1977: p. 79) explains 'that the big difference in average IQ between the two groups of children at the age of four and a half was due to their different experience since they left the institution.' The parents of the adopted children spent more time reading to and playing with their children.

Tizard was also able to examine a very small number of children placed for adoption at the later age of four and half years. The numbers are too small to draw any firm conclusions, but these much later placed children did not show the same intellectual recovery found in the children placed at the age of two years.

'Indeed, of the children who left the institution after the age of four and a half, one – the first to go – increased in IQ, whilst ten out of fourteen decreased in IQ. This figure includes [the restored, adopted and fostered children] ... The finding may not, however, be a chance one; it may be more difficult to accelerate the intellectual development of children after the age of four or so than earlier.'

(Tizard, 1977: p. 228)

A later study followed these same children through to 16 years of age (Hodges and Tizard, 1989a). An additional feature of this study involved the use of a comparison group of non-institutional children matched for both the children restored to their birth parents and those adopted. The children adopted before the age of four continued to perform better (mean IQ 114) than both those restored to their biological parents (mean IQ 96) and those who had remained in institutional care (mean IQ 96). Within the adopted group, children placed with middle class parents achieved higher scores than those placed with working class parents.

In terms of academic achievement, late-placed children do better than children who remain with or who are restored to their disadvantaged biological families. On the other hand, they do not do quite as well as their non-adopted socio-economic counterparts or indeed, adopted children placed as babies. Jerome (1993: p. 292), for example, found that in a clinical population of adopted children, those placed after six months scored six points lower on full IQ tests than those adopted before six months. Hodges and Tizard (1989a) found that at 16 years of age, ex-institutional children performed slightly less well academically than their matched comparisons. Comparing children who remained in residential care with those who left to be adopted, Triseliotis and Russell (1984: p. 77) report more higher level qualifications for the adopted group than the residential group. When a group of children adopted as babies are compared with a group of late-placed children, Howe (1997) observed that whereas 81% of baby-adopted children passed at least one national certificated exam before the age of 17, this figure dropped to 43% for late-placed children.

Social, emotional and behavioural adjustment

It is in the area of psychosocial adjustment, personality and relationships that early life experiences appear to have most impact on later development. A large number of studies have explored the extent to which, if at all, adversity prior to adoption affects children's social relationships and behaviour. There is broad agreement that late-placed children are perhaps not as socially skilled or as confident as their non-adopted peers, but there is less consensus about the level of disturbance.

A common reaction amongst researchers is to express surprise that so many late-placed children appear to develop relatively 'normally'. Kadushin (1970) talked to the parents of 91 young adolescents who had been placed for adoption when they were at least five years old. He categorised 74% as successful, 11% fairly successful and 15% unsuccessful. Triseliotis and Russell (1984) also found that around 80% of late, 'high risk' adoptions were evaluated as positive or fairly positive by the adult adopted people themselves. In Kadushin's (1970: p. 213) view 'the children studied turned out to be more "normal," less "maladjusted" than they had any right to be, given the trauma and insults to psyche experienced during early childhood.' He felt that there was a tendency to overestimate the importance and power of the past.

Overall, though, the balance of opinion seems to be that late-placed children enjoy a better level of psychosocial adjustment than those who remain in institutional settings or home situations of adversity but not as good as the general population of children (Hersov, 1990: p. 498). Indeed, Moffitt (1987) found no relationship between age at placement and such matters as rates of admission to psychiatric hospital and offending behaviour, though she does argue that there are inherited components that contribute to both these behaviours. However, it must be noted that the adopted children in this study were raised in a nursery. The late-placed group were not adopted so much as a result of prolonged parental abuse or neglect; their delayed placement was because they had, for whatever reason, spent a long time in residential care.

> 'There was little or no contact between the adoptees and their biological parents; in almost all cases, the decision to place the infant for adoption was made prenatally, and the adoption agency separated the infants from their mothers at birth and placed them in babies' homes, a case of privation rather than deprivation. Differences in the character of early life experiences may have a profound bearing on subsequent behaviour and development rather than the lateness of the adoption *per se*.'

> (Moffitt, 1987; p. 348)

The majority of studies find that children adopted after the age of six months tend to show higher levels of anxiety, insecurity and antisocial 'externalising' problem behaviour during adolescence (for example, Brown, 1959; Witmer *et al.*, 1963; Humphrey & Ounsted, 1963; McWhinnie, 1967: p. 260). Kotsopoulos *et al.* (1993: p. 395) concluded that 'better psychosocial functioning was associated with adoption during the first six months of life.'

In their comparison of children initially placed in nurseries with a view to being adopted (who were eventually either adopted as babies, fostered or returned to birth parents), Bohman and Sigvardsson (1990) compared their behaviour at various ages. The 'fostered' group were placed at a mean age of nine months. By the time they were seven years old, 70% had been adopted. Compared to the baby adopted and non-adopted children in general, they showed much poorer levels of psychosocial adjustment at all ages. In adolescence, rates of criminal behaviour, alcohol and drug use, aggressive behaviour and general 'maladjustment' were much higher in the late-adopted group than the baby-adopted group.

However, the picture is not uniform. Seglow *et al.* (1972: p. 76–77), comparing early and late-placed children at the age of seven years, found no differences in social adjustment scores outside of the school setting. But in school, age at placement did appear to make a difference to adjustment scores. Levels of 'maladjustment' increased sharply for children placed after the age of six months, rising even higher for those placed later than 12 months.

Tizard (1977) compared children who had been raised in an institutional setting for at least the first two years of life before either being 'restored' to their biological parents, fostered, adopted or left in the residential home. In the nurseries, the children were cared for by a large number of staff. Unlike more recent groups of late-placed children, Tizard's group appeared not to have been so much the victims of long inflicted abuse, neglect or rejection by their parents although they did languish in children's homes for most of their first two years. Their physical care was good, but the children were unable to form strong selective attachments. They tended to respond to all adults in a friendly, but uncommitted way. These points are emphasised because it may be that an institutional environment has rather different implications for a child's psychosocial development than an abusive, neglecting or rejecting one. By the age of four and half years, both the restored and adopted children were seen as attention-seeking, 'over-friendly' and talkative. The children restored to their biological parents found themselves in homes that were materially and socially less rich. Compared to the adopted children, they tended to be more tense, twitchy and unhappy. They showed less concentration during testing and were more inclined to be clingy and less easy to manage (Tizard, 1977: p. 94). A small number of adopters were having problems but at this age most seemed to be coping well.

By the time the children were eight years old, the adopted group began to show fewer adjustment problems than their restored counterparts. They had formed good attachments with their new parents. Those who had returned to live with their biological parents were much less affectionate and not so attached. However, 'both adopted and restored children tended to be less popular with other children, more aggressive and more solitary than their classmates' (Tizard, 1977: p. 131). In general, school social life seems to be a particular problem for late-placed children. Although they perform well intellectually, interpersonally they have more difficulties than either their classmates or 'working-class children' who had grown up with their own families. In Tizard's study, ex-institutional children, whether adopted or restored, were more often described as unpopular, disobedient, quarrelsome, restless, solitary, liable to tell lies, to be resentful when corrected, and to seek attention from teachers. About half of the children placed at two years old, and more than half the restored children were so described (Tizard, 1977: p. 108). Out of the restored children, 66% compared with 15% of the adopted children had been referred to a mental health specialist because of their behaviour.

Followed through to 16 years of age, many of these antisocial behaviours continued but whereas the adopted children showed some improvement, the restored children generally became worse. There was still evidence of anxiety, hostility, irritability and restlessness in the ex-institutional children, whether restored or adopted, but both teachers and parents described more problems in adolescence amongst those children who rejoined their birth families (Hodges & Tizard, 1989a). The 'restored' children had higher rates of referral to mental health services than adopted children. They wanted less involvement in family discussions and identified less with their parents.

The adopted children showed a number of similarities with the restored group, both finding relationships with peers to be a source of difficulty. Friends were less likely to be seen as a source of emotional support. And both sets of ex-institutional children still appeared attention-seeking, wanting the interest and approval of adults. 'Thus,' conclude Hodges & Tizard (1989a: p. 73), 'whilst there was no evidence of a long-term effect of early institutionalisation on IQ, there was evidence that, as a group, the ex-institutional children had more behavioural and emotional difficulties than comparison children...'

However, failures and successes in these cases are always relative. Tizard reminds us that although all ex-institutionalised children have interpersonal problems, the children restored to their biological families exhibit them to a more marked degree and at greater frequency.

In their study, Triseliotis & Russell (1984) interviewed two groups of adults: one who had been placed for adoption between the ages of two and eight years, and another who had spent the larger part of their childhood in residential care. The adopted people had been placed in public care on average at a younger age than their residential counterparts. They had also lived with their birth families for a shorter period (12 months versus 53 months). The mean age at placement of the adopted group was 41 months, with an average of 30 months in care prior to adoption.

Over 33% of the adopted children and 70% of those raised in residential care said they had experienced emotional and behavioural disorders during their childhood either after their adoption and during their stay in long-term institutional care (Triseliotis & Russell, 1984: p. 86–87). Echoing the views of the teachers in Tizard's research, these adults also recognised that making friends and mixing with their peers at school had been difficult. But again the problem was higher for the residential group (28%) than for the adopted group (16%).

In their prospective study of boys placed after the age of five years, Rushton *et al.* (1995: p. 689) describe their pre-placement experiences and reasons for entering care prior to adoption. The majority had suffered neglect and/or abuse. Around half had a parent suffering a psychiatric illness and/or very poor material circumstances and/or parental marital discord. At least three of these were present for two thirds of the boys. Immediately after placement adopters reported conduct problems, emotional problems, difficulties with peers and attachment problems. By the end of the first year, the mean number of problems had halved, although overactivity and attachment difficulties (separation anxiety, few demonstrations of affection) remained at original levels. After five years, a third of the of the boys had a high number of problems including social relationship and attentional problems, and oppositional behaviour.

Eight years after placement (adolescence for most boys), of those 81% placements which had not 'broken down' there was a marginal upswing in problem behaviour. 'The majority of the boys developed affectionate relationships with their new parents but difficulties in relationships with peers and overactive/restless behaviour proved more persistent' (Rushton *et al.*, 1995; p. 693). Using parental judgements of the boys' behaviour, about half appeared to be making good to satisfactory adjustments. The half that were not so well-adjusted showed a variety of problem behaviours including insecurity, stealing, poor concentration, restlessness and aggression.

In a larger study of 'special needs' late-placed children, Rosenthal & Groze (1994) surveyed around 300 families and their children (mean age 10.2 years) and then again three years later (mean age 13.5 years). Although a majority of parents still felt positively about their relationships with their children at the older age, the percentage of negative replies had increased by about 10% from the earlier study when the children were aged ten years.

Antisocial behaviour and maladjustment, particularly during adolescence, appear to rise at a higher rate amongst late-adopted children than socio-economic controls and children adopted as babies or the general population (for example, see Versluis-den Bieman & Verhulst, 1995). According to Triseliotis & Russell (1984: p. 74, 127), a quarter of their late-placed children had received a police warning and/or appeared before a court for some criminal offence (usually shoplifting or house burglary) before the age of 16. Rates were slightly higher for the children who had grown up in children's homes. A similar figure of just under 30% contact with the police for a criminal offence was reported by Howe (1997) in his group of late placed children. These figures are *higher* than for non-adopted children whose parents are from similar socio-economic backgrounds as the adopters but *much lower* than for children raised in either children's homes or by parents similar to the adopted children's birth parents. For example:

'The proportion of adoptees and residential people appearing before a criminal court did not differ much, but residential people were more likely to reappear. The latter were also more likely to be heavy drinkers, to be referred for psychiatric help in adult life, and to report emotional problems at interview.'

(Triseliotis & Russell, 1984: p. 186)

Increased criminal behaviour amongst late-adopted children was also found by Mednick and his colleagues in their Danish studies (CIBA, 1996: p. 134). But in the Swedish studies, curiously, prolonged institutional care only increased the risks of criminality in women but not in men (Cloninger & Gottesman, 1987; Bohman, 1996).

In spite of the difficulties experienced by many late-placed children, Triseliotis & Russell (1984: p. 158) are keen to emphasise the successful side of adjustment for these children. Using a measure of the adult's present 'quality of life', they assessed that 40% of the adopted people were free of any of the nine handicaps identified. In contrast, only 10% of the residential people were free of the same handicaps. Looked at another way, 25% of the adopted adults had three or more handicaps, a figure which rose to 60% for the residential group. This more optimistic re-framing of the picture, particularly when compared with ex-institutional children who returned to their biological families, is also borne out by the findings of Hodges & Tizard (1989b).

Psychiatric clinic studies of adopted children

Late placement does appear to pose an increased risk of mental health, behavioural and psychiatric problems in adopted children over and above the slight extra risk of behavioural disturbance shown by all adopted children. Adopted children in general and late-adopted children in particular appear to show more antisocial, externalising, acting-out, conduct disordered behaviour than non-adopted control populations. However, some studies report only modest and subtle differences between early-adopted, late adopted and non-adopted clinical populations (Jerome, 1993).

In a large survey of 1314 children attending an out-patient psychiatric clinic, 5% were found to be adopted (Menlove, 1965). In general, the adopted children were more aggressive and hyperactive than a control group, behaviour which was particularly pronounced in those placed after the age of six months. Similarly, Ounsted (1970) and Offord *et al.* (1969) found proportionally higher numbers of referrals to mental health clinics for children placed older than six months. Cohen *et al.* (1993) compared a group of adopted children who had attended a mental health clinic with a matched group who had not. The mean age at adoption was significantly older for the clinic group (33.3 months) than for the non-clinic group (15.4 months).

However, there are hints that rates of psychiatric problems among late placed adopted children, though high compared to baby-adopted children, are still lower than for children raised in residential institutions or those restored to their biological families after a period in public care (for example, Tizard, 1977: p. 222). Triseliotis & Russell (1984: p. 123) noted that at interview adults raised in residential care were far more likely to report emotional or behavioural problems than the late-adopted people.

Humphrey & Ounsted (1963: p. 605) also observed a particular symptomatology associated with the late-adopted children attending their Oxford clinic:

> '...there is no difference in symptomatology between children adopted *early* and those brought up mainly by their own parents [the control group] ... Equally, there are no significant differences between early and late adoptees *with the exception of stealing, lying, cruelty to animals and destructiveness of property*, which were much more common in the latter group ... We were particularly impressed by our finding that more than one in two of the children adopted later had stolen, compared with one in four of those adopted early.'
>
> (Humphrey & Ounsted, 1963: p. 605, emphasis added)

Similarly, in a five-year follow-up study of children referred to a psychiatric clinic, Kotsopoulos *et al.* (1993) found that better psychosocial functioning was associated with those who had been adopted during the first six months of life. At follow up, a trend was observed in which those adopted under the age of six months were least likely to have a psychiatric diagnosis. Those adopted after the age of six months had poorer levels of adaptive functioning.

Von Knorring, Bohman & Sigvardsson (1982), using the Swedish adoption data, observed that children placed between 6 and 18 months were more likely to experience a 'reactive neurotic depression' in adulthood. Anxiety and acute depression most often occurred following the loss or departure of a partner. Out of those adopted late in Triseliotis & Russell's study (1984: p. 125), 11% had been referred to the psychiatric services as an adult, although the figure rose to 25% for those raised in residential care.

Rates of satisfaction

Many studies ask both adopters and their grown-up adopted children to rate their level of satisfaction with the adoption. Satisfaction, of course, does not necessarily correlate with behaviour, disturbance or levels of adjustment. Parents may express considerable satisfaction with the progress made by a 'special needs' child, even though his or her behaviour remains difficult or disturbed. Levels of satisfaction tend to correspond with the quality of relationships experienced between parents and their children. In turn, many observers believe that the character of parent–child relationships is a product of the child's attachment style. Late-placed children's relationship history is one of forming, breaking and re-establishing attachment relationships with old and new carers (see Rushton & Mayes 1997 for a review of forming fresh attachments in childhood).

After one year in placement, Quinton *et al.* (in press) observed that 43% of 61 late-placed children had made a good relationship with both new parents, while 30% were said to have a satisfactory relationship with one parent.

Kadushin (1970) judged the success of children placed between the ages of 5 and 11 years old in his study by the level of satisfaction expressed by the parents when the children were aged between 12 and 17 years old. Rates of satisfaction with the overall adoption experience were: 59% extremely satisfying, 19% more satisfying than dissatisfying, 9% about half and half, 10% more dissatisfying than satisfying, and 3% extremely dissatisfying. A more recent study by Rosenthal & Groze (1994) looked at children whose mean age at adoption was 4.7 years. When the children were 13, the impact of adoption on the family was said to be very positive or mostly positive in 69% of cases. In 21%, results were judged 'mixed', leaving 3% categorised as negative. Looked at another way, 57% of parents thought that they 'got along' very well with their child, leaving 34% who said they got along 'fairly well', 6% 'not so well' and 4% 'very poorly'.

Tizard also posed the question of parental satisfaction as a measure of success in the adoption of late-placed children. She found that:

'If the measure of success is the parents' satisfaction with the adoption, only three of the twenty-five couples whom we visited when the children were eight expressed reservations so serious as to amount to dissatisfaction. Sixteen couples were unreservedly delighted with their child; the remaining six would not for one moment have parted with him, but they had gone through periods of disenchantment or difficulty in which they had experienced doubts about their decision.'

(Tizard, 1977: p. 212)

Triseliotis & Russell (1984: p. 137) asked adult late-adopted people and residentially reared people whether they felt that their experiences of childhood care had been helpful. Out of the adopted children, 70% said that their experience of adoptive family life had been beneficial, but only 40% brought up in a children's home said the same. Mixed feelings were described by 25% of the adopted people and 40% of the institutional group. However, 5% of those adopted and 20% of those reared in residential care thought the experience had actually been harmful. To some extent, this was reflected in the level of happiness reported by the two groups. Out of the adopted group 93% said they currently felt happy or fairly happy with their lives, while only 67% of the residential said they felt the same way.

Elements of happiness and satisfaction were also picked up by Triseliotis & Russell (1984: p. 116–117) in their enquiries about the quality of people's relationships in adult life. About half of both adopted and residentially reared people had married at least once at the time of the interview. The residential group tended to marry younger. They said they had a desire to have a home and family of their own. Of those who had married, 18% had divorced or were separated. Of those currently married, 32% expressed some dissatisfaction, leaving 68% expressing considerable satisfaction. Of the adopted people who had married, 24% had divorced or were living apart. Of those who were married and living together at the time of the interview, nearly all of them said that their relationship with their spouse was satisfactory. The authors offer no control baseline for these findings, but it does seem that initially at least, marriage breakdowns are high for both groups. However, whereas adopted people's relationships seemed to improve, a substantial minority of the residential group continued to experience problems in their intimate dealings with others.

The researchers then went on to ask people about the relationship they had with their own children, if they had any. Adopted people who were parents reported that they related well with their young children. In contrast, residentially reared parents tended to experience some anxieties about their parenting role, particularly in the first year or so. Summarising these findings, Triseliotis & Russell write:

'On matters of social and personal adjustment, significantly fewer adoptees (16 per cent) were classified as 'disturbed' compared with residential people (48 per cent) ... Overall, less than a quarter of adoptees and almost three-fifths of residential people were facing either serious material, social or personal problems. Adoptees who were facing such problems would also express 'mixed' or 'negative' feelings about their adoption blaming their current situation on the outcome of their adoption. The single factor that appeared to point to some relative social and personal stability in the current lives of some residential people was the extent to which they felt they experienced caring and good relationships with the staff.'

(Triseliotis & Russell, 1984: p. 156–157)

The authors conclude that the late-adopted people were coping much more successfully with adult life than the residential group. They believed that the opportunities to form good, stable and close relationships in adoptive family life helped late-adopted people reverse many of the major developmental setbacks experienced in early life.

So, although it is acknowledged that many late-placed children exhibit difficult and demanding behaviour, particularly during adolescence, in many cases relationships between parents and their children appear to improve as they enter their late teens and early adulthood. Howe (1996b) reports that in his sample of all late-placed children, only 46% of adoptive parents retrospectively described their relationship with their child at the age of 16 as positive. However, evaluations of these same relationships when their child was an adult (aged 23 years and over) saw this figure rise to 75%.

Overview of outcome studies of late-placed children

Researchers have compared the development of late-placed adopted children with

(1)   the general population of non-adopted children;
(2)   baby-adopted children;
(3)   children reared in residential institutions;
(4)   children reared in residential institutions and then 'restored' to their biological families.

Whereas the development of baby-adopted children is broadly the product of their genetic inheritance and (in most cases because of selection procedures) interactions with a good environment, the basic formula for late-adopted children is more complicated. Late-placed children's development after placement is the result of interactions between (1) genetic inheritance, (2) an initially adverse environment, and (3) a later favourable environment. Those who believe that children's trajectories along particular developmental pathways can be altered if their social environment changes argue that the effects of a good second environmental experience (adoptive family life) can substantially undo the psychosocial damage caused by early life adversity. In contrast and without denying the benefits of a good adoption, the 'early experience' lobby believe that children pay at least some developmental price for suffering poor quality care in the first few years of life. Our review of the research allows us to judge the strengths of these two positions.

On most measures, late-adopted children perform slightly worse than the general population of non-adopted children and children adopted as babies (that is, under six months). On the other hand, their overall levels of adjustment are much better than those of children who remain in institutional settings and children who have been returned to and raised by their disadvantaged birth families.

Perhaps not surprisingly then, the research evidence appears to lend support to both arguments. It seems clear that disturbance and neglect in the early years do have some long-term negative impacts on personality and social development. On the other hand, the degree and extent of the psychosocial upset is not as great as that experienced by children whose environment remains adverse, suggesting that good levels of developmental recovery are possible and that outcomes are not as bad as sometimes feared if children are placed in a positive, restorative social environment.

More specifically, it appears that in the case of physical development, recovery, if affected in the early years, is likely to be very good. Cognitive development also appears to be capable of strong recovery, particularly if children are placed in a new, stimulating environment before the age of two years. Compared to children who remain in or who are returned to materially and socially poor family environments, late-adopted children from similar families of origin appear to gain anything between 10 and 15 full IQ points over their non-adopted counterparts. However, there are indications that their scores do not quite match those of baby-adopted children, hinting that a small intellectual deficit is suffered if placements out of adversity are delayed. Of course, this interpretation ignores the possibility that late-placed children might have parents who are not as cognitively competent as the parents of baby-adopted children (the reasons for the children being placed for adoption tend to differ between the two groups). The reason for the slightly lower IQ scores of late adopted children could therefore be the result of inheritance, early environmental adversity, or a combination of the two. Some studies suggest that children placed older than four or five years old from poor psychosocial environments tend to show less cognitive recovery.

In general, the socio-emotional development of late adopted children is not as positive as that of either baby-adopted children or matched controls of non-adopted children of families of similar socio-economic status as the adopters. However, it is much better than that of children raised in either institutions or socio-economic adversity. Although by no means all late-adopted children show the full range of developmental problems, rates of these behaviours do tend to be higher for this group than for those placed as babies. The profile of behaviours also tends to be distinctive of late-adopted children and differs in its overall make-up from those problem behaviours found in non-adopted children raised in families in which social and material life is poor. There is a bias towards 'externalising', oppositional and antisocial behaviours, particularly in adolescence. They appear most pronounced in the context of school and in relationships with peers. The following behaviours and personality traits are those most frequently used to describe and identify tendencies in late-adopted children:

- Insecure and anxious
- Attention-seeking and demanding
- Restless
- Poor concentration
- Unpopular with peers and relationship problems with peers
- Lying
- Hostility, anger and aggression
- Oppositional behaviour

● Conduct disorders including criminal behaviour
● Improved social adjustment in early adulthood

It has to be emphasised that although a significant minority of late adopted children will manifest many of these behaviours in full measure at particular times during their childhood, the majority will develop only mild versions, if they appear at all. Considerable help and support is required by parents of the more difficult, demanding and angry children. There seems no denying that some children are badly affected by poor quality early life experiences. Rejection, neglect and abuse prior to placement appear to heavily impair some children's ability to develop along normal social and emotional pathways. This remains the case even when they subsequently find themselves in positive, caring environments. It is in the field of close relationships that these children find the most difficulty, whether with parents or peers.

Many observers describe the children as 'angry'. And as they act out their anger, they often find themselves getting into trouble with parents, teachers and the police. In some circles, these children have been diagnosed as suffering a 'reactive attachment disorder'. However, many commentators point out that the diagnosis should be reserved for only gross disturbances in social relationships displayed by a very small number of children who have experienced extremely inadequate parenting and multiple changes of carer (for example, see Rushton & Mayes, 1997). But whatever the label or the numbers, this particular group of late-adopted children prove particularly difficult to parent.

It is possible to identify three interesting developmental divisions within the broad category of late-placed adoptions. *These are based on the different character and quality of the children's pre-placement experience.* At least three types of early life experience can be discerned in adoption research:

(1) Institutional care: no experiences of close, regular intimate relationships and therefore no experience of sustained and personalised rejection, abuse or neglect in relationship with a prime carer.
(2) Good quality care with main carers during the first year or two of life before the relationship takes a turn for the worse and the child experiences loss, abandonment, rejection, abuse and/or neglect in the subsequent years before being placed for adoption.
(3) Continuously poor quality care and loss, rejection, abuse and/or neglect during the years prior to being placed for adoption.

Many late-adopted children also appear to underperform at school. Academic achievements appear to be adversely affected by the relatively poor levels of psychosocial adjustment that many of these children display, even though their levels of cognitive competence are generally a little above average.

Nevertheless, the percentage of parents reporting satisfaction with their adoptions are generally high, typically ranging between 70 and 80%. These figures often do not include the views of parents of children whose placements 'broke down' or were disrupted. Disruption rates increase with increasing age of the child at placement, varying from around 10% for children under ten years old at placement to 20–40% for children aged over ten years of age at the time of placement. Combining disruption rates with developmental outcome measures and parental satisfaction rates produces slightly reduced rates of 'success'. A very crude product of these three measures suggests that around 55–60% of all late-placed children neither disrupt nor receive a negative evaluation by their parents.

Given the deprived backgrounds of many of these children prior to adoption, these rough and ready figures are encouraging. However, it is apparent that adopting 'special needs' children requires skilled parenting and the unflagging interest and support of a variety of post-adoption services. As they grow older and enter adulthood, those who enjoy the continued support of their parents see further improvements in their levels of psychosocial adjustment. The different behavioural profiles generated by late-placed children with different psychosocial backgrounds hint at the importance of early experiences in personality formation and the development of social competence.

Chapter 6

Older Children Placed for Adoption: Pre-placement Environmental Influences on Development

Late-placed adopted children bring with them three conditions that might influence the quality of their social and emotional progress once adopted. The quality of their ante-natal history is often worse than that of baby-adopted children. Second their natural temperaments remain present both before and after placement. Finally, they have a history of pre-placement relationships that will have helped form aspects of their early personality, behaviour and relationship style.

We have already considered the complex interactions between genes and environment in Chapter 3. The subtle interplay between temperament and social relationships is more complex in the case of late-placed children. They move out of one social environment with its particular array of actions and reactions into a completely new environment, which soon generates its own array of actions and reactions. However, adoption research so far has not been able to unravel these highly complex, two-phase gene–environment interactions. We must just take it that the principles and ideas introduced in our earlier discussion of behavioural genetics continue to operate and influence children's development once they find themselves in new families.

Environmental influences on late-placed children

The pre-placement factors that have proved much more amenable to study are environmental.

The basic question is: Which pre-placement experiences, if any, appear to affect late-placed children's subsequent behaviour and development? More specifically, researchers have wondered whether particular pre-placement experiences might be acting as either risk or protection factors in children's post-placement development, or whether they are simply neutral and have no bearing either way.

In finding answers to these questions, we should also be able to consider the extent to which developmental recovery is possible for children adopted beyond infancy. Two assumptions are generally and reasonably made: (1) that most late-placed children experience poor quality care and relationships prior to their placement, and (2) that these experiences adversely affect their psychosocial development, at least up to the point of placement. Here the question is: if these children are then placed in a totally new environment in which the quality of care and relationships are good, can they overcome the negative developmental effects caused by the initial adversity? Is developmental recovery possible?

As in the previous chapter, three types of answers are given to these questions:

(1) Some people believe that socio-emotional development remains impaired, even after placement in a well-resourced, well-functioning adoptive family. *This position states that early psychosocial environments have considerable impact on the long-term development of children's personality, behaviour and relationship styles.* If this is the case, then developmentally we should expect late-placed children to be more like children who remain in birth families where emotional and social adversity continue to be present with the result that rates of problem behaviours and adjustment difficulties are higher than normal.

(2) Others argue that full developmental recovery is possible. *This position states that later life experiences continue to have a major influence on psychosocial development and that they are quite capable of reversing any developmental setbacks suffered in the early years.* If this position is true, then developmentally we should expect late-placed children to be more like other children raised in socially and emotionally advantaged families showing low rates of problem behaviour and adjustment difficulties.

(3) A third group takes the middle ground, recognising that although a good placement allows huge strides to be taken in terms of improved adjustment and social competence, nevertheless the adversity suffered in the first year or so leaves a psychological legacy that can be seen in increased rates of some, but not all problem behaviours and adjustment difficulties. *This position states that early life experiences are particularly important in laying down basic personality structures that make it more difficult for later life experiences to influence personality, behaviour and relationship styles. However, new relationships can and do have a major effect on these basic psychological structures although echoes of the original deleterious effects of poor quality care will still be present and found in children's current ways of behaving and relating.* Developmentally, we should expect these

children to be less well-adjusted than children raised from birth by socially and emotionally competent parents, but better adjusted than children who have been raised in continuously poor functioning families.

Pre-placement experiences and older-placed children's development

We shall consider the impact of four pre-placement factors on children's post-placement development:

(1) Biology and inheritance.
(2) Age at placement and number of moves prior to placement.
(3) Quality of pre-placement care and close relationships.
(4) Children's pre-placement behaviour.

Biology and inheritance

Many researchers investigating late-placed adopted children acknowledge that genetic predisposition may account for such behaviours as emotional instability. But they also concede that to design a study in which temperament can be separated from early environmental influences is exceedingly difficult. The usual conclusion is to agree to leave the matter open whilst recognising its potential for explaining some behaviours.

Where associations have been found, they often conflict and confuse. For example, Triseliotis & Russell (1984: p. 171–176), in contrast to the Danish studies, but using much smaller numbers, found no significant association in alcohol abuse, antisocial behaviour and psychiatric illness between adopted children and their biological parents. The only positive finding to emerge in their work suggested that those raised in residential care who developed a psychiatric illness were more likely to have a 'disturbed' parental background and have had parents who were heavy drinkers or alcoholics.

However, using larger numbers Mednick, in dialogue with symposium colleagues, makes the following points:

Denno: Sarnoff Mednick, didn't you show that people who were left in the adoption institution [residential nursery prior to being placed] were most likely to become criminal?
Mednick: Yes, level of criminal offending was elevated among offspring placed at a later age. But within each age of placement we found the genetic relationship that we noted for the entire sample.
Rowe: But the question is: Why were they transferred later? Were they difficult babies?
Mednick: We have an idea about this, but we haven't published it. I

went with a social worker and read the case reports of the children who were up for adoption but were never placed. Every weekend (at least in the 1930s) Danish people who wished to adopt would visit the orphanages and pick children. Those children who were not placed had a 7.5% rate of schizophrenia. That is a high rate of schizophrenia. This means that the adoptive parents are able to tell which of these small children is going to become schizophrenic! Children whose selection by an adoptive parent is delayed may be less attractive physically and behaviourally.'

(CIBA, 1996: p. 134)

The point being made is that babies who are not chosen early (and therefore placed late) inherit characteristics that are not only intuitively unappealing to prospective adopters but can be associated with increased rates of antisocial behaviour in later childhood. These children therefore suffer a double blow. Their inherent characteristics and dispositions put them at greater risk of behaving antisocially. These same characteristics ensure they are the children who will be chosen last which means that they stay in residential care the longest. Prolonged stay in care deprives children of continuous, selective close relationships. The socio-emotional poverty of this experience further disturbs their psychosocial development, adding to the risk of them becoming poorly adjusted in later childhood.

This is an example of a complex gene–environment interaction that appears to compound the developmental difficulties experienced by some children. Indeed, one could hypothesise that many late-placed children are, in this sense, self-selecting as late placements. On this reasoning, late-placed children are not representative of all children who experience adversity in early childhood. Part of the reason that their biological parents may find caring for them difficult and why, for example, they might experience several foster parent breakdowns, is that their inherited character and temperament may be more difficult to parent than that of children from similar family backgrounds who either never enter the public care system, or if they do, return home. Thus, many late-placed children may have qualities that

(1) result in the failure of their biological parents to care for them effectively,
(2) make them hard to look after by foster carers and other substitute carers,
(3) delay their placement in adoptive families,
(4) increase the risk of them developing difficult social behaviours,
(5) having brought about an extended period of unsettled and disturbed early life experiences, further increase the risk of them developing behavioural, emotional and psychiatric problems as a result of that disturbance.

Age at placement and number of moves prior to placement

On the face of it, older age at placement and many changes of carer prior to adoption might be expected to lead to more disturbed and less adjusted behaviour. But the evidence is not entirely clear cut on these matters. Generally, there is an association between age, number of possible moves and quality of care. What is less clear is which one or combination of these is responsible for increasing rates of problem behaviour in late-placed children. For example, although late age at placement may be associated with an increase in the number of children showing some adjustment problems, it may be the quality of pre-placement relationships that actually affects subsequent development and not the age at placement as such. Barth and Berry (1988: p. 72) make a similar point approaching it from another angle. 'Children's characteristics associated with older age and adoption instability include their behavioural and emotional problems, the experience of pre-adoptive multiple placements, and previous adoptive placements.'

In her analysis of similar data, McWhinnie (1967: p. 42) also recognises the problems of interpretation. She cites research that said if a child experiences more than one change of home before being placed, the chances of a successful adoption are reduced. This study, she observes, did not control for age and the doubt remains that maybe age rather than number of moves could be the controlling factor. Confirming these suspicions a number of other studies (for example, Fratter *et al.*, 1991: p. 42; Rushton *et al.*, 1995: p. 692), using more sophisticated designs, have concluded that having experienced multiple caretakers or multiple moves, in itself, does not appear to be associated with breakdown. For the remainder of this section, we shall concentrate on age and the number of moves as pre-placement variables in post-placement outcomes.

One of the most regular findings is that the rate of 'disruption' of adoptive placements rises with increasing age at placement (for example, see Barth & Berry, 1988; Fratter *et al.*, 1991: p. 35). Breakdown rates range between 5 and 15% for children placed under ten years old but rise steeply, sometimes reaching 40–50% for children placed after the age of 12 or 13 years.

Levels of psychosocial maladjustment, particularly with boys, also appear to increase with rising age at placement (for example, Jaffee & Fanshel, 1970). Although this does not mean that children placed very young (for example, as babies) are immune from problem development, rates of problem behaviour appear to increase as older children are adopted. By the same token, we also have to keep reminding ourselves that by no means all late-placed children will become difficult. Those who are placed late, after multiple moves and whose adjustment and behaviour are good, developmentally speaking, are equally interesting. The qualities they possess and the care they experience might provide strong clues about why some late-placed children's adjustment and development are relatively problem-free compared to others.

An example of the general trend of older age at placement/poorer adjustment qualified by exceptions, is given by McWhinnie:

'Taking the two extremes of adjustment, this gave the higher proportion placed under 16 weeks amongst the well-adjusted than amongst the poorly adjusted. On the other hand it remains significant that 3 children placed as early as 4 weeks were later severely maladjusted and that of the 5 not placed until they were at least a year old, 2 later made a good adjustment ... After the age of two, however, there was clear evidence of feelings of insecurity in the child resulting from such late placement.'

(McWhinnie, 1967: p. 214, 260)

Again using small numbers, Tizard (1977: p. 178) observed that more of the children who had been longest in institutional care and who were adopted late or restored to their biological families showed more difficult behaviour than the children who had spent less time in the nursery before placement. These later-placed children tended to have 'very poor concentration, especially at school; they had more tics and nervous habits than the children who left the institution earlier, and more of them had temper tantrums.' It was not the age at placement that affected developmental outcome, believed Tizard, so much as the type of care and the length of that care. The exception to this was IQ scores. While the children adopted between the ages of two and four years raised their IQs, those placed after the age of four and half years had not raised their IQs since leaving the institution.

Humphrey & Ounsted (1963: p. 603) also identified differences in IQ scores depending on age at placement, but using different age boundaries. In higher socio-economic status adoptive families, children placed before the age of six months had a mean IQ score of 119, while those placed after six months had a mean score of only 107. In contrast, the IQ of those adopted by 'working class families' did not appear to be sensitive to age at placement (100 and 99 for early and late-placed placements respectively). Similar IQ differences, though not quite so marked, were also obtained by Jerome (1993: p. 292) between those adopted before and after six months.

Although Kadushin's (1970: p. 208) study of late-placed children showed 'a greater degree of psychic health and stability than might have been anticipated given the nature of their backgrounds and developmental experiences', age at placement did seem to affect adjustment. Like many other studies, the capacity of these children to develop good interpersonal relationships seemed to be related to successful outcomes. 'The older the child was at the time of placement ... the greater the likelihood of less favorable outcome' (Kadushin, 1970: p. 208).

Quality of pre-placement care and close relationships

Perhaps one of the strongest associations to emerge from research is that between children's experience of poor quality care and relationships before placement and developmental impairment after placement. Studies that have been able to control for age at placement and the number of moves before adoption, find that it is not age or moves as such that prelude disturbance, but rather poor quality care prior to being placed.

The adoption of older children represents the loss and re-establishment of attachment relationships. Prior to adoption, the majority of late-placed children will have formed either a secure or an insecure attachment with their main carers. These relationships are then 'lost' through either separation, abandonment, rejection or neglect. The children have to form new attachment relationships with their adoptive parents. Within this 'process' are various developmental opportunities and risks. For example, *poor quality relationships* with biological parents may place children at some long-term developmental risk. The *loss* of close relationships, whatever their quality, can also be a source of great anxiety. This places further stress on children's emotional integrity. And finally, the *emotional demands* that both late-placed children and adopters place on each other as they attempt to establish closeness can be high. There is therefore no guarantee that the children's new attachments will be relaxed and secure.

Most studies of late-placed children recognise that what happens before adoption appears to have an impact on what takes place after adoption. For example, Thoburn (in Fratter *et al.*, 1991: p. 42) found that of children placed aged five to eight years old, those with a history of 'institutionalised' care suffered a disruption rate of 30% compared to a rate of only 13% for those described as non-institutionalised.

Examinations of late-adopted children report that, in general, a history of child abuse is associated with instability and poorer social development after adoption (Boneh, 1979; Zwimpfer, 1983; Nelson, 1985; Kagan & Reid, 1986). Kadushin (1970) observed that the majority of his late-placed children had been raised in large families in which they suffered physical and emotional neglect. Thoburn (in Fratter *et al.*, 1991: p. 43) found a high disruption rate of 41% for children with a history of deprivation and abuse compared to 30% for those with no such history. In a small study, Sack & Dale (1982), looked at 12 cases of children who had been physically abused and neglected *during their first two years of life and up until the time they were removed*. The children's average age at adoption was five and a half years. They developed patterns of behaviour described as 'intermittently provocative' and 'punishment seeking'. All the adoptive parents said that they found their behaviour provocative, bewildering and very difficult to handle: 'Whenever we try and reward him for something, he immediately stops doing it'; 'He wants to prove to us how bad he is' (Sack & Dale, 1982: p. 445). The researchers also report that the children exhibited considerable separation anxiety when their parents went away for more than the usual amount of time, even though the parents complained that they could never 'get close' to their child.

Children who have been sexually abused may present parents with very particular problems. These children may 'act out' sexually or behave 'seductively' – with their adopters, siblings, friends – behaviours which parents can find upsetting and hard to handle (Powers, 1984 cited in Bagley, 1993; Macaskill, 1984). It seems then, that an '*absence* of any experience of good parenting', whether at home or in substitute care, places children at risk of a poor outcome (Rushton *et al.*, 1995: p. 692).

Neglect and rejection featured in the pre-placement lives of most of Humphrey & Ounsted's (1963) late-placed psychiatric clinic population. However, contrasting clinic with non-clinic adopted children, Cohen *et al.* (1993) found that 29.4% and 18.8% respectively had a history of abuse, although this was reported as not reaching statistical significance.

One possible refinement is that if the quality of the early relationship environment has long-term developmental consequences, then different types of initial adverse environments might propel children along different developmental pathways. The particular social and emotional content of relationships that are impersonal, inconsistent, hostile, indifferent and dangerous are likely to differ. Such differences might lead to a variety of adaptive strategies and behavioural consequences. Thus, pre-placement adversity may not itself be an undifferentiated experience. If early care experiences are related to psychosocial development after adoption and if such experiences vary, then we might expect to see a variety of developmental pathways being taken through post-placement childhoods.

In a study of parent-reported descriptions of 211 adopted children, Howe (1996b; 1997) used a simple classification of pre-placement types of care and relationship experiences to examine post-placement outcomes. Three groups were defined:

(1) *Baby-adopted children* placed before the age of six months with no adverse care experiences prior to being placed.
(2) *Good start/late-adopted children* who experienced non-adverse care for their first year of life or up until the time of placement, whichever was the shorter. In the case of children placed after their first birthday, prior to separation from their biological parents they experienced adverse care, usually in the form of rejection and/or neglect.

(3)   *Poor start/late-adopted children* who experienced adverse care
       during their first year of life or up until the time of placement,
       whichever was the longer.

At the time of interview with parents, the adopted children were
young adults. The adoptive parents were asked to report any experiences of problem behaviour when their children were adolescents.
'Within-group' comparisons were made. The baby-adopted and good
start/late placed groups both showed relatively low mean problem
behaviour scores (0.7 and 0.6 out of a maximum of 10, respectively).
The poor start/late-placed children had a significantly higher mean
problem behaviour score of 2.2 out of 10. Similar patterns were found
in the reported rates of 'angry and hostile' behaviour towards parents
and other family members (18% for baby adoptions, 20% for good
start/late placed children, and 44% for poor start/late-placed children),
and referral rates to psychological and psychiatric services in adolescence (16%: 15%: 39%, respectively).

However, when parents were asked to say whether or not they
believed that their child felt significantly anxious or insecure during
adolescence, the majority of both the good-start/late-placed and poor-
start/late-placed children reported high levels of insecurity in the
children. Insecurity also expressed itself as low self-confidence. Thus,
although both groups of late-placed children were seen as anxious and
insecure, the way they expressed these feelings resulted in different
kinds of behaviour. The insecurity of the good-start/late-placed children tended to lead to anxious-to-please and compliant behaviour. In
contrast, insecurity in the poor-start/late-placed children was more
likely to result in angry, oppositional behaviour. This suggests that
different qualities of early care propel children along different developmental trajectories.

But even this refinement fails to pick up some of the more subtle
differences within each of the three groups. Howe (1997) was also able
to identify two sub-groups within each of the three main groups that
seemed to buck the group's prevailing trend. For example, although
75% of baby-adopted children showed *no* serious problem behaviours
during adolescence, 25% did express high rates of 'externalising'
problem behaviours. A similar picture emerged for the good-start/late-
placed group with 65% exhibiting *no* serious problems in adolescence
and 35% who did. Matters are reversed in the case of poor-start/late-
placed children. 72% showed high levels of problem behaviour, but a
significant minority (28%) of this psychologically vulnerable group
showed *no* significant problem behaviours during adolescence.

These findings remind us that although we might detect behavioural
trends and tendencies in adopted children from different backgrounds,
the exceptions can be as interesting as the rules. We might speculate
that adoption in itself may place a developmental stress on some

children, as witnessed in the case of baby-adopted children who exhibit higher than expected levels of externalising problem behaviours. We might also deduce that children who experience poor quality care and relationships during their first year or so of life are put at a developmental disadvantage, no matter how good their subsequent care (the poor-start/late-placed group). Even so, a substantial number of these late-placed children achieve relatively problem-free childhoods. This is a powerful reminder that other factors clearly can come into play, serving to 'protect' some ostensibly vulnerable children from psychosocially impaired development.

Interesting, and something that we shall consider later, are the lower breakdown and disturbance rates described for late-placed children with either major learning difficulties or severe physical disabilities (for example, Macaskill, 1984; Wolkind & Kozaruk, 1986; Thoburn *et al.*, 1986; Glidden, cited in Rosenthal & Groze, 1994). The majority of these children experienced a range of pre-placement stresses, but something about either them or their relationship with their adoptive parents seemed to offer some protection against disruption and behavioural maladjustment. Some combination of the high level of the physical needs of the children and the knowledge, expertise and commitment of the adopters seems to produce good secure attachments and low problem outcomes.

Quality and character of children's behaviour prior to placement

Children's behaviour, seen as a 'pre-placement variable' is closely linked with the quality of pre-placement care. Certainly, it is reasonable to believe that poor quality care can lead to poor behaviour. On this reckoning, it is not so much that difficult conduct prior to adoption is associated with poor outcomes. Rather, it is poor quality early care that leads to both pre-placement problem behaviour and post-placement misconduct. But as always in social relationships, there is something of a chicken-and-egg quality to the argument. We can also risk the thought that children whose behaviour is difficult are likely to experience poor quality relationships with their parents. This approach places the origin of the difficulties within the children themselves (say, temperament, organic problems in brain function, hormonal excesses) and not the relationship between children and their parents. These alternative pathways need to be borne in mind as we consider the linkages between children's pre-placement behaviour and their progress after adoption.

On the whole, the evidence suggests that children who display significant behavioural problems before placement are the most likely to experience behavioural difficulties after placement. Several studies report higher disruption rates for children who had either emotional problems, behavioural problems or already experienced an adoption disruption before they were placed (Barth & Berry, 1988: p. 93; Borland *et al.*, 1991; Fratter *et al.*, p. 1991: 42). The problem behaviours most likely to be described were social misconduct and relationship difficulties with other people. The children typically exhibited behaviours of lying, cruelty, fighting, threat, disobedience, running away, aggression, delinquency, stealing and vandalism. Their desire for adult approval was generally low. Some children seemed unable to receive or give affection. A few had eating disorders. Barth & Berry (1988: p. 156) found that the degree of external behaviour problems before adoption was a better predictor of disruption than age at placement (Barth & Berry, 1988: p. 156).

Conclusion

Historically, a majority of studies have examined the association between pre-placement variables and adoption breakdowns rather than subsequent psychosocial development. There is broad agreement that the higher the number of 'special needs' that children have prior to placement, the higher the risk that the adoption will disrupt. Previous adoption breakdowns and the presence of externalising problem behaviours and emotional difficulties increase the risk of the adoption breaking down. Foster parents who decide to adopt after having gained experience and understanding of their children appear more likely to 'succeed', at least in terms of keeping their children through to adulthood. Support also comes from research that finds that adoption agencies which prepare parents thoroughly before they adopt have lower disruption rates (Cohen, 1984; Borland *et al.*, 1991: p. 21). Information, group support, full knowledge of the children and their background and what to expect, all help parents understand and cope with late-placed children.

The major pre-placement factor that seems to underpin all the others is the quality of care and close relationships experienced by late-placed children before they join their new adoptive families. Neglect, rejection and abuse lead to behavioural and emotional problems. In turn these upset children's ability to cope with people in general and new close relationships in particular. The longer children remain in situations of social and emotional adversity, the more disturbed their behaviour is likely to be. Thus, although problem behaviour, emotional disturbance and later age at placement are associated with increased rates of disruption and disturbed psychosocial development, early and prolonged poor quality care appear to lie behind these factors. We also looked at the possibility that poor quality pre-placement care itself is not an undifferentiated experience. Different kinds of adversity might project children along different developmental trajectories. Institutional privation, neglect, physical abuse, sexual abuse and hostile rejection may each produce a particular developmental psychopathology in the pre-adopted child. Adopters of late-placed children will therefore find themselves parenting not simply a child of adversity but more specifically, a neglected child, a rejected child and so on.

However, we must remember that a significant minority of late-placed children, many of whom began life in adversity, show good adjustment. Although they might appear prone to suffer a little insecurity and anxiety at times of stress, their childhoods are broadly problem-free. Why, then, do some late-placed children run into severe developmental difficulties while others manage to reach adulthood without major mishap? Do some children bring strengths of temperament or personality with them to the adoption? Or does their adoption provide them with relationships that helps them overcome the disturbing effects of their pre-placement care? Or is it some combination of the two?

The present chapter and our earlier discussion of gene–environment interactions have considered some of the possible developmental strengths and weaknesses that children might *bring with them* to their adoptions. Naturally optimistic and sociable children might be resistant to the damaging effects of negative social experiences. Some late-placed children might have been able to establish good-enough self-images and levels of social competence during their first year or two to protect them against later adversity. On the other hand, children with difficult temperaments or those who have experienced particularly hostile and rejecting relationships with their biological parents may possess few skills or emotional resources to cope with the demands of the new relationships in their adoptive family. The next chapter considers possible *post-placement experiences* that may contribute to late-placed children's psychological development and the outcome of their adoption.

Chapter 7

Older Children Placed for Adoption: Post-placement Environmental Influences on Development

Proponents of the strong line on developmental recovery argue that good quality post-experiences can overcome most, if not all, of the psychological damage caused by early traumas and adversities. They cite adoption as a powerful example of the ability of children to return to normal developmental pathways given a propitious environment. Their belief is that most adopters do in fact provide effective, compensatory parenting. However, the growing volume of outcome research on late-placed children has tempered these initially very positive pictures painted by some of the more optimistic advocates of the adoption of older children. Certainly, many children fare much better than those who remain in situations of social and emotional stress. But, it also has to be recognised that a significant number of late-placed children do exhibit levels of disturbance and behavioural upset much higher than would be expected for children of families of similar social backgrounds to those of the adopters.

Post-placement environmental influences on older-placed adopted children's development

This mixed picture has the potential to provide clues about what might help and hinder normal development. The environmental variety and complexity inherent in late-placed adoptions offers opportunities to examine some of the possible factors that might be playing a significant part in the growth of behaviour and personality. Children arrive in various states of social, emotional and behavioural wellbeing. And once they have been adopted, they find themselves living with new parents, siblings and friends. A number of adoption studies have looked at the relationship between outcome and the characteristics of the new adoptive environment. Most attention has been paid to the adopters themselves – as people, as parents, as personalities. Some research has also considered late-placed children's relationships with their adoptive siblings as well as other matters surrounding the adoption including 'telling', contact with birth-relatives and the possible significance of being placed transracially. We shall examine eight elements of the post-placement environment and their impact, if any, on late-placed children's development, behaviour and quality of relationships:

(1) Adoptive parents' characteristics.
(2) Adoptive family's characteristics.
(3) Parenting style of adopters.
(4) Siblings.
(5) 'Telling' and the provision of autobiographical information.
(6) Transracial adoptions.
(7) Contact with biological parents.
(8) Post-adoption support.

Adoptive parents' characteristics

Much interest has been taken in the age of the adopters and whether or not this has a bearing on the outcome. Triseliotis & Russell (1984: p. 50) report that adopted people themselves tended to be less satisfied in those cases where adoptive parents were aged 46 years or older at the time of placement. Some children said that they felt emotionally distant from 'old' parents. Other researchers suggest that the chances of a placement breaking down are slightly higher for younger parents than older parents, whether or not they are satisfied. One explanation is that older parents 'have more life and parenting experience and can thus withstand the turmoil of adolescence better' (Berry & Barth, 1990: p. 223). But reminding us that the analysis and interpretation of adoption outcomes is rarely simple or straightforward, Borland *et al.* (1991) found that childless couples were more successful in parenting children who were placed with them under the age of ten years, while experienced parents seemed to cope best with the more disturbed children who arrived after their tenth birthday. Overall, however, the evidence on adopters' age, experience and outcome remains patchy and inconsistent, suggesting that not too much should be read into these matters in themselves.

There is some consistency in the finding that parents with higher academic qualifications and more time in education tend to do less well with late-placed children. Disruption rates, for example in Barth & Berry's (1988: p. 94) work, were highest for new parents with college degrees and lowest for those with only basic high school education. This is echoed in studies which describe increased levels of dissatisfaction and adjustment problems amongst children adopted by families of higher social and economic status and educational background (Jaffee & Fanshel, 1970; Triseliotis & Russell, 1984; Rosenthal & Groze, 1994).

Adoptive family's characteristics

The quality of relationships between family members is often reported as an important factor in determining children's development. The processes involved in selecting and preparing adopters might be expected to filter out people who experience personal, marital or family instability, factors known to correlate with child disturbance. Such selection processes on the whole seem reasonably successful in identifying parents with good personal and social resources. Even parents whose adopted children have been referred to mental health clinics appear to enjoy better levels of adjustment, psychological health and marital accord than the biological parents of non-adopted children seen in the clinical setting (Cohen *et al.*, 1993). Adoptive families who cope best with 'special needs' late-placed children are more cohesive, have more flexible roles and family rules, and tend to display fewer symptoms of psychological disturbance (Sack & Dale, 1982; Cohen, 1984; Nelson, 1985; Tienari *et al.*, 1990; Cohen, *et al.*, 1993). The mutual support of family members, including fathers who are prepared to become actively involved in child care as well as support mothers, helps both children and adults gain in emotional strength (Westhues & Cohen, 1990). In general, it appears to be the positive, warm, open, responsive and reciprocal quality of family relationships that helps children develop good levels of adjustment, high self-esteem and relatively problem-free behaviour (Bagley, 1993).

Barth & Berry (1988: p. 125) report the interesting finding that families who were in regular contact with nearby living relatives had lower disruption rates than those who did not have relatives living within easy, regular visiting distance. This appears to be part of a general finding that families who enjoy social support – say from each other, relatives, friends, fellow church goers – appear to cope better with their adopted children.

Parenting style

The incorporation of late-placed children into adoptive families is most successful in those cases in which parents are prepared to make a major commitment of time and energy (Tizard 1977: p. 216). Adopters who appear to have personal problems (for example, non-consummated marriages, failure to adjust to infertility, lack emotional warmth) may find it hard to 'bond' with their children and outcomes may therefore be more unfavourable (Kadushin, 1970; Ounsted, 1970).

The association between high social and educational status of adopters and poorer outcomes is often explained by the stress and guilt induced in their children because of high parental expectations and the pressure this places on children. Parents who value and encourage 'instrumental goals' such as educational success rather than 'expressive goals' such as caring and warmth in relationships are less likely to raise well-adjusted and relaxed children (Triseliotis & Russell, 1984: p. 80–81). Late-adopted children most value warm parenting laced with much support, encouragement, openness and honesty about the adoption coupled with an unconditional acceptance of their strengths and weaknesses.

Parents who find it difficult to sustain a warm, giving, unconditional relationship with children who continue to be needy, demanding and difficult are less likely to succeed. The lack of positive interaction and reciprocity can prove a disappointment to some parents. They begin to feel detached and even alienated from their children. Adopters who feel ineffective may become discouraged and ultimately dissatisfied (Nelson, 1985). In contrast, parents who expect and accept their children to have some behavioural and emotional problems as a result of early adversity and stress, enjoy more successful outcomes (Smith & Sherwen, 1983, and Cohen, 1981, cited in Barth & Berry, 1988: p. 71). Patience, tolerance and flexibility in the face of awkward and needful behaviour appears to underpin the most effective parenting of late-placed children. These qualities can extend to other areas of parent–child relationships. For example, Hodges & Tizard (1989b: p. 95) observed that adopters 'spent more time playing with their children, spent more time with them in 'educative' pursuits and involved them more in joint household activities' than either the biological parents of 'restored' children or, indeed, other middle-class parents of non-adopted children.

Many of these themes are nicely captured by Rushton *et al.* (1995: p. 692). They rated adopters in terms of their consistency, sensitivity, flexibility, warmth and understanding in their parenting behaviour. They found that 'The presence of two or more of: positive mothering, positive fathering and definite adoption plans, 1 month into the placement was strongly predictive of a better outcome 8 years later' (Rushton *et al.*, 1995: p. 692). Matters are further refined by taking into account the degree of pre-placement adversity experienced by the adopted boys. Slightly less positive parenting and increased ambivalence about the adoption were more likely if the boys had experienced poor quality care prior to their adoption. Less positive parenting was associated with poorer outcomes. However, if the children had high adversity background but nevertheless did receive positive parenting, they also showed moderate to good outcomes. 'That is, *all* the children with poor outcomes had a combination of higher pre-placement adversity and lower levels of positive parenting at the start of their placement' (Rushton *et al.*, 1995: p. 693). In other words, pre-placement adversity increases the risk of less positive parenting by adopters, but if the adopters can rise above this and provide positive parenting, late-placed children, whatever their pre-placement history, are much more likely to enjoy a good developmental outcome.

Summarising the adoptive parent and family factors associated with positive outcomes, Triseliotis *et al.* (1997: p. 33–34) list: absence of other young children when placing young children, not overstressed as a family, strongly motivated to provide a home for a child, tolerance of difference, flexibility of roles and rules, realistic expectations about possible difficulties, inclusive attitude towards the family of origin including acceptance of contact, and willingness to receive support from outside.

Siblings

There are several dimensions to adopted children's sibling environment and its relationship to outcome. Siblings can be either biologically or non-biologically related. That is, they can be other children of an adopted child's own biological parents or they can be the biological children of adoptive parents. Siblings can also be other non-biologically related children adopted by the adopters. Thus, it is possible for an adopted child to live with siblings, some of whom are their full-blood or half-blood brothers or sisters, some to whom they are not biologically related but have also been adopted by the same family, and others to whom they are not biologically related but who happen to be the birth children of the adopters. Siblings can vary in number. Some may be older or younger than the adopted child. Unravelling the impact of siblings on outcomes is not easy and the findings appear mixed. Simplified, we might consider three types of sibling environment:

(1) the presence of biologically related brothers and sisters;
(2) the presence of other, non-related adopted children;
(3) the presence of children born to the adopters.

Much attention has been paid to the advantages and disadvantages of placing sibling groups together. This is a complex issue and is often decided on grounds that are pragmatic rather than developmentally ideal. The physical and emotional ability of adopters to take two or more brothers and sisters is often limited. One member of a sibling group may have particularly high levels of need that will dominate family life and deprive others of time and attention. Results concerning the success of sibling group placements are spread across the spectrum. A few early investigations suggested that disruption rates were higher for sibling group placements (Boneh, 1979 cited in Festinger, 1986: p. 3; Kadushin & Seidl, 1971). Wedge & Mantle (1990) found that children placed with a sibling were neither more nor less likely to experience breakdown than those separated form a sibling.

A number of more recent studies have edged towards drawing more optimistic conclusions. They incline towards finding that placement stability tends to increase if two or more siblings are placed together (Kagan & Reid, 1986; Barth & Berry, 1988; Fratter *et al.*, 1991: p. 38;

Strathclyde Permanency Study cited in Borland *et al.*, 1991). The pre-servation (rather than the breaking) of sibling relationships may be a source of emotional continuity and so be acting as a protective factor. In other words, as Bagley (1993: p. 63) observes 'sibling groups should never be broken up simply in order to make placements easier.'

The presence of adopters' biological children appears to put baby-adopted children at some increased risk of problem behaviour, but the picture is less clear cut in the case of late-placed children. Barth & Berry (1988) found no relationship between disruption rates and the number of children in the family. But couples adopting adolescents did experience higher breakdown rates if there were biological children in the home (Berry & Barth, 1990). In general, these researchers found that families without birth children had a better record of coping with the more demanding children. Other studies have also reported gen-erally lower success rates when the adopters have birth children as part of the family (Wedge & Mantle, 1990). However, Thoburn *et al.* (1986) found that larger families with grown up children and relatives able to provide additional support were well represented among those who had successfully reared late-placed special needs children.

When the presence of other adopted children is added to the picture, the results remain inconsistent. Barth & Berry (1988: p. 127) found that disruption rates increased significantly if other adopted children were present. However, when only children placed as adolescents were considered, these differences disappeared (Berry & Barth, 1990). In other studies, the composition of the total sibling environment had no discernable bearing on outcomes for late-placed children, including disruption rates (Festinger, 1986: p. 30), rates of problem behaviour (Howe, 1997), and the development of emotional or psychiatric problems (Triseliotis & Russell, 1984: p. 50).

'Telling' and the provision of autobiographical information

It is now accepted as good practice that children should be told that they are adopted from as young an age as seems appropriate. Very young children, although they seem quite happy to announce that they are adopted, appear to have no real understanding of what this means. Not until the age of eight or nine years do children begin to realise the full implication of what it means to have been adopted. Adolescence, again, marks another psychological level of understanding and may be one of the most important times for parents and children to discuss adoption. 'Telling' therefore should not be a one-off event. Indeed, children's understanding of what it means to be adopted changes as they grow older. Therefore, information and discussion about being adopted should be a natural and relaxed part of the adoption process throughout childhood.

There is not a great deal of direct research on the relationship between 'telling' and developmental outcome. When it is considered, it tends to be seen as a feature of the adopters' parenting and relationship skills. If these skills are poor, then discussion about adoption becomes confused. It appears as another manifestation of the problems that some parents have in relationships with their children. Some parents, having 'told' their children that they are adopted when they were very young, never raise the topic again. Others do not give their children all the background information which they have in their possession. Some children sense that adoption is a sensitive subject for their parents and may suppress their thoughts and feelings about the matter. Thus, it can be difficult to unravel issues around 'telling' from more general parent–child relationship problems. The more strained and difficult relationships are between adopters and their children, the more problematic and badly handled is the subject of adoption and being adopted.

A small number of researchers have addressed issues surrounding telling, the provision of personal information and identity. Most researchers report that children want to know about their backgrounds; cultural, racial and ethnic heritage; genealogy; and reasons for being adopted. The provision of such information is believed to be closely linked with the formation of a clear and secure identity and self-concept (Triseliotis *et al.*, 1997: p. 38). Over the years, Triseliotis has produced a steady stream of valuable studies in this area. In their look at late-placed children, Triseliotis & Russell (1984) found that satisfaction levels increased the more open, complete and reflective were discussions about the adoption. Adopted people wanted to know as much as possible about their biological parents, other family members, origins, background and general circumstances before being placed, including the reasons for being taken into care. Failure to get a clear picture of these matters often seemed to add to children's confusion. But parents who went to the other extreme, insisting that being adopted should be publicly acknowledged at all opportunities, also upset children:

> 'When I was young my mother used to introduce me as her adopted daughter ... I hate being introduced as that, it used to screw me up. She was trying to bridge a gap and make it easy but I hated it.'

> (Triseliotis & Russell 1984: p. 97)

'Yet in spite of these strongly held and expressed views,' continue Triseliotis & Russell,

> 'no direct association was found between the disclosure and timing of adoption and the sharing of background information and genealogical information and a number of variables concerning satisfaction/dissatisfaction with the experience. Adoptees, however, who said that there was no discussion concerning their adoption and

their background were more likely than the rest to receive psychiatric help in childhood and in adult life.'

(Triseliotis & Russell, 1984: p. 107)

As in the case of baby-adopted children, the fact of being adopted can be a risk factor in itself and the less well adopters handle this, the more negative the impact on the adoption outcome. Versluis-den Bieman & Verhulst (1995) believe that the combination of adolescence and being adopted, particularly for late-placed, overseas and transracially placed children, can be especially difficult.

The general view is that although adopted children express clear and definite views about the need for and value of 'telling', the quality of relationships with their adopters is much more important in determining the overall level of satisfaction. Although many children and adopters appear to find talking about origins and backgrounds a difficult topic, it does not necessarily upset the good quality of their relationship and the success of the outcome.

Transracial placements

The routine placement of black children in countries where the majority ethnic community is white is a relatively recent phenomenon, particularly in Western countries. The scale of placements began to increase during the 1960s and 1970s with the increased willingness of white couples to adopt black children. It seemed preferable to place black children in care for adoption with white families rather than see them languish in public care. The growing practice of intercountry adoptions further added to the volume of placements that saw children moving from one racial and cultural background to another. However, the political significance and symbolism of black children being raised by white parents soon generated fierce critiques of what came to be known as transracial placements. The practice had powerful echoes of old oppressions and injustices. Black social workers began to mount philosophical, cultural and political arguments against the value, appropriateness and rightfulness of transracial adoptions. The campaign proved to be very effective and it soon became orthodox policy to vigorously seek same-race placements for both white and black children. This required improved and imaginative recruitment practices to attract more black parents to adopt black children. The results continue to be successful, and it has become progressively easier to place children from minority ethnic backgrounds with matched families.

The debate has also made people realise that definitions of race, ethnicity, culture and identity are far more complex than was previously understood. The complexities and subtleties of race and mixed parentage, religion and class mean that even same-race placements are fraught with political, religious and cultural problems. Nevertheless, in spite of some of the difficulties of definition and even though policies and practice are changing in the direction of same-race placements, there is still research interest in assessing and evaluating the outcome of transracial placements psychologically as well as morally. Even this activity, though, is fraught with political problems. The issue finds itself squarely in Humean territory where empirical questions of what *is* the case do not logically lead to political answers which say what *ought* to be the case. In practice, the two questions often become confused and psychological claims are made on the basis of political beliefs and political positions are argued from empirical evidence. Rushton & Minnis (1997) have reviewed both positions in a very clear, comprehensive and helpful paper at the end of which they reach a number of eminently balanced conclusions. They recognise the different strengths of the two perspectives and this section benefits from their careful and sensitive treatment of a tricky area of theory and practice.

Studies that have examined rates of placement breakdown, having controlled for things such as age, find no differences between transracial placements and white same-race placements (McRoy & Zurcher, 1983 cited in Triseliotis *et al.*, 1997: p. 168; Barth & Berry, 1988; Berry & Barth, 1990; Charles *et al.*, 1992; Thoburn *et al.*, 1997). Subtle differences can be detected when results are further analysed. For example, Thoburn in her analysis found that 'when other variables are held constant, neither having two black nor two white [biological] parents is significantly associated with outcome, but being of mixed parentage is a risk factor in that it is associated with negative outcomes' (in Fratter *et al.*, 1991: p. 40).

A similar picture emerges for psychosocial and behavioural development. Satisfactory outcomes range between 70–80% for black children placed transracially, success rates similar to those achieved by late-placed white same-race adoptions (for example, Gill & Jackson, 1983; Simon & Alstein, 1977; 1987; Silverman & Feigelman, 1981; Bagley, 1993). Similarly, in their study of 1538 transracially placed 'international adoptees', Versluis-den Bieman & Verhulst (1995: p. 1425) concluded that 'transracial adoption is not related to later maladjustment.' As with white same-race late-placed children, problem behaviour and adjustment difficulties appear to be related to early life adversity and poor pre-placement care and not, for example, being black in a white family (for example, see Silverman & Feigelman, 1981). In other words, breakdown rates (which are the same for minority ethnic children whether raised by same-race or transrace parents) appear to be governed by child related factors. Experienced parents of either the same or different ethnic backgrounds to their children experience the same demands and difficulties when parenting children whose pre-placement care has been very deprived, abusive and damaging (Thoburn *et al.*, 1997).

Results are less clear on the ability of transracially placed black children to develop a positive racial identity. White parents of black children who take a very pro-active and sensitive line in ensuring that their children are exposed and introduced to black communities and culture appear to have some success in helping their children achieve a positive black identity. Those who take no such action are much less successful. These observations are not necessarily incompatible with Simon and Alstein's (1987: p. 140) finding that as young adults, the transracially adopted people in their studies remained firmly committed to their adoptive families.

On measures of self-esteem, again the evidence records no significant differences between same-race and transrace adoptions (Gill & Jackson 1983; McRoy *et al.*, 1982; Silverman & Feigelman 1990; Thoburn *et al.*, 1997). Low self-esteem in late-placed children appears more to do with adverse early care than skin colour (Thoburn *et al.*, 1997). Several researchers in this field are keen to point out that self-esteem and racial identification do not have to be related. Reviewing the work of McRoy and others, Silverman & Feigelman write:

'Perhaps their most interesting quantitative finding on racial identi-fication was the absence of any relationship between measures of racial identification and self-esteem. This data suggests that self-esteem and racial identity are not inextricably bound as is sometimes asserted. They appear, in fact, to be independent dimensions. It implies that a transracially adopted black child might develop a positive sense of self without an exclusive identification with the black community.'

(Silverman & Feigelman, 1990: p. 197)

Bagley (1993: p. 55) reminds us that the development of self-esteem is largely derived from the quality of parenting a child receives. Two dimensions of good parenting are recognised. The first is the provision of love and warmth. The second factor is independent of the first, but equally important. It involves a mixture of authoritative (but not authoritarian) parenting, consistency or norms and rules, fairness, a 'coherent and ego-enhancing account of a child's own identity (wher-ever that is relevant); and consistency and continuity of key figures in the socialization process' (Bagley, 1993: p. 55). Triseliotis *et al.* (1997: p. 171–172) also note that transracially placed children appear to be as well adjusted as matched samples of white children placed with white parents, possibly 'suggesting that the quality of parenting may be the paramount factor, rather than racial matching.'

Thus, all else being equal, the prevailing view is that black children should be placed with matched black families, although devel-opmentally transracially late-placed children appear to suffer no greater risk than white same-race placed children.

Adoption has always found itself walking a fine line between the social and the psychological, the personal and the political, the developmental and the cultural. The placement of children from minority ethnic groups has heightened all the standard issues surrounding the movement of children between families, between classes and between countries. The way such tensions get resolved reflects the direction of the prevailing political climate, the niceties of which are delicately captured by Rushton & Minnis who conclude:

'On the basis of our own political and value judgements, we believe that transracial placements continue to be difficult because the social context is a racist one. Therefore, despite the fact that the limited research evidence tends to give positive support for transracial placements, we find ourselves continuing to argue that ethnically matched placements will be in the best interests of both the child and the community in most instances.'

(Rushton & Minnis, 1997: p. 11)

Contact with biological parents and family

In similar vein to the demand for same-race placements, considerable political pressure has built up over recent years for some form of contact to be maintained between adopted children and their biological families, at least in most cases. The arguments for these 'open' adoptions is based on a mixture of evidence drawn from anthropological studies (it seems to work well in other cultures), the unresolved feelings of loss experienced by many (but by no means all) birth mothers and the belief that developmentally children benefit by not severing all ties with their biological parents and family.

In fact, studies that examine the long-term outcome of adopted children *either maintaining or breaking contact* with birth relatives are few and far between. The drive for more open adoptions has received most of its impetus from political arguments based on notions of rights, honesty and openness as a philosophy that should underpin all human relationships. The evidence that such philosophies and the practices based on them is actually beneficial to children's psychosocial development is largely missing. However, adoption practices, so often spurred along by strong political rhetoric rather than carefully garnered psychological findings, has become enthusiastic about the rights and the merits of increased openness in adoption. This further shift away from the secrecy that has so often surrounded adoption and the idea of a 'clean break' has been broadly welcomed by adoption agencies and their workers, although less is known about the views and feelings of adoptive parents.

The battle lines between open and closed adoptions began to be sharpened after the work of Goldstein, Freud & Solnit (1973; 1980) first appeared. These authors felt that unless children placed for adoption made a complete break from their biological parents, they would suffer a sense of impermanence in their key relationships. As a result they would not feel secure and good attachments to their new parents would be threatened. Developmental wellbeing was promoted by having a continuous relationship with one set of 'psychological' parents only. All contact with non-custodial parents should therefore be stopped. Literal interpretations of the 'permanency' movement in child welfare work generally took these arguments to mean that children should be clearly and unambiguously raised by only one set of 'psychological' parents, be they the children's biological parents or adoptive parents, but definitely not both.

The counter-argument saw the value of openness and contact, particularly for older children placed for adoption (Ryburn, 1994). Children, it was said, are quite capable of handling multiple relationships. A full picture of who they are, from whence they came and to whom they are related helps adopted children avoid confusion, speculation and the spread of misinformation. The anxieties caused by feelings of loss and separation, rejection and abandonment are also reduced if children remain in some form of contact with their biological family. Meaningful relationships can be maintained. Openness cuts down insecurity. It allows children to feel more positive about themselves. Their self-image can be good. The experience of 'dual psychological parenting' poses no great problems for late-adopted children (Thoburn, 1996).

Two main kinds of contact can be identified: indirect contact (letters, photographs, current information); and direct contact (periodic face-to-face meetings between adopters, adopted children and members of their biological families). Although there is very little work on the long-term outcomes of open versus closed adoption, the indications are that contact, particularly in the case of late-placed children, generally appears to be a good thing (for example, Ryburn, 1994). Each case, of course, has to be considered on its merits. For example, contact may be much more problematic and 'contra-indicated' in cases where the child has suffered sexual abuse or severe physical abuse.

Older-placed children not only have clear memories of their birth families, many of them also enjoy maintaining some form of contact with them (Thoburn *et al.*, 1986; Sorich & Siebert 1982; Hill *et al.*, 1989). They seem perfectly able to handle the variety of relationships involved. And assuming that adopters offer competent parenting, relationships within the adoptive family not only remain secure but can often be strengthened by children's contact with birth relatives. A number of studies in this field also suggest that when late-placed children are not allowed or encouraged to maintain contact, problematic behaviour and adoption breakdowns are more likely (Borland *et al.*, 1991; Wedge & Mantle 1991; Fratter, 1996). Lower disruption rates and higher levels of adoptee satisfaction have been described for adoptions where contact has been maintained (Eldred *et al.*, 1976; Thoburn in Fratter *et al.*, 1991: p. 45). One interpretation given to these findings is that contact acts as a 'protection' factor in late-placed children's development.

Contact does not mean that children wish to return to their biological parents. Rather, the message appears to be that whether the quality of relationships with their biological parents was good or bad, they have been and remain important people in the children's lives. They should not be denied or ignored. 'Some of the evidence ... suggests that older children who are pressurized to abandon existing meaningful relationships with members of their birth family, or any family for that matter, may find it difficult to attach themselves to a new family' (Triseliotis *et al.*, 1997: p. 76).

Of course, for some children, the experience of contact can be difficult, but even in these cases, the children often recognise that openness is a more realistic and ultimately healthier route down which to go. 'I knew where I stood,' said one young man in Fratter's study (1995 cited in Triseliotis *et al.*, 1997: p. 79), 'I knew who was the better mother.'

At the end of their useful review of contact, Triseliotis *et al.* conclude that although the studies of contact are small in both scale and number, they:

> '... seem to suggest that olde_ children, especially, are able to distinguish between different types of relationships and to have the capacity to relate to more than one set of parent figures simultaneously. It does not follow that the relationships with each of these is the same, as different satisfactions seemed to be derived from each. The same studies also suggest that, overall, the children found contact useful because of the direct explanations they had from their birth parents about why they couldn't keep them.'

> (Triseliotis *et al.*, 1997: p. 79)

Post-adoption support

Not only are disruption rates lower if adopters are well-prepared by social workers (the provision of full background information and realistic expectations about the child), they are also reduced if post-adoption support is provided (Kagan & Reid 1986; Barth & Berry 1988). Bagley & King (cited in Bagley, 1993: p. 63) add that support is particularly important and effective in the placement of children who have been sexually abused. Thus, along with the support of family and friends, professional as well as financial support also appear to help adopters cope, particularly in the case of difficult children (Borland *et al.*, 1991: 25, p. 27).

The quality of post-placement environments and outcomes: parent–child interactions

Late-placed children arrive with their own history of relationships, ingrained behaviours and burgeoning personalities. These established characteristics interact with and influence the adopters and other family members. As we have seen, whether or not a placement breaks down or problem behaviours develop depends on the quality of these parent–child interactions. The interactional skills of both late-placed children and their adoptive parents can be either good or poor. We might therefore anticipate four basic combinations of parent–child relationship skills that might influence placement outcomes:

(1) interpersonal skills of both child and adopters are good;
(2) skills of child are good but those of adopters are poor;
(3) skills of child are poor but those of adopters are good;
(4) skills of both child and adopters are poor.

The origins of the children's and parents' relationship competences can be many and various, but it is worth recognising a few, particularly as some can be influenced by the practices of adoption workers. It also has to remembered that children with easy temperaments and good interpersonal skills can raise adopters' level of parenting just as children with difficult temperaments and demanding behaviours can lower the parenting skills of other adopters.

Providing adopters with knowledge about their children and preparing them for what to expect appears to help parents understand the needs and behaviours of late-placed children. This can make parents more patient, tolerant and accepting. Similarly, the provision of practical and emotional support, whether by family, friends or adoption workers, seems to give adopters the strength and opportunity to think about their children and their relationship with them in a less anxious and agitated way. Adopters need deep emotional resources as well as practical parenting skills.

On top of whatever behavioural and personality characteristics adopted children bring with them to their placement, they also have to handle the fact of being adopted. As well as their adoptive family, they have experiences and memories of their birth family. The feelings of loss, rejection and hurt that so often affect adopted children can easily upset their ability to handle close, emotionally significant relationships. This is why many people believe that contact with biological relatives is developmentally helpful. In many cases (though by no means all), contact and openness help dispel the secrecy, the confusion and the feelings of rejection that frequently appear to lead to such difficult and demanding behaviour by adopted children.

Finally, the concept of *resilience* may help us to understand some of the different outcome patterns associated with late-placed children. In spite of early life adversity, environmental risks or poor placement experiences, some children seem to emerge psychologically relatively unscathed. They are able to cope appropriately and competently with most normal social relationships. Resilience turns out to be a fairly complex and subtle attribute. It is certainly not to be seen as a fixed quality that somehow shields the individual from all adversity throughout life. It is perhaps sufficient to note at this stage that children display huge variation in their response to stress and adversity, and the variety of outcomes reported for late-placed children might in part be explained by variations in individual resilience. But even so, as Rutter (1995a: p. 77) reminds us: 'No-one has absolute resistance to stress and often "escape" from damage is relative and not complete.'

Children's resilience may derive from a number of inherited and environmental sources. Fonagy *et al.* (1994) identify a wide range of defining attributes of resilient children that include: easy temperament; high IQ; a sense of humour; absence of early separation and losses; a good, warm relationship with at least one caregiver; availability of good social support; and interpersonal empathy and awareness. It can be seen that this brief list ranges over the three basic inputs that we have been examining – inherited characteristics, pre-placement experiences, and post-placement experiences. At the end of her analysis of late-placed children, Tizard reached similar conclusions:

> 'There seem ... to be three possible mechanisms – the 'problem' children may have been more genetically vulnerable than the others, and/or they may have had different experiences within the institution, and/or they may have had different experiences after leaving the institution ... Whatever the explanation, and it seems likely that a number of factors were involved, the children's difficulties tended to begin early and to persist. The most difficult children at eight had usually been identified as such in the nursery; there was a marked tendency for the children who gave the most difficulty in their new homes at four and a half to be still seen as difficult at eight.'

> (Tizard, 1977: p. 225–226)

Conclusion

As we have seen, children who arrive in their placement having experienced at least some good quality care in their early life, who have few behavioural or emotional problems, whose temperament is easy, and whose self-esteem is good are easier to parent. Placed with skilled parents, the outcome for these children is likely to be good. And even those adopted by less competent parents may interact in such a way that the adopters' deficiencies do not undo the resilience acquired by the children. Only if the skill and sensitivity of the adopters is very low may some of the vulnerabilities that nearly all late-placed children bring to placement increase the risk of a poor developmental outcome.

However, the experiences of perhaps the majority of late-placed children leave them vulnerable to the rigours and demands of social relationships. They join families after a history of abuse, neglect or rejection. They have rarely enjoyed care by a parent that has been either long-term or consistently warm and responsive. In some cases, the children's own difficult temperamental make-up may have exacerbated relationships with their parents that were already stressed and poor. For late-placed children, major experiences of loss and separation are the rule rather than the exception. One consequence of such early adversity is to produce behaviour that is difficult. As we have heard, if these low-resilience, high-vulnerability children are placed with families in which warmth is low, stress levels are high, understanding and tolerance limited, flexibility rare, and structures uncertain and inconsistent, the adoptive family environment is one that increases the risk of a poor developmental outcome and in some cases, the breakdown of the placement. Particularly difficult and demanding children may, of course, tax the skills of parents who would otherwise cope well with less needy and less problematic children.

On the other hand, place these same children with skilled, experienced and responsive parents and we see an increase in resilience and decrease in vulnerability. This picture squares with the work of Werner & Smith (1982) who tracked a number of high-risk children. About 10%, in spite of childhood adversity, managed to develop into well-adjusted adults. A range of factors seemed to contribute to this minority group's positive outcome. These included: smaller family structure; the opportunity for some good quality interactions (moderate attention given to the child); clear, fair and consistent household rules; and a low number of stressful events encountered. Late-placed children who transfer from biological families low on these protective factors to adoptive families high on these factors might therefore expect to achieve a degree or more of developmental recovery.

Chapter 8

Heredity, Environment and Adoption Outcomes

The next step is to tidy up, simplify and organise what we have learned so far about the various associations found between adopted children, their experiences and the success or otherwise of their placements. It will give us a clearer idea about the main behaviours and developmental characteristics of adopted children and link them to various features in both their pre-placement and post-placement world. This will place the many observations made about adopted children and their development into some loose order. Categorising observations is a preliminary step towards developing theories that account for the various developmental routes taken by adopted children between placement and early adulthood. Although the exercise captures only the most regular and pronounced observations, it has the attraction of allowing through only those findings that persistently appear in adoption outcome studies. Such an approach deliberately tolerates a wide range of research designs. It is therefore both interesting and reassuring that although there may be disagreement over methodology and many of the fine empirical details, there is a great deal of consensus over the broad features of the adoption outcome landscape.

The success or otherwise of placing children for adoption has taken two basic forms:

(1) The first looks at the psychosocial development of adopted children. A placement is regarded as a success (*a positive outcome*) if the child is seen as well-adjusted, has relatively few problem behaviours and displays social competence at home, school and with peers. Placements which disrupt and breakdown clearly fail. Breakdown has been used as a extreme measure of non-success, particularly in the case of late-placed children. By the same token, not to break down, again particularly for late-placed children, can be taken to indicate a relatively positive outcome.

(2) The second criterion is based on the views of those involved – adopters and adopted children. People may be more or less satisfied with the adoptive experience. To express satisfaction is taken to indicate *a positive outcome*. Although there are cases in which different evaluations are made by parents and children,

there is sufficient agreement in the majority of instances for this measure to be seen as reasonably robust.

There is also a high degree of accord between the developmental measures and the levels of satisfaction. Well-adjusted children have parents who feel very satisfied with the adoption; poorly adjusted children either feel dissatisfied themselves or have parents who feel a measure of dissatisfaction or disappointment.

The pre-placement and post-placement factors can now be correlated with the two categories of positive outcomes and poor outcomes. In addition, two further refinements might be made by way of organising the observational material: (1) factors can be associated with either genetic inheritance or environmental experience; and (2) outcomes can relate to either baby-adopted children or late-placed children. Baby-adopted children will be looked at first.

Factors associated with outcomes for baby-adopted children

For most children adopted as babies the outcome, whether looked at emotionally, socially or educationally, is very good. Compared to children born to biological parents of similar background and character but who remain with their parents, adopted children do extremely well. Across a whole variety of measures, rates of success for adopted children are much better than those for the biological comparison groups. However, compared to non-adopted children raised in families with similar socio-economic characteristics to those of adoptive parents, rates of success for adopted children are slightly worse. We have, therefore, an interesting picture that hints at the influence of both inheritance and adoptive family life on adopted children's psychosocial development.

Given that (1) certain temperamental characteristics such as high inhibition (high threshold of arousal) increase the risk of some children behaving antisocially, (2) these temperaments might be heritable, and (3) more adopted children than non-adopted children in socio-economically advantaged homes have a biological parent who has behaved antisocially, it might be expected that more adopted children would exhibit problem behaviours than non-adopted children. To a small extent this appears to be the case, but the frequencies are not as great as might be expected if genetic risk factors alone were accounting for problem behaviours. Similar observations can be made for the expected and observed occurrences of psychiatric illnesses in adopted children. We might therefore conclude that being adopted offers some protection. In contrast, the environment of children who remain with their socio-economically disadvantaged biological parents does not appear to protect them to anything like the same extent. Indeed, many features of their environment (high criticism/low warmth parents, material poverty, emotional stress, lack of support) are indicators of high risk.

The relative strength of inherited and environmental risk and protection factors will influence the level of psychosocial adjustment achieved by particular adopted children. Parents giving up their children for adoption have higher rates of antisocial behaviour and antisocial personality disorders. These carry 'significant *hereditary loadings*'. All traits interact with the environment and are capable of bringing about changes in the way other people respond to individuals with those traits. The expression of temperamental and personality predispositions can also be influenced by the environment. The attributes of the social environment therefore matter a great deal in determining how certain inherited predispositions are shaped and expressed.

Clinicians and outcome investigators have tended to concentrate on adopted children's post-placement *environmental* experiences. They tell us which environmental characteristics appear to affect children's development for better or worse. Two environmental factors in particular have been identified as highly influential in adoption outcome: first, the actual experience of, meaning and interpretation given to being adopted poses a potential psychosocial risk for adopted children, and second at the specific level, adoptive families, like non-adoptive families, will vary in the quality of social relationships they offer children. Parent–child relationships are especially critical, although as children grow older sibling relationships increase in importance.

Table 8.1 describes the inherited and environmental factors and experiences that have been most frequently associated with either a positive outcome or a poor outcome.

The presence of particular factors or experience does not mean that the placement will inevitably lead to either a positive or a poor outcome. It is simply that the rates of either a positive or a poor outcome are higher if that particular factor or experience is present. Even though rates are higher if the factor or experience is present, it is merely relative to the rate recorded if the factor or experience is not present. It could still be that the rate of the poor outcome behaviour is relatively small. For example, we might observe a rate of offending behaviour of 12% for adopted children (with non-criminal adopters) who have a biological parent with a criminal record, a figure which drops to only 3% for adopted children who do not have a biological parent with a criminal record. This also means, of course, that 88% of children (with non-criminal adopters) who have biological parents with a criminal record do not commit criminal offences.

Thus, for each adopted child, we have a balance of risk and protection factors and experiences that tip the developmental outcome towards either good psychosocial adjustment or poor psychosocial

Table 8.1 Factors and experiences associated with positive and poor outcomes in baby-adopted children.

	Positive outcomes	*Poor outcomes*
Heredity (pre-placement factors)	Easy temperament	Difficult temperament Inhibited temperament (high threshold of arousal) Psychiatrically ill biological parent Biological parent has a criminal/alcohol abuse record
Social environment (post-placement experiences)	*Parents:* warm, empathic, sensitive, accepting, responsive, interested. Stable, non-conflictual marriage *Family:* expressive; thoughts and feelings communicated accurately, openly and effectively; stimulating environment Other adopted (not necessarily biologically related) *siblings*	*Parents:* Unresolved feelings about infertility; inappropriately high expectations; low warmth/high criticism parenting; anxious parenting; intrusive, power-assertive control strategies 'Insistence on difference' *Family:* disturbed, conflictual relationships Presence of *siblings* who are the biological children of adopters Implications of *being adopted* perceived negatively by the child i.e. to have been 'rejected' by one's biological parents

adjustment. Furthermore, as genetic predispositions and the psychology of being adopted are, in a sense, pre-givens, the main variable that appears to influence outcome is the quality of social relationships generated within adoptive family life. The interaction between (1) good/poor parent–child and family relationships, (2) easy/difficult child temperaments, and (3) the psychological risk of being adopted, create a number of possible developmental pathways for adopted children. Each pathway is associated with a particular outcome profile which may be judged overall to be either good or poor.

In these examples, genetic dispositions are having some active or reactive impact on the social environment. We can, of course, reverse the direction of influence. Skilled, open, responsive and empathic parents can develop strong, supportive relationships with children whose innate temperaments are disposed to be difficult. Their children are helped to develop good coping strategies. The result is that these adopted children show better levels of adjustment than similar children who remain with their poorly skilled biological parents. In contrast, insensitive, inattentive adoptive parents wrapped up in their own needs, can create anxiety and insecurity in children who might otherwise approach life positively and confidently.

We have seen that the research evidence finds that the majority of children adopted as babies achieve good levels of social and emotional adjustment. Thus, if we know that all children who are adopted have to adjust to the psychosocial stresses associated with adoption and that rates of inherited risk factors (for example, biological parents who have a history of antisocial behaviour or mental health problems) are higher for adopted children than non-adopted children from similar socio-economic backgrounds, we can conclude that in the majority of cases, adoption is acting as a protective experience against these inherited and experiential risks. Bohman & Sigvardsson (1990: p. 104–5) reached this conclusion in respect of adopted children's vulnerability to crime and heavy drinking. They observe that the high frequency of criminality and alcohol abuse in biological parents was not seen in their adopted children. Adoption 'largely reduced the risk of social incompetence and maladjustment. This conclusion is supported by the comparison with the children who were taken back by their biological mothers or who had grown up in foster homes. Among these children, maladjustment and school failure were common and persistent.' More importantly, the element of adoption that is providing the protection appears to be good quality parent–child relationships.

Nevertheless, it has to be remembered that given the generally high socio-economic standing of adoptive families, higher than expected numbers (though still small overall) of adopted children experience adjustment problems. In this minority of cases, the research suggests that the risks associated with inheriting difficult temperamental and personality traits and/or the condition of being adopted itself are either too high to receive protection from the parent–child relationship or that the quality of parent–child relationships are themselves poor and so fail to offer protection – indeed, they may even contribute to the risk.

Factors associated with outcomes for late-placed children

The situation here is more complex. Whereas we might simplify the developmental pathway taken by baby-adopted children as a product of the *interaction* between their *genes* (G) and the *environment* (E) of their adoptive family $(G \leftrightarrow E)$, it is not possible to offer such a straightforward picture for late-placed children. Not only do they have inherited traits, these traits interact at different times with radically different environments. However, we might simplify environments into the pre-placement environment covering all experiences prior to adoption (E^1) and the post-placement environment generated by the adoptive family (E^2). Interactions between genes and the first environment (E^1) lead to certain developmental outcomes, which then interact with the second, post-placement environment of the adoptive family (E^2). So, interacting with the second environment of the adoptive family are: the child's genetic characteristics, which continue to be present $(G \leftrightarrow E^2)$; and whatever behaviours and personality dispositions emerged from the first, pre-placement gene-environment interaction $(G \leftrightarrow E^1)$. This might be represented as:

Developmental Outcome of Adoption $= [(G \leftrightarrow E^1) \leftrightarrow (G \leftrightarrow E^2)]$.

These symbolic representations of what is going on are only a crude attempt to convey some of the complex psychosocial interactions that take place over time for children placed at older ages with adoptive parents. They are a reminder that unravelling the various influences on late-placed children's development is not easy and simple formulae are not possible. Those who believe that complete developmental recovery is possible appear to rule out the continued influence of pre-placement experiences. In effect, they argue that outcome at any stage in children's development is simply a product of genes and sufficient exposure to the current, prevailing environment, that is $(G \leftrightarrow E^2)$. The evidence presented in this book suggests that pre-placement experiences continue to have some influence on post-placement development, although the quality of the post-placement environment is capable of having a big impact in its own right.

In terms of mapping the associations between child and placement factors, and poor and positive outcomes for late-placed children, the inherited characteristics of children are present both before and after placement. In their interactions with the social environment, these characteristics will certainly influence the pre-placement outcome. However, because of the difficulties of design and interpretation, outcome research on late-placed children has rarely considered the part that heredity might continue to play in development, although it has considered physiological conditions such as the presence of physical disability. In effect, this means that outcome research on late-placed children has tended to look at the variables in children's pre-placement and post-placement environments that are associated with poor and positive outcomes. Table 8.2 describes the main associations.

Again, as with baby-adoptions, for each adopted child, we have a balance of risk and protective factors that tend to tip the developmental outcome towards either good psychosocial adjustment or poor

Table 8.2 Factors and experiences associated with positive and poor outcomes in older children placed for adoption.

	Positive outcomes	*Poor outcomes*
Social environment (pre-placement experiences)	Adoption by foster parents Good quality care experienced during first 12–24 months	Adverse care experienced throughout much of childhood prior to placement including abuse, neglect and rejection Institutional care up to and beyond 12–24 months Problem behaviours particularly externalising problem behaviours Older than 8–10 years at placement
Social environment (post-placement experiences)	*Parents:* warm, fair, accepting, realistic expectations, encouraging, mutually supportive and consistent *Family:* flexible roles and rules, open and expressive communication patterns *Sibling* group placements *Emotional support* from extended family and local community *Contact* with birth relatives Support of *post-adoption services*	*Parents* (particularly if college educated): high, unrealistic expectations Implications of *being adopted* perceived negatively by the child i.e. to have been 'rejected/failed' by one's biological parents

psychosocial adjustment. Children bring to their new families the behaviours, personality styles and relationship patterns formed within their pre-placement environment. Outcomes will therefore depend on how deep and entrenched are the pre-placement patterns and how strong and influential are the post-placement experiences. It is therefore difficult to interpret outcomes. For example, how can we tell what has helped bring about a positive outcome? Effective adoptive parenting? A resilient child? Benign pre-placement care? Simply being removed from an adverse environment? Conversely, we might wonder what might have contributed to a poor outcome? Incompetent adoptive parenting? A deeply damaged child, not susceptible to the belated appearance of good quality care? A child with serious behaviour problems who drains the resources of parents who would have no difficulties coping with a non-problem child?

As with baby-adoptions, we also know that there is some risk associated with being adopted itself. Children, particularly late-placed children, have to think about what it means to have been placed for adoption by their biological parents. As they grow older, they realise with increasing clarity that their parents had prolonged experience of caring for them, *and then chose to give them up for adoption.* The conclusion that some children draw from this realisation is that there must have been some negative quality about them which brought about their rejection. This feeling can intensify if the biological parents either kept a brother or a sister or went on to have more children whom they did not place for adoption.

One of the strongest features to emerge from outcome studies of late-placed children is the importance of close relationships for adopted children and their psychosocial development. Triseliotis *et al.* (1997: p. 36) write that '. . . the evidence suggests that the quality of this relationship [with the adoptive mother] is possibly the paramount factor which appears to over-ride all other considerations and factors, including colour and ethnicity.' The quality of such relationships, both before and after placement, has a deep bearing on behaviour and personality. Parenting, the quality of family life, and emotional support both inside and outside the family appear as the most important variables associated with poor and positive outcomes. These findings are extremely interesting on at least two counts. First, how important is the quality of close relationships in early childhood on the long-term development of personality and social competence? Second, can later relationships influence and modify the impact of earlier relationships on personality development and social understanding? Thus, adoption studies take us to the heart of matters concerning human social development. While:

(1) baby adoptions provide a natural experiment on the parts played by nature and nurture in development,

(2)   late-placed adoptions offer a natural experiment on the influences
       of early care experiences on the growth of personality, behaviour
       and relationship style.

As a result of more than 50 years of adoption research, we now have
a sense of what are the key factors that are influencing adoption outcomes in particular, and children's development in general. They
mostly revolve around *the quality of close relationships that children
experience both before and after placement*. Relationships carry
information about what the participants mean to each other, or believe
that they mean to each other. People also interpret these meanings in an
attempt to understand themselves, others and their relationships. A
sense of who one is forms in relationships. Depending on the character
of these close relationships, self-images and self-understandings, self-
esteem and self-efficacy can veer towards either the negative or the
positive.

   Positive outcomes have been associated with parenting (both before
or after placement) that shows empathy, acceptance (of the child for
what she is and her biological parents for what they are), confidence,
consistency, and reliability. Such parenting promotes understandings of
self that are positive. There is undoubtedly a psychology of adoption
that also has a major bearing on outcomes. To be adopted can be
interpreted as either to be loved and wanted (by one's adoptive parents)
or not to be loved and not wanted (by one's biological parents).
Successful outcomes seem more likely in cases where the positive
connotation is being made.

Risk and resilience, vulnerability and protection

The fact there are statistical associations between some environmental
variables and poor outcomes does not necessarily mean that the variables themselves are the risk factors or causally related to the outcome
in some direct way. The variables themselves may not be the risk agents.
Poverty, for example, is associated with certain diseases and illnesses,
but it is not material deprivation as such that causes the disease. Rather,
rates of smoking, poor diet or psychological stress may be higher in
poor households and these constitute the risk agents. For example:

   '. . . it is now apparent that relative subnutrition in early infancy (as
   indexed by low weight at birth and during the first year of life) is
   associated with a much increased risk of coronary artery disease and
   heart attacks in middle-age (Barker, 1991). The mechanisms are not
   fully understood but it seems likely that the early subnutrition may
   increase the organism's susceptibility to unduly rich diets in mid-life.
   Note that it is being *under*-weight in infancy that predisposes you to
   heart disease, whereas it is being *over*-weight in middle age that

creates the risk. The lesson is that risk factors may operate in different ways at different age periods.'

(emphasis original, Rutter, 1995a)

Unravelling the relationship between environmental factors and outcomes in adoption studies is helped by understanding the nature of risk and protection. So, in psychosocial situations, exposure to a risk may bring about a psychological dysfunction or some kind of social maladjustment. For example, the loss of a close love relationship – say the death of a spouse – can directly precipitate depression. However, as Rutter (1990: p. 186) points out, the continued lack of a close relationship (rather than its sudden loss) constitutes a *vulnerability factor* (rather than a direct risk factor) if other life stressors are met. The lack in itself may not be a risk. It only renders individuals vulnerable to psychological dysfunction if they subsequently experience stressful or adverse events, such as the failure to keep a job or the onset of a serious illness.

Brown *et al.*'s (1986) study of depression in women also makes these distinctions. The loss of a parent in childhood only makes adult women vulnerable to depression if they are also exposed to the subsequent risk of not receiving warm, affectionate parental care by their carers. Such losses create feelings of helplessness (inability to control key emotional experiences) and low self-esteem. It is the emotional vulnerability created by these feelings coupled with the risk of later affectionless care that lead to the depression. Parental loss is not associated with depression if children subsequently receive good quality emotional care: that is, they do not experience the risk variable of poor quality care.

Other characteristics and aptitudes serve to *protect* individuals against the disturbing consequences of risk environments. These protective mechanisms operate in a variety of ways including avoidance of the risk, immunity to the provoking agent, and positive cognitive processing of the negative experience. Many of the most effective protective mechanisms promote self-esteem and feelings of self-efficacy in the individual. Some factors in themselves do not protect individuals directly against risk, but they might increase people's positive self-evaluation of themselves or their effectiveness so that when they experience a setback or a hostile experience, their view of self is not too deeply disturbed.

Garmezy (1985, cited in Rutter 1990: p. 182) identified three broad sets of variables that operate as protective factors:

(1) personality features such as autonomy, self-esteem, and a positive social orientation;
(2) family cohesion, warmth, and absence of discord;
(3) the availability of external support systems that encourage and reinforce children's coping efforts.

Reworking these factors into the more subtle notion of protective mechanisms, Rutter (1990: p. 202; 1995a) produces the following five predictors of protective processes:

(1)   reduction in the personal impact of the risk experience,
(2)   reduction of negative chain reactions,
(3)   those that promote self-esteem and self-efficacy,
(4)   those that open up positive opportunities,
(5)   the positive cognitive processing of negative experiences.

Each predicts resilience.

People who are exposed to a risk but who manage to continue functioning adaptively might be said to show *resilience* in the face of that particular stress or adversity. Resilience is not just a matter of possessing some constitutional strength that equips some people to resist stress, adversity and other kinds of social assault. It is also an indication of how people perceive, conceive and respond to hazards. Resistance to stress can never be absolute. Levels of resilience for any one risk will vary between individuals (Rutter, 1990). For example, children of mentally ill parents are at increased risk of developmental impairment themselves. But by no means all such children will be adversely affected; many escape relatively unscathed. Research on differences in temperament strongly suggests that children with difficult temperaments respond less adaptively to stress and adversity. Finally, the way people either view, approach or negotiate risk situations can also lead to more or less effective outcomes (Rutter, 1990: p. 181–182).

The search for protective mechanisms rather than protective factors provides greater insight into how some individuals remain resilient in the face of adversity. Thus, although we have risk indicators, perhaps the more important concept is that of risk mechanisms – the processes that take place making some people susceptible to the risk.

'In summary, the crucial difference between vulnerability/protection processes and risk mechanisms is that the latter lead directly to disorder (either strongly or weakly), whereas the former operate indirectly, with their effects apparent only by virtue of their interactions with the risk variable.'

(Rutter, 1990: p. 188)

These distinctions between risk and resilience, protective and vulnerability factors provide a number of insights that begin to help us understand why different environmental experiences are associated with either positive or poor outcomes in adoption.

Let us take being adopted itself. It has been strongly implied throughout the presentation of the outcome studies that in some aspects being adopted appears to protect children against some risks and that at other times it seems to increase their vulnerability. Clearly, adoption itself cannot be both a risk and protective factor. It is when we examine matters in more detail that we begin to see that it is certain processes experienced within adoption that affect children's vulnerability or protection. For example, adoption has been shown to offer some protection against committing criminal offences for children who might otherwise be at risk because their biological parents have a criminal/ alcohol abuse record. Clearly, relationships within the adoptive home must be providing certain experiences that help children deal positively with temperamental traits, which under different circumstances could lead them to behave antisocially.

We have also seen that being adopted can carry a negative message, thus appearing in the research as a risk indicator. To be adopted can be interpreted by children to mean that their biological parents could not or would not care for them. Children can feel anger towards their biological parents for rejecting them as well as anger with their adopters for somehow being the instruments that facilitated this rejection. The feeling that they were not wanted can also be interpreted as being unwantable, unlovable or even bad. This reduces self-esteem and self-worth. Matters can be further compounded by the sense of unresolved loss of the biological parents experienced by many adopted children. These increase children's vulnerability to the minor risks experienced in all close relationships, including doubts about being loved and valued. Parents who do not handle this vulnerability well or children who also have difficult temperaments that create irritable, hostile and coercive responses in others, may, inadvertently, amplify the children's doubts about being loved and feelings of low self-worth. In response, children's behaviour may grow worse. There is anger at being rejected coupled with a provocative attitude. Downward spirals can easily set in once relationships get beyond a critical point. Because many adopters feel that they have dealt with the 'telling' of adoption in earlier childhood and no longer see it as a basic issue, they can find themselves out of emotional phase with their adopted adolescent children. The vulnerability of being adopted increases for children who connote being 'given up' by biological parents negatively. This may lead to difficult behaviour which is not fully understood by parents. They react to the poor behaviour rather than the emotional confusion. Their responses add to the risks present in vulnerable adolescents' social and emotional environments.

If there is a risk element in being adopted that works via children's negative interpretation of what it must mean to be given up by one's biological parents, then this might explain why openness and contact might be associated with more positive outcomes. Contact might act as a protective process, in effect by removing the risk of negatively interpreting the biological family's apparent decision to reject the adopted child. However, the feelings and reactions of the adoptive parents might also enter the balance of the equation. If they are relaxed and accepting of the biological family (by no means an emotionally easy thing to do) and able to facilitate open contact, then adopted children are both removed from a risk (apparent rejection by their biological family) and engaged in positive, protective relationships with their adoptive parents.

On the other hand, contact with biological parents might unsettle some adopters, making them feel anxious, threatened and without full entitlement to or control of their children. Thus, although the adopted children are able to avoid the risk posed by closed adoptions, they are exposed to the risk of having adoptive parents who do not feel easy with contact. For them, the children that they love might also represent a source of hurt and emotional discomfort. In sharing their love with others, children who are loved by their adopters might cause them pain. Adopters who have not adjusted to their own infertility or who had unloving parents themselves might find the practice of open adoption emotionally difficult. In such cases, the gains of avoiding one risk might be outweighed by the losses of being exposed to another.

It is within relationships that children build up models of themselves and other people. Relationships that are experienced as indifferent, hostile or rejecting produce low levels of self-esteem, self-worth and self-efficacy. Children do not see themselves as valuable or effective social players. They therefore remain vulnerable when they find themselves in environments of risk and adversity. The result can be behaviour which is maladaptive and antisocial. This can trigger a negative chain reaction of critical and coercive responses by others that amplify the social risks. The origins of self-esteem and self-efficacy may explain why not all late-placed children experience adjustment problems. Two protective processes might be identified.

Children who enjoyed good quality care for at least the first year or two of life may have been able to build sufficiently positive and robust views of self to enable them to resist the undermining effects of later poor quality parent–child relations, say in the case of a lone mother who then marries a man who rejects his step-child. 'To that extent, secure, harmonious parent–child relationships provide a degree of protection against later risk environments' (Rutter, 1990: p. 206). This does not mean that the rejected child will not suffer emotional upset within the context of the rejecting relationship. However, it might mean that the child blames the parents for the deterioration rather than herself as someone essentially unlovable and bad. If the child is then placed with adoptive parents who are warm and accepting, she is once more able to respond confidently and securely. It might also be the case that a child with good self-esteem produces more positive reactions in those with whom she interacts, again suggesting that good-quality early care associated with successful outcomes is the source of the protective mechanism of high self-esteem.

In contrast, late-placed children who experienced few, if any prolonged good quality parent–child relationships will enter new relationships with low self-esteem, self-worth and self-efficacy. Their feelings about self will be poor and their views of others will be that they are not to be trusted and that they may be a source of rejection and hurt. Indeed, to be adopted itself is proof that those who should have been the children's carers, could not or would not look after them. This is not a recipe for easy relationships or problem-free behaviour. It is also likely to bring out the worst in others. This merely confirms, at least as far as the children are concerned, that the world of others is a hostile, difficult place. This mechanism might explain why some late-placed children's developmental profile is poor.

However, we also know that many late-placed children with long histories of persistent neglect, abuse and rejection are able to show significant developmental recovery. One possible explanation is the ability of children to reflect accurately and realistically about the adverse character of their upbringing so that they no longer believe that there is something about them which is unlikeable and socially ineffective. Self-esteem is re-established. It is important how we handle and interpret bad relationship experiences, particularly when we are young. The adverse, painful experience is 'cognitively processed' thereby reducing its negative impact. So, for example, children begin to recognise that their mother was psychiatrically ill, or that she was the victim of a violent partner, or that the stresses of poverty and a large family simply ground down a parent. Children understand that the problems were not of their making. They see that there was not something terrible about them that was to blame. The protection gained by reducing the impact of the risk can arise out of later positive experiences. Warm, enhancing adoptive parenting can supply late-placed children with experiences that allow them to re-evaluate their earlier negative relationships with their biological parents not as due to their failings as a child but rather as a consequence of problems experienced by their parents. Similarly:

'... the loss of a love relationship (through rebuff, bereavement, or separation) is important not so much because a loss is painful in itself but because it causes people to question their own ability to maintain relationships. The concept of 'neutralization' suggests that if the threatening life event is accompanied or followed by some other event that counteracts this damage to self-esteem or self-efficacy, the risk should be reduced.'

(Rutter, 1990: p. 204)

Thus, it is not the warm, loving relationship with adoptive parents that provides the direct protection. Rather it is the opportunities that such relationships provide that allows children to see themselves as lovable, socially effective and able to control what happens to them (rather than see themselves as passive and helpless). Resilience can be increased if people feel in control of their lives and 'become effective in shaping what happens to them' (Rutter, 1995a: p. 79). Initial models of self and others can therefore be modified as people experience themselves in new relationships. Using this protective process and the development of a more secure sense of self, they can then review earlier negative experiences and the reasons for being adopted (both potential risks) as the product of other people's failures and difficulties rather than as an indication that they themselves are of low value, interest and regard as far as other people are concerned. They can also approach new situations with increased emotional and cognitive confidence. The challenges of new situations and social relationships are less likely to be experienced as threatening and disturbing with the result that behaviour is less problematic and social adjustment much higher.

This analysis highlights the value of secure and supportive relationships in providing protection against future risks. In adoption, such relationships may be experienced in the pre-placement environment (in the form of good quality care in the first years of life) and/or in the post-placement environment (in the form of good quality adoptive parenting). Both experiences are associated with positive outcomes. Indeed, there is strong evidence that good intimate relationships at any time in life boost people's feelings of worth and potency.

Using Rutter's (1995a) types of protective mechanisms, we might also expect adopted children, otherwise thought to be vulnerable, to increase self-esteem and self-efficacy if they experience 'task success'. Accomplishments at school, sport, music, a hobby, skill or pastime can translate into positive feelings of self-esteem and self-efficacy. This gives people more confidence to deal with demands and challenges leading to improved social success. However, adoption outcome studies have rarely explored these variables directly. We only know that the better adjusted and behaviourally problem-free children produce higher rates of academic success than children who show poor adjustment and problem behaviour. We could also interpret these findings to suggest that academic success protects children from maladjustment and anti-social behaviour. 'Turning points' in adolescence often occur in the field of personal relationships and task accomplishments and may help children shift into a more adaptive developmental trajectory.

Adoption outcome studies and the problems that analysts have in interpreting the findings illustrate the wide variation in how people, including children, respond to stress and adversity. Though not talking about adoption in particular, but children's development in general, Rutter (1995a: p. 85) summarises matters of risk, resilience and recovery in seven points. Individual variation, he says, derives from:

(1)   personal characteristics, including temperament,
(2)   in part from previous experience,

(3) in part from the ways in which the individual copes with negative experiences,
(4) in part through indirect chain effects stemming from the experience and how it is dealt with,
(5) in part by subsequent experiences,
(6) in part the way people cognitively process or think about and see themselves as individuals.

Adoption outcome studies remain peculiarly well placed to illuminate matters of risk, resilience and recovery in human growth and development.

Chapter 9

Attachment, Relationship-based Theories and Adoption Pathways

Making sense of what is observed and looking for patterns in the findings of research takes us into the realm of theory. Theories help us make sense of what we see. They organise what we know. They suggest relationships between one set of events and another. Underlying mechanisms that account for disparate arrays of facts point to deeper orders that possibly govern appearances. Without theory, the world would seem arbitrary, contingent, lacking pattern.

Although those with post-modern inclinations may indeed accept that there really are no fundamental principles to be found and that all relationships are indeed contingent, others who proceed scientifically by measuring, observing and collecting data, believe that both the physical and social world are ordered and that the order is a product of natural rules. Those who theorise do not claim to have discovered *the* truth but merely possible and interesting ways of organising what we know. If it helps clarify what might be going on, albeit provisionally, partially or provocatively, a theory serves a purpose. Theories and the models associated with them stimulate research, provoke debate, and set up a dynamic, productive relationship between observation and fact. In setting out to link the scatter of empirical findings by the use of possible causal mechanisms, theories challenge investigators and practitioners to examine the plausibility of the order proposed and the rules that are said to generate that order. Concepts help give shape to the field of enquiry. Theories inject energy.

The observations, findings and classifications reported by researchers therefore invite explanation. Theorists, when presented with a field of facts, ask: What is going on here? Why do things appear this way (rather than that)? Are there regularities that link and connect features and events? Thinking theoretically encourages people to operate at several levels simultaneously. One of the first things that theorists in many fields try to do is classify the information that they have. They devise taxonomies in which things are categorised according to qualities and characteristics they have in common. This is a very suggestive exercise. It is premised on the idea that for things to be alike in some way, they must be determined by similar rules and experiences. This can sometimes provide powerful clues about what the underlying principles might be, but just as often the classification can mislead and send the theorist off into a conceptual cul-de-sac.

For example, chemists long wondered about the whys and wherefores of the natural elements. Throughout the nineteenth century they sought to classify them according to their physical and chemical properties, that is the way they appear and behave. Out of this emerged the periodic law. Recurring patterns were observed in the properties of the elements. The inert gases for instance, such as neon and argon were placed together; the reactive metals sodium and potassium seemed to have a lot in common; and so on. Once having made the classification it then becomes possible to ask: What determines this order? Why should some gases be chemically inert? Why are sodium and potassium so reactive? This pushes the theorist to look for some underlying mechanism that accounts for the variety of surface properties and behaviours. As far as the chemists were concerned, it seemed that the number of protons and the way electrons are configured provided a very neat and elegant formula for arranging the elements into family groups whose members had much in common. This classification became known as the 'periodic table' in which elements are grouped according to the degree of similarity in their physical and chemical properties.

Not too dissimilarly, in adoption outcome studies we have an array of facts; we possess observations; we find associations; we observe regularities. Is it possible to classify the behavioural and psychological properties shown by adopted children? And if it is possible, can a theory be found that accounts for both the properties possessed and the logic of the classification?

One way of approaching the task is to look for observations, reflections and asides made by researchers that seem unusually persistent, insistent and widespread. These may tell us what is important. They might also point to some of the mechanisms and processes that are influencing the behaviours. As we have seen, one of the most frequently mentioned factors said to be important in understanding outcomes in adoption is the quality of relationships that children have had with their main carers. For children adopted as babies, this has been almost exclusively with their adoptive parents. But late-placed children will have experienced close and important relationships with at least two sets of prime carers: their biological parents and their adoptive parents. The quality of both pre-placement and post-placement relationships are thought to have a major bearing on overall development.

It is within relationships that children experience processes that will give them protection against or make them vulnerable to subsequent exposure to environmental risks, including handling the knowledge that they are adopted. One possible way, therefore, of trying to order and make sense of what we know about adopted children and their development is to use our knowledge of how relationships with prime carers help shape and form children's personality, social understanding and interpersonal behaviour.

Attachment theory has shown itself to be very useful to child welfare and adoption workers. It offers a framework that classifies different behaviours and relationship patterns. It also suggests various psychological mechanisms that explain why we might see these different behaviours and relationship patterns. Attachment and relationship-based theories of personality development are just one of a number of possible ways of organising what we know as a result of adoption outcome studies. Theories are suggestive and provisional; they can be improved and developed, or superseded by theories that explain more and brook fewer anomalies and exceptions. But insofar as attachment theory manages to encompass and organise a large swathe of placement outcome findings, it can be seen as a provisionally useful and relatively effective theory, at least for the while. Relationship-based theories help adoption workers and adoptive parents make sense of many behaviours that otherwise might seem puzzling and perverse (also see Brodzinsky, 1993 for 'a stress and coping model of adoption adjustment' in which the primary assumption 'is that children's adjustment to adoption is determined largely by how they view or appraise their adoption experience and the type of coping mechanisms they use to deal with adoption-related stress').

The classification used by attachment theorists to explain parent–child relationships and personality development will be used to organise the various developmental pathways taken by adopted children as described by adoption researchers. But before outlining the classification adapted to adoption, we need to say a little about attachment theory and the central part played by 'inner working models' in guiding children's approaches to handling close relationships.

The development of social understanding and psychosocial competence in children

Although biological and innate temperamental factors play a large part in the development of personality and social competence, there seems little doubt that the relationship environments in which children find themselves have a profound effect on their socio-emotional progress. More specifically, the quality of early relationships can be important for later personality development. In most families, including biological families and baby-adopted families, children remain in continuous relationship with their key family members. It is not always clear therefore whether, say in the case of adolescent children, outcomes and behaviours are the result of early or current parent–child relationships. Late-placed children, of course, offer a different story. Their history of parent–child relationships has been discontinuous; the people who comprise their current social environment are totally different from those who made up their early social environment.

The quality of relationships generated by parents and carers will also vary from family to family. Adverse relationship environments upset children's ability to develop social understanding and to cope with other people. Feelings of self-esteem and self-efficacy are likely to be low as a result of such experiences. Children who fail to develop a good understanding of their own emotional make-up, other people and the social situations in which they find themselves find social life difficult. We need, therefore, to consider the growth of personality within parent–child relationships (for more extensive treatments of this topic see Dunn, 1993; Howe, 1995a; Rutter & Rutter, 1993).

Rutter, reviewing research in this area, writes:

'... it seems that the postulate that a lack of continuity in the loving committed parent–child relationships is central has received substantial support ... What has stood the test of time most of all has been the proposition that the qualities of parent–child relationships constitute a central aspect of parenting, that the development of social relationships occupies a crucial role in personality growth, and that abnormalities in relationships are important in many types of psychopathology.'

(Rutter, 1991: p. 341 and 361)

For most children, their closest relationships are generally with their mother or father but they can extend to older siblings, grandparents and other familiar adults. Children can have multiple attachments but these are limited in number. Not all attachment figures are treated equally. The mother figure is generally preferred in times of stress (Belsky & Cassidy, 1994: p. 377). The quality of relationships *between* parents and others can be as influential as those between the child and his or her parents. For example, parents who quarrel or prefer a younger sibling can upset a child's emotional development. And it must be remembered, too, that parents bring their own psychosocial histories into current relationships, including those with their partners and children. In this way, the psychosocial environments that parents generate and in which children learn to understand themselves and others can be transmitted across the generations.

Attachment theory is broadly seen as a theory of personality development arising out of Bowlby's work on children's close relationships with their prime carers (Bowlby, 1979, 1988). Attachment behaviour is a biological response that ensures children seek close proximity to *selected* adults when their level of anxiety begins to rise. Being in close relationship with one or more adults brings a number of potential benefits to the child. The food supply can be maintained. It provides a safe, protective environment for infants when they are vulnerable, particularly when they experience physical or emotional upset, anxiety, fear or danger. Equally important, attachment relationships with selective attachment figures offer experiences that allow children to learn about and become able to handle family life and the social world. And as language facilitates communications about such experiences and exchanges, children will learn to speak and pick up the cultural habits and expectations of their community.

Children who feel securely attached learn to recognise and handle their own and other people's emotions, develop social empathy and learn to behave morally and with a conscience. They learn to trust others, cope better with stress and frustration, and develop feelings of self-worth and positive affect (Fahlberg, 1994: p. 14). They develop positive expectations of themselves and others. Children who feel insecure remain in a constant state of mild or severe anxiety, tension and emotional arousal. Their attention is on their own internal emotional state. This blocks them from processing external experience, including learning about social relationships in a relaxed, exploratory manner.

To function appropriately and effectively, children need to make sense of their own and other people's behaviours, reactions, emotions, intentions, needs, desires and beliefs. The development of social and emotional understanding is crucial if children are to become effective, knowledgable and competent social players – in short, become socially literate. The more coherent, responsive and stimulating are the social relationships in which children find themselves the more they will be able to learn about and understand (1) themselves, (2) other people, and (3) the relationship between them. As Frith (1989: p. 169) says, 'the ability to make sense of other people is also the ability to make sense of one's self.' It is therefore extremely helpful in terms of children's psychosocial development for them to be in relationships where they can build clear models of themselves and the part they play in interpersonal life.

Internal working models

In order to make sense of other people and social relationships, infants generate inner mental representations – internal working models – of the self, others and the relationship between them. The concept of the internal working model is central to attachment theory. Such mental models help individuals organise their expectations about other people's availability and responsiveness. The models themselves arise out of children's relationship and caregiving experiences. Not only do they lay down structures that influence people's personality, they also guide how they perceive, interpret and respond to other people. Put very simply, the infant has expectations of:

(1) whether or not at times of stress and anxiety their caregiver is likely to be available and respond with warmth and concern,

(2) whether or not they themselves are someone about whom other people care and are likely to respond with love and attention, and

(3) whether or not they see themselves as someone who is effective in close social relationships in terms of having needs met, notice taken, feelings understood or thoughts appreciated.

If internal working models of the self, others and the relationship between them develop within close relationships, we can see that the quality of these intimate relationships will influence how children view both themselves and other people. The more adverse the child's relationship history and experience, the more insecure and anxious they will feel in current relationships and the more negative, devalued and ineffective they will view themselves. In this sense, external relationships become mentally internalised (Howe, 1995a: p. 24).

The internal working model mediates the influence of early relationship experiences.

'On the basis of their experiences, individuals develop different representational models – that is, different beliefs about themselves, different expectations about others, and different sets of conscious and/or unconscious rules for organizing and accessing information about feelings, experiences, and ideas related to attachment – and these lead to particular kinds of interactions with new social partners and have long-lasting consequences for personality and close relationships.'

(Belsky & Cassidy, 1994: p. 381)

Internal working models therefore represent the beginnings of social understanding. The infant's emotional bond toward the mother or selective attachment figure is an intimate relationship with another social being. It acts as a prototype for all subsequent close relationships. It therefore provides the first 'working mental model' upon which later relationships are perceived, developed and conducted, and to that extent there can be a self-fulfilling quality in the way children and adults conceive others and their relationships with them. If the child's relationship with his or her mother is rich and reciprocal, responsive and empathic, then the child will be able to build working models of the self, others and social relationships that are coherent and positive. But if the child's close relationships are unpredictable, insensitive and unresponsive, he or she will build more negative models of the self, others and social relationships in which people are seen as less responsive and less available.

Insecurely attached children develop negative expectations of other people. They will begin to react defensively as a way of coping with the confusion, rebuff and anxiety that insecure attachments spawn.

Rejection, neglect, unavailability and maltreatment produce internal working models that see (1) other people as unavailable, untrustworthy and a source of emotional pain, and (2) the self as unworthy of love and sensitive treatment. Not being able to make sense of one's own emotional states or those of others is confusing and anxiety provoking. The social world and one's self in it are therefore modelled as unreliable, erratic and unresponsive. Thus, those children who are least able to handle and process anxiety are the ones most likely to experience the highest levels of social stress and confusion. The absence of strong, well organised mental models means that the world of relationships and other people remains frustrating and puzzling.

Moreover, working models of attachment established in early relationships are carried forward into new relationships where they guide perceptions, interpretations and behaviour. This is part of the reason why attachment theorists place such importance on internal working models. It is clear that if children's understandings and expectations of themselves and others are developed in early, prototypical relationships and these models influence interpretations and responses in later relationships, this way of approaching matters should be particularly useful when trying to make sense of behaviours of late-placed children. It suggests that new, close relationships with adoptive parents will not be experienced and handled without reference to earlier close relationships. The more emotionally significant and demanding the current relationship, the more earlier relationships and the inner working models developed to represent and cope with them will be brought into play. Late-adopted children therefore may not be responding to the external, objective qualities of their new relationships. They may be reacting (and defending themselves) according to what they expect to experience in close relationships as well as how they expect to be viewed by others. Reacting to others on the basis of one's inner emotional condition rather in terms of what people actually appear to be saying and doing, can be difficult for both parties. There is always the likelihood that behaviour guided by inner working models developed in insecure, high anxiety attachments will eventually bring about feelings and behaviours in others that confirm the model and the psychological defences that go with it.

Classification of attachment styles

The quality of relationships that children and adults have with other people, particularly those with whom there is an attachment relationship, will depend on the other person's physical and emotional (1) availability, (2) sensitivity, (3) responsiveness, (4) reliability, and (5) predictability. Attachments figures who are warm and attentive create secure attachment relationships. Relationships that are inconsistent, cold or confusing increase levels of anxiety producing attachments that feel less secure.

In practice, researchers have recognised four basic dyadic attachment styles (Ainsworth *et al.*, 1978; Main & Solomon, 1986). Attachment theory helps us to understand the way children and adults behave and react in relationships. The continuity of attachment experiences and associated psychosocial behaviours throughout the life span is not yet borne out by research. However, there is compelling clinical experience that sees each of the four attachment/relationship styles underpinning much of human relationship behaviour throughout the life cycle. This does not forbid change; indeed children and adults who experience major changes in their close relationship environments may develop different types of emotional understanding and social competence. Mental internal models can be revised within the context of new significant relationships. The choice of a sexual partner, a placement with new parents in adoption, or improved mental functioning in a previously psychiatrically ill mother can all set up new social environments that have the capacity to modify the individual's internal working model, and views about the self and others.

Each attachment type witnesses children needing to develop an internal working model of and psychological adjustment to the relationships in which they find themselves. The different internal working models also have their correlates in various adult personality types. Four types of attachment experience have been described:

(1)   secure attachments,
(2)   insecure, ambivalent attachments,
(3)   insecure, avoidant attachments,
(4)   disorganised attachments.

(Fuller versions of these categories can be found in the pioneering works of Ainsworth *et al.*, 1978, and Bowlby, 1988; also see Main & Solomon, 1986; Belsky & Cassidy, 1994; Howe, 1995a for introductions to attachment theory.) A small number of children, particularly those raised in large residential nurseries from a very young age, may have had no opportunities to develop selective attachments. Being cared for by large numbers of care workers on a shift basis means that children raised in institutional environments can become 'non-attached'.

Put crisply, *securely* attached children enjoy consistent, attentive and reciprocal relationships with their main carers. They develop inner working models in which they see other people as positively available and themselves as loved and likable, valued and socially effective. *Insecure, ambivalently* attached children experience parenting that is inconsistent, unreliable and emotionally neglectful. They need to increase the demands they make on their carers in a struggle to gain their love, interest and attention. They are only intermittently successful in this ploy. Their ambivalence arises out of their simultaneous need for and anger with their prime attachment figures. *Insecure, avoidantly* attached children experience parenting that is hostile, rejecting and controlling. They experience little warmth or love in the relationship. Their anxieties are rarely acknowledged and they receive little comfort; their emotional needs remain largely unmet. They understand that they are neither loved nor lovable. The psychological tactic is to retain physical proximity but avoid emotional intimacy with the attachment figure. Insecure children with *disorganised* attachments experience their parents as frightened, frightening or dangerous. As their parents are the source of their anxiety, they have a dilemma. It is difficult to approach the attachment figure for comfort and understanding as he or she is the cause of the anxiety. However, there is no-one else available to help them with their distress. The result is a disturbed, disorganised response in which the child is left alone with their feelings of upset and helplessness.

Each of the four attachment styles is appropriate when seen in the context of the particular parent–child relationship. As an attempt to deal with raised levels of anxiety, they make psychological sense as *adaptive strategies* given the character of the relationship in which they find themselves. The internal working model associated with each attachment pattern represents the child's attempt to handle the emotional anxiety generated by the parent's level of availability and responsiveness. Therefore each attachment pattern is a *defensive manoeuvre* mounted by the child as he or she tries to control his or her level of anxiety. To that extent, different attachment behaviours are adaptive responses to the psychological situation in which children find themselves. It is only when children step outside that relationship and use the experience and the mental model to understand and relate with other people, that their behaviour and relationship becomes maladaptive and dysfunctional.

Children in secure attachments see other people as a resource and potential source of safety and comfort. In the face of anxiety they adopt a positive *approach* response towards parents.

If the attachment style is one of ambivalence, children make an *approach response against* the parent whose attentiveness and interest is unreliable, unpredictable and uncertain. At the same time they are drawn towards their attachment figure, they exhibit *resistance* and anger, not knowing whether their needs will be recognised, understood or met. Ambivalently attached children therefore *increase their attachment behaviour* in a desperate attempt to gain interest and attention ('fight').

Children in avoidant attachment relationships cope with anxiety by an emotional *moving away* from others; they avoid intimacy and have no faith in the benefits of close relationships. These children *decrease attachment* behaviour as a way of trying to cope with raised, but unrecognised distress and anxiety ('flight').

Disorganised attachments witness behaviours in which the child's psychological defensive strategies become confused and muddled. They are not sure whether to approach or avoid other people. In effect, these children have *no strategy* at all with which to deal with their anxiety. The result is an emotional *standing still* or *agitation* ('freeze').

We shall use the attachment categories along with the defensive strategies and internal models associated with them to rework and reorder the findings of adoption outcome studies. Using an attachment perspective to organise what we know in adoption research allows us to recognise five patterns of adoption:

(1)   Secure patterns.
(2)   Anxious patterns.
(3)   Angry patterns.
(4)   Avoidant patterns.
(5)   Patterns associated with children with a history of no selective attachments.

Each pattern describes a suite of distinctive behaviours and relationship styles. The following five chapters will describe each pattern in more detail and suggest possible links with children's pre-placement and post-placement experiences. An extended case example will complete each chapter.

The case examples are taken from my own research in which I interviewed 120 adoptive parents whose children had to be aged 18 years or over at the time of the interview. Of the adult-adopted children, 211 fell into this category representing both baby-placed and late-placed children. Parents were asked to report on their own experiences as well as the behaviour and character of their children from the time of placement. Both quantitative and qualitative data were collected. (Fuller versions of the methodology and analysis can be found elsewhere: Howe, 1995b, 1996a, 1996b, 1997).

Chapter 10

Secure Patterns

Children feel valued and understood when parents or prime attachment figures interact with them in a warm, attentive and caring manner. Mothers, for example, who are sensitive to their children's needs and emotional states respond accurately and appropriately. This 'good enough' parenting enables children to build a reliable, useful picture of how 'relationships and other people work'. They learn to understand the part they play in social interaction. In this way, relationships become reciprocal and synchronised. Other people are seen in a positive light. They can be trusted. They are available and responsive. The self, therefore, is understood to be of interest, relevance and value to other people. Children learn to see themselves as socially effective, potent and lovable. Self-esteem, self-efficacy and confidence grow in such environments.

Secure attachments

Secure attachments free children to explore the environment beyond the parent–child relationship. They can play in relaxed and contented fashion, engage in 'pretend' games, and resolve crises in either real or fantasy situations. Such opportunities provide further experiences in which secure children can learn about the world. These children are usually sociable and well-liked by their peers. They cope reasonably well with the conflicts, upsets and frustrations of everyday social life. To this extent, secure children understand and recognise the nature of their own as well as other people's feelings and so they cope well and appropriately with social relationships.

As they progress through childhood and into adolescence, children are able to form close, mutual, stable, trusting and harmonious relationships. They are capable of humour and self-disclosure. Levels of shared interest and reciprocity remain high and mutually satisfying. The needs of both partners in relationships – whether with friends, siblings or lovers – are met. The stresses and conflicts of everyday life are handled reasonably well. Problem-solving skills and planning capacities are generally good. Both children and adults can concentrate and sustain work/play activities for long periods. People's self-images tend to be good. Other people are approached positively and seen as potential resources. Autonomous–secure individuals are reasonably realistic and accurate about their own strengths and weaknesses (Main, 1994). In terms of psychosocial development, secure attachments therefore act protectively.

Although for most children, secure selective attachments are made with one or both of their parents, this does not rule out the possibility of some insecurely attached children forming close, effective relationships with people other than their parents. Other people, at different times during childhood, might include an aunt, a schoolteacher or even a friend's mother. In the case of late-placements of course, children previously in insecure attachment relationships with their biological parents have the chance to experience competent, caring parenting from their adopters. We might also presume that some children with certain temperamental characteristics (such as having an innately positive, sociable, easy going outlook) might succeed in engaging the support and interest of caring and concerned people if their own parents are unable to respond with warmth, interest and consistency.

For a variety of reasons, therefore, some children who experience early adversity and who might be expected to develop anxious attachment styles and insecure personalities, nevertheless manage to enjoy good quality relationships with people other than their biological parents. As a result, such children find their developmental trajectory shifting from a negative to a positive course. These alternative relationships allow children to develop inner working models in which they can begin to conceive of themselves as likable and socially effective. This raises self-esteem and self-efficacy, both of which are thought to offer children protection. Late-placed children who exhibit secure patterns of development might therefore be expected to have one or more of the following:

(1) an easy temperament;
(2) good-enough parenting in the first year or two of life;
(3) skilled, warm, accepting parenting from their adopters;
(4) a talent or accomplishment that is well-regarded and raises self-esteem;
(5) a good positive relationship with, for example, a sibling, friend or teacher.

Thus, as far as adoption is concerned, we might expect the majority of adopted babies to follow a secure developmental pathway leading to a good adjustment. And as it is still the case that most adopted people were adopted as babies, secure attachment patterns should predominate. The research evidence seems to support this. Positive outcomes and levels of satisfaction run very high for children placed as babies. The rigours of preparation, assessment and the selection of

adopters ought, perhaps, to ensure a significant bias towards competent parenting and secure attachment patterns. Children join their
parents during the first weeks or months of life, and so arrive with very
little pre-placement relationship history of an adverse nature.

Developmentally speaking, then, securely attached adopted children
have relatively trouble-free, 'normal' childhoods. There will be the
usual ups and downs that all children experience at home, at school,
with parents and with friends. But the general pathway is straight.
Parents report on the experience of adopting in warm, positive terms.
Children have good self-esteem and self-regard. They report that they
felt loved, wanted and valued.

Temperamentally, secure children will cover the full range, though
with late-placed children we might expect higher rates of easy, sociable
temperaments. At school they generally try their best. Academic successes will broadly reflect their cognitive abilities. Educational and
occupational outcomes will therefore match children's innate talents
and abilities, whether these are physical or intellectual, social or artistic.
We are as likely to see mechanics and engineers as doctors and lawyers;
nurses and hairdressers as surveyors and police officers. On the whole,
because these children are not distracted and disturbed by undue levels
of emotional anxiety, they are likely to realise their potential.

Table 10.1 summarises the behaviours, progress, achievements and
personality attributes that broadly characterise adopted children who
have experienced secure attachments.

Case examples

Emma

Nigel and Pam Hartley had already adopted a baby boy before they
adopted Emma. She was born to a 19 year old Catholic nurse. The birth
mother had emigrated from Ireland to complete her training in London.
She had a brief relationship with a young car factory worker by whom
she became pregnant. She felt that she could neither go home to raise
the baby, cope on her own in London, or have an abortion. In the end
she decided to place the baby for adoption. In approaching Nigel and
Pam, the adoption agency wrote describing Emma and her birth family:
'Although her background is not as good as your adopted son's, we
wonder if you might be interested in adopting a baby girl. On her
father's side she comes from a family of car workers and so if you
would rather wait for a baby of higher degree, do not hesitate to say so.'
This both amused and outraged Nigel and Pam who had no doubts
about taking Emma; indeed the letter made them feel all the more
determined to adopt the little girl. She was born slightly premature and
spent a couple of weeks in hospital before going to foster parents. She
was placed with her adoptive parents when she was 11 weeks old.

Table 10.1 Secure children: behaviours, characteristics, achievements and personality.

General:	Positive feelings of self-esteem, self-efficacy and self-confidence
	Good social understanding and empathy
	Socially competent
	Capable of reciprocal behaviour
	Trusting of peers and adults
	Have friends
	Cope well with change and transitions
School years:	No major behavioural problems at home or school
	Generally constructive and competent at play and work
	Able to concentrate
	Achieve potential or thereabouts
	No serious lying
	Relatively trouble-free, 'normal' adolescence
	Little or no criminal behaviour
	No referrals to mental health services (child psychiatrist/ psychologist)
Late adolescence/early adulthood:	
	Capable of independent behaviour
	Leave home smoothly (college, work, partner, marriage)
	Relatively stable career/jobs
	Adult relationships conducted competently
Evaluation:	View of adoption by adopted person: positive and satisfactory
	Views of adoptive parents: positive and satisfactory.

Her parents described her as 'a gorgeous little baby.' She quickly put on weight and was rarely ill. Pam remembered her as an easy, good-natured child 'who got on well with everybody'. Although she always had a number of friends, she maintained a close friendship with one particular girl that lasted right through to adulthood.

At school Emma worked reasonably hard, but initially made slow progress. She fell behind with her reading at her first school. With help from a remedial teacher she improved rapidly. Her teachers described her as 'a delightful child; no trouble'. In adolescence she continued to be a pleasure to parent. 'She's a chatty individual. She went through a funny punk phase when she was about 17 which I must admit I wasn't very keen on. At one time she dyed her hair bright purple and wore lots of scruffy clothes, you know, with slits in her trousers and studs on jackets, that sort of thing. We tried to grin and bear it! Anyway she seemed to grow out of it. We laugh about it now, especially when we look at some of the photos we took of her then!'

Emma's academic achievements were modest but acceptable. She left school and went to University where she studied history. Again, she never shone particularly brightly, but managed to gain a lower second class degree whilst thoroughly enjoying her time at college. Emma then decided to take a secretarial course which lead to her first job working for an oil company. Aged 25, she met and married Alan. Two years later Emma had her first baby, a daughter whom they named Lucy, followed two years later by a son, Jack. Although she lives some distance away from her adoptive parents, visits and telephone calls are regular and frequent. There is great delight on all sides with Emma's children.

Throughout her childhood Emma had expressed mild curiosity about her background, but never seemed urgently interested in learning more about her birth parents. She knew all that her adoptive parents knew and that seemed to suffice. However, after the birth of Lucy she began to wonder a little more about her birth mother. Pam and Emma discussed whether or not she might seek further information about her background. With the support of her adoptive parents she decided to initiate a search. Counselling was received and Emma was surprised how quickly thereafter she located her birth mother. After an exchange of letters and a telephone call, birth mother and daughter agreed to meet. The reunion went well. Emma learned that Mary, her biological parent, had married and given birth to another daughter.

Nigel and Pam also met Mary with Emma. 'I must say it was an odd experience,' recalled Pam. 'I suppose if I'm honest I had felt anxious when Emma went to see her natural mother. We chatted politely and exchanged a number of photographs of Emma when she was a baby. We got some pictures of Mary's daughter who of course is Emma's half-sister. I told her a lot about Emma – when she was a little girl, at school, you know, the whole growing up thing.' Eighteen months have passed since Emma first met her birth mother. The frequency of contact has dropped and communication is now mainly around Christmas time and the grandchildren's birthdays. Pam says that Emma seems very matter-of-fact about the contact, accepting it as a natural part of her life. In spite of Pam's initial apprehensions, the contact appears not to have affected the warm mother–daughter relationship that she felt they had always enjoyed. 'We're really just carrying on as before,' reflected Pam. 'Mary's there. Emma keeps in touch with her but not as often as I think Mary would perhaps like. I don't know. Emma's satisfied her curiosity but doesn't seem to want to make any more of it other than a friendly contact. Their lives have followed very different routes and maybe there's not a lot in common.' Both Emma and her adoptive parents view the adoption with the utmost pleasure and satisfaction.

Ben

Ben's mother was a young, lone parent who struggled to look after him for the first year. Although the health visitor said his mother seemed to love him, she was often depressed and his physical care suffered. When he was ten months old, she placed him with his father who was living with another woman. Two months later Ben was admitted to hospital suffering malnutrition. After gaining weight he was returned to his mother. However, four months later she took him to the local day nursery and left him there with a note pinned to his coat that said 'I cannot look after Ben. Please put him in a home.' He was placed in a residential nursery. The staff described him as 'a very sad little boy.' He stayed in the nursery until he was four years old, after which he was placed for adoption with Joanne and Oliver Maitland.

Joanne said that it took Ben a while to calm down. He was easily excited but 'even then I found him a warm, outward going, affectionate little boy.' His sociability extended to school. 'Mind you,' added Joanne, 'Ben has always had a strong play instinct. Work comes second!' Although teachers felt he could work harder, they said he was a 'delight' to have in the class. That did not stop them insisting that he take school work home to finish. His mother said that he hated that, and it was the one thing that caused us to argue. Ben was very good at most sports. He played for the school's football and cricket teams. 'He did manage to just pass a few of his exams when he was 16, which was a surprise ... and a great pleasure I must say. He was very pleased with himself.'

When Ben was 12 years old, Joanne was suddenly taken into hospital and stayed there for a week. 'Poor old Ben was distraught. He packed his bags and made contingency plans about where he was going to live. He thought I was going to die, you see. He was very frightened at the thought of losing me and when I got home he told me all about his worries.'

After a short period in the school's sixth form he left to attend a work training scheme at the local college. He experienced a variety of jobs, mainly in the area of gardening, horticulture and landscaping. His record of attendance and general commitment were only just acceptable, but he eventually scraped through his training and found a job working in commercial greenhouses. Oliver said that Ben enjoyed the work and was well-regarded by his employers. But sadly, the firm ran into financial difficulties and Ben was made redundant. He is now 22 years old and is unemployed, though he is actively looking for work as a gardener or landscaper.

For the last 18 months he has been in a close relationship with a girl. 'She's a very sensible, steady type and she's had a good influence on Ben. He's an intelligent boy who doesn't always apply himself.' He has now left home and lives with his girlfriend in a rented house in the same town as Joanne and Oliver, and pops over to see them a couple of times a week. 'He's a very easy going young man; a very relaxed person' said Joanne. 'I actually think he's quite gifted at relationships and with people. And he always seems to land on his feet. I often think he'd work very well with old people. I'm enormously fond of him and he's been a great support to me over the years.'

Chapter 11

Anxious Patterns

Loss of and separation from primary attachment figures is deeply unsettling for young children. However, the way infants react to and grieve such losses will depend on the quality of the attachment relationship. The way people mourn is a product of their past relationship and loss history on the one hand and the quality of their current social relationships on the other (Parkes, 1986; Parkes & Weis, 1983). We shall be looking at how ambivalently and avoidantly attached children respond to loss in the next two chapters, but here we need to consider a number of variations on the theme of loss and separation in the lives of children who have had some experience of good quality close relationships in their early years.

The quality of pre-placement care

Some delayed and late-placed children do experience reasonably good quality care before they reach the age of 12 months. They can be subdivided into three groups.

(1)   Good quality pre-placement care
(2)   Poor start/delayed baby adoptions
(3)   Good start/late-placed children.

Two involve reasonably good quality parental care followed by a major loss of that care. The third group describes babies who experience several months of impersonal or inconsistent care before being placed with their adoptive parents, usually by the time they are about six or seven months old. Two of the groups show patterns of mildly insecure behaviour throughout childhood and we shall be looking at these in more detail. But first we need to acknowledge a rare group of late-placed children who maintain secure attachment patterns both before and after placement.

Good quality pre-placement care

This first group, psychologically speaking, is relatively straightforward. Children who have been well cared for by their parents and enjoyed secure attachment experiences can, in the long run, adjust reasonably well to the loss of one or both parents. 'Grief', says Fahlberg (1994: p. 133), 'is the process through which one passes in order to recover from a loss.' Of course, it is normal for children who have suffered a loss to experience grief reactions. The grieving process would be expected to pass through the following phases:

(1) an initial sense of shock and disbelief,
(2) pain and yearning,
(3) possible feelings of anger and resentment,
(4) this is followed by depression and withdrawal,
(5) a final phase of adjustment, reorganisation and resolution.

For example, when Simon was six and Jessica was four years old, both their parents died in a car crash. The family had been very friendly with and close to their next-door neighbours, Angie and Charles Arlott and their older children. It was eventually agreed by all concerned that Simon and Jessica could be adopted by Angie and Charles who were keen to have the children. Naturally both brother and sister grieved heavily for their parents. But the strength of their early attachment experiences meant that they trusted adults and assumed their emotional availability. They had also established good self-esteem and a feeling of social competence. Their inner working models of themselves and others allowed the children to represent and understand relationships in an essentially positive light. They were therefore able to approach their adoptive parents in a trusting fashion. After a period of mourning and transition, Simon and Jessica were able to develop secure attachments with Angie and Charles. They recovered and adjusted well. They were bright and able children who eventually went on to study at university.

The remaining two 'early secure' patterns describe adopted children who show mild anxiety and insecurity throughout their placements.

Poor start/delayed baby adoptions

The first of these is seen in some children placed as 'older' babies – typically between five and eight months of age. Their early care is physically good but impersonal. Many are placed initially in residential nurseries. If there is uncertainty about whether or not the birth mother will relinquish her baby for adoption, the child might be 'held' in a nursery until it is clear which way the decision is going to fall. The babies generally receive adequate physical care, but they are unable to form close, emotional attachments to any one nursery nurse. Their ability to form robust inner working models of themselves and others is frustrated, and if they continue to experience 'serial caregiving' it might be expected that they will develop the dysfunctional behaviour patterns of non-attached children. However, the children who are eventually placed for adoption, find themselves, albeit belatedly, in a highly responsive, attentive, good quality social environment with carers who are constant. Many theorists believe that full-blown selective attachments develop during the first seven to eight months of life. Babies adopted after the age of five months but before seven or eight months, therefore have the chance to experience good quality psychosocial care while still within the timeframe of this allegedly sensitive period.

We might speculate that the basic inner working models that form within this eight-month period of brief residential care followed by intimate parental care achieve most, but not quite all of what children who experience continuous, uninterrupted secure parental care achieve. Put colloquially, the mental representations achieved by these children suggest that other people are available – eventually; and therefore the self is lovable and effective – probably. Although attachment behaviour triggered by feelings of anxiety and distress now brings the children into reliable, reciprocal parent–child relationships, historically the strategy has not always brought such positive results. Residues of earlier versions of the inner working model that formed within the psychosocially limited environment of the nursery still remain. There are therefore vague, lingering doubts about the availability and responsiveness of other people that continue to lightly disturb self-esteem and self-efficacy. Insecure behaviour can still be spotted. Feelings of anxiety can be aroused when the social environment once again is experienced as unreliable or unavailable. For this group, experiences of close relationships start off poor but get better.

Good start/late-placed children

The second group of mildly anxious and insecure adopted children initially set out on a different developmental pathway. For at least the first year of life, they enjoy good quality care. They are able to develop secure attachments and establish non-defensive, positively orientated inner working models of themselves and their relationships with other people. However, after this early benign phase, matters take a turn for the worse. The children's relationships with their main carers becomes increasingly negative. The children suffer physical and emotional neglect, abuse, hostility or rejection. During the first phase of good parent–child relationships, the children are able to lay down reasonably robust and positive senses of self. Self-esteem and feelings of social competence begin to establish themselves. Possessed of a core of positive self-regard and social effectiveness, children are able to conclude that when things go wrong, then it is not some negative quality possessed by them that has wrought the new situation (for they have been loved and understood); rather it must be something amiss with other people that has brought about their change in fortune. To be on the receiving end of hostile feelings is not pleasant and it is upsetting, but for the time being the children's sense of a good self remains intact. The initially responsive care experienced by these children provides sufficient protection to allow them to develop some resilience when faced with the later risk of deteriorating parent-child relationships. Nevertheless, sustained neglect and hostility will take a toll and even the strongest spirits will begin to feel less secure.

Examples of this pattern include children born to lone, often young mothers. If they choose to stay at home with their own parents, the mothers might expect to receive material and emotional support. The strains of motherhood are thereby lessened. All of this bolsters the quality of parenting so that the babies are able to form secure attachment relationships. It is often the case that the maternal grandmothers share in the care of the babies. In these examples, not only do the mothers gain in confidence and competence because of the help and experience provided by their own mothers, but also the babies may form secure attachments with their second carer. However, if the young mothers decide to leave home and live on their own, or if they form a new sexual relationship and set up house with their partner, as far as the children are concerned, this represents a radical change of social environment. If mothers find coping on their own stressful, this may adversely affect their relationship with their children. Indeed, the children might be blamed for the mothers' difficulties.

Mothers who leave home to live with a boyfriend require their children to develop a new relationship with their stepfather, whereas previously children had an exclusive relationship with their mothers, they now have to share her with someone else. If mothers and their new partners have more children, family life changes even more drastically for the first-born children. Difficult behaviour in response to this fast changing social world may set off a chain of negative reactions. Stepfathers might become increasingly irritable and angry with their stepchildren; they might favour their own sons or daughters. Mothers, also tired and exasperated with their oldest children's mounting emotional demands and dissatisfactions, might also be drawn into feeling hostile towards them. Loss of intimacy and having to share their mother's love and attention with partners and younger half-siblings is calculated to *increase attachment behaviour*. Children's behaviour becomes more attention-seeking, demanding and difficult. In the end, both parents feel they can no longer cope with or control these children. The final rejection sees the children being looked after by foster parents before being placed for adoption, typically aged around three, four or five years old.

For this group, experiences of close relationships start off good, then get worse, before finally returning to good again with a new set of parents. As far as the children are concerned, after the experience of losing a warm, loving relationship first time round, the adult world can never again be entirely trusted or taken for granted. The strategy is to make sure that attachment figures are not lost again. The basic relationship style is therefore one of anxious compliance: to keep parents engaged and thinking well of you. However, the children's insecurities will lead to anxious, immature behaviour that will occasionally get them into social difficulty and thus, potentially on the wrong side of their parents. The basic pattern describes children anxious to ensure that they do not lose the love and care of their adoptive parents while at the same time regularly getting themselves into mild social scrapes that they fear might threaten the love and availability of their carers.

One more variation on the theme of 'good start/bad finish' in children's pre-placement experiences can be recognised. Although some psychiatrically ill mothers may be well enough for a while to provide good quality, warm, attentive, loving care, the onset of a major mental health problem can upset the secure start enjoyed by their children. As their mother's illness progresses, children can be neglected or abused, feel confused or frightened. In effect, the availability and responsiveness of the children's mothers is lost. In extreme cases where there is little prospect of the children being cared for by their mothers, adoption becomes the recommended route.

For example, Edmund and Elizabeth were cared for reasonably well by their mother and father – Sam and Maureen Wiseman – up until the age of six and four years respectively. But then their mother's behaviour gradually became more bizarre and unpredictable. Their father left the family and contact with him was lost. Maureen was admitted to psychiatric hospital on a number of occasions. The children were placed in short-term foster care. The last time she looked after the children before they were finally received into care and placed for adoption, she had become increasingly obsessed about the cleanliness of the house. Along with Edmund and Elizabeth, she began to sleep in the garden shed for fear of making the house dirty. The furniture was either burned, sold or destroyed so that bit by bit the house became uninhabitable. Maureen finally broke down altogether and was admitted into a long-stay psychiatric hospital.

Although the children of psychiatrically ill parents do not experience active rejection by stepfathers and birth mothers, the sequence of 'good care → poor care → good care' is similar to that described above and leads to similar behaviour patterns.

Patterns of behaviour, personality and relationship style

The inner working model that underpins these children's understandings and expectations of themselves and others forms within attachment relationships that are basically secure. However, in the cases of both the poor start/delayed baby adoptions and the good start/ late adoptions, the children also experience some trauma, sufficient to unsettle the otherwise positive outlook they have on themselves and others.

The poor start/delayed baby adopted children only experience high quality, reciprocal care during the second half of their first year. In contrast, the good-start/late-placed children find that their initially positive representation of the availability of attachment figures is put under severe strain when the quality of their parental care subsequently deteriorates. Nevertheless, in both cases, the children experience sufficiently 'good-enough' early attachments to allow them to develop an essentially positive view of themselves and others. Such a view means that at times of distress and anxiety, when attachment behaviour is triggered, the children are able to implement a positive approach response towards their carers. Other people are seen as potentially available, and the self is seen as potentially effective in securing a positive response.

However, the levels of confidence, self-esteem and self-efficacy are not quite as robust as those achieved by children who enjoy unbroken secure attachments. The delayed start or the later loss of a secure attachment relationship mean that other people's availability and interest cannot be quite taken for granted, and the self may not always seem to be effective in ensuring that needs are going to be met. So, a frisson of anxiety and insecurity troubles the generally positive character of these children's underlying inner working model of self, others and social relationships.

The prime unconscious aim of children who follow this pattern is to ensure that they never again lose their primary attachment figures. Having found caring parents after a poor start or having lost them after a good start and then being placed, these children are determined to hang on to the safe and secure relationship provided by their adoptive parents. In the case of the good start/late placed group, it is as if they are saying: 'Look, I have experienced a happy secure relationship and I liked it. But then I lost it through no fault of my own. It has happened before and so it could happen again. I am now enjoying good quality care once more, and so I'm definitely not letting go this time.' The children have the capacity to trust adults, engage in reciprocal behaviour, and give as well as take emotionally. Although mildly insecure children are reasonable confident of their parents' love, they never quite assume its unconditional availability in the way that totally secure children do. Their anxiety levels rise when they perceive that their parents' good will, love or emotional availability are in danger of being lost. The availability of parents is perceived to be most at risk when the children's behaviour causes parents to get cross. As these children often act out their anxieties, they do tend to exasperate their parents from time to time.

All of this makes the children in this group essentially home-centred. The fear of losing close and important relationships means that they remain alert to their parents' mood and availability. They can be oversensitive. They spot indifference and rejection even when they are not present or intended. These children are keen to 'fit in' and try their best. They want to please and get things right. Anxious and *compliant* behaviour often go hand in hand. For example, Catherine, adoptive mother describing her daughter's early behaviour said:

> 'When she was little, Elsa would rush around wanting to know what she could do to help. She'd try to be one step ahead of me all the time. "I've made you a cup of tea mummy' or 'I thought it was going to rain so I brought the washing in off the line." If she got something wrong, like she broke a plate or spilt a drink, she seemed to fall to pieces. She seemed almost ready to pack her bags and be ready to be sent off. She just couldn't handle herself if she thought we were going to tell her off.'

Harmonious situations see the children at their most relaxed; tension and conflict make them feel unsettled and nervous. There is a great need to be loved, wanted and accepted. These behaviours mean that these children are very loving and generous. At Christmas and on birthdays, mildly anxious children are the ones most likely to buy the biggest card or spend all of their pocket money on a present for Mum. They are tender and caring with small, vulnerable animals and pets, and not a few contemplate careers in one of the helping professions working with either babies or animals. The children's rather transparent vulnerability, keenness to be loved and wish to feel secure makes them easy to love, though not always easy to parent.

Times of transition and possible separation revive old feelings of insecurity. It is at such moments that the children become anxious, agitated, clingy, tearful, demanding, inconsolable and attention-seeking. Most parents report that levels of disturbance and upset increase when it is time to change school or a house move is contemplated. Mothers or the children themselves going into hospital recharge old separation fears. In the middle years, the prospect of spending a few days away from home is not viewed with great pleasure. Trips away with the school, the guides or scouts raise levels of anxiety. 'When the school said they were going to take the children off to France for a week,' remembered Rita, 'Tim got all excited and said he couldn't wait. But as it came nearer the time to go, he got more and more anxious. I could tell. He'd get upset and cross at the slightest thing. And when it was about four or five days to go, he said he didn't feel well and wondered whether he should really go to France. I knew exactly what it was. We didn't pressure him, and we finally agreed that maybe traipsing off to Rouen could wait till another day.' Children often take days or weeks to settle themselves down after a major upset or change in routine.

Testing situations increase anxious behaviour beyond the normal.

The fear of failure leads to avoidance. For example, school sports days where there is competition and the possibility of losing are not approached in a relaxed mood, even by children who are quite athletic. Running shoes will suddenly be lost or an ankle 'sprained'. Academic examinations are even more threatening. Irritability increases, despairing moods become more frequent. And when the exams finally arrive, panic and doom are the order of the day. The children tend to underachieve academically, at least while at school. However, many of these adopted people, once they feel finally secure and confident, make good educational progress in their later teens and early adult years. A lack of self-confidence and a great need for reassurance seem characteristic.

In their eagerness to be liked and accepted, mildly anxious children are prone to behave in a rather immature way with friends, who themselves are more likely to act younger than their years. There is a tendency to show-off and be silly, behaviour which can get them into mild trouble. Gary, aged 12 years, was dared by his friends to write 'bugger off' on his teacher's car using a felt tip pen. He carried out the dare but was caught by another teacher just as he finished writing the last letter 'f'. Young adolescent girls can find themselves unable to say no to sex with boyfriends for fear of losing them. Keeping in with friends is more important than remembering to bring books home or complete homework. Socks, training shoes and sweaters regularly go missing. Poor concentration and a general scattiness are reported by parents and teachers alike for many of the children. However a few, particularly girls, maintain an 'anxious-to-please' attitude. They work hard, often with great neatness and are rewarded with good results.

When children realise they have 'gone too far' in some way, the children are desperate to make amends. The aim then is to recover their parent's love and acceptance as quickly as possible. There is that lurking anxiety that mum or dad might stop loving them. And although they do get into silly trouble, these are not children who commit criminal offences. They are well-meaning.

When they reach late adolescence and early adulthood, the prospect of becoming independent is an unsettling thought. It is often the case that mildly anxious children are the last to leave home. Leaving home feels like the threat of a major loss and separation. There are lingering worries that when they move out there may be nothing to connect them to their parents who therefore might no longer be available. It is as if these children need to spend a few extra years at home to confirm feelings of trust and permanence. Having arrived late, they intend to leave late. When they do try and move out, many children need several trial goes before they finally succeed. Thus, while brothers and sisters may go to college or hunt for flats or plan to get married, these children typically stay at home often until their mid-twenties. Nevertheless, as the years tick by, feelings of trust and the acceptance of secure, loving relationships increase and confidence grows. Belief in their own lovability continues to gain ground.

Parents of this group of children speak warmly of the adoption. There are never regrets; indeed the children's slight vulnerability encourages parents to feel protective. These are sensitive and responsive children and great pleasure is taken in their upbringing. Table 11.1 summarises the major behavioural characteristics of the mildly insecure child.

Table 11.1 Mildly anxious and insecure children: behaviours, characteristics, achievements and personality.

General:	Mildly insecure and anxious
	Over sensitive
	Low self-confidence
	In need of lots of reassurance
	Clingy when young
	Compliant
	Anxious-to-please
	Well-meaning
	Very loving
	Sentimental
	Slight immature behaviour
	Attention-seeking
	Proneness to act silly or daft and show-off
	Easily led
	Impulsive
	Home-centred
	Dislike of changes of routine
	Heightened anxiety at times of loss and separation
School years:	Slightly poor concentration
	Avoidance of testing and challenging situations
	Under achieve academically
	Friendships with equally immature peers
	No record of criminal behaviour
	Unlikely to be referred to the child psychiatric psychological services
Late adolescence/early adulthood:	
	Tendency to delay leaving home and establish independence.
	Susceptibility to become overinvolved and anxious in relationships
	Reluctance to take too much responsibility in work situations
Evaluation:	View of adoption by adopted person: positive and satisfactory
	Views of adoptive parents: positive and satisfactory

Case example

Andrew

Julie was 17 years old when Andrew was born. She had a somewhat stormy relationship with her mother but decided to live at home after her son's birth. Andrew's father was a young man in the army who seemed frightened by Julie's pregnancy. He soon disappeared from the picture. Initially mother and daughter were united in their interest and love for the baby. They went out shopping together for a pram and baby clothes. However, after four months, Julie felt that her mother was interfering too much. Julie began to go out more at night time, leaving Andrew with his grandmother. She told Julie that she should stay at home; she had got herself pregnant and so could not expect to live a carefree life; she had responsibilities. They started to quarrel. Julie found a new boyfriend, Gary, a man three years older than herself. When Andrew was ten months old, Julie left home to live with Gary in a small flat, taking her son with her. He would often be left on his own in a cot at night while his mother and stepfather went out. Several times he was farmed out to be looked after by his mother's friends for a few days or a week.

Julie soon found herself pregnant by Gary. Her second baby, Liam, was born when Andrew was 21 months old. Julie and Gary argued and shouted a great deal, mainly about how much time and money Gary spent on drink. Andrew became more and more fretful, whiney and demanding. His stepfather said he could not stand the noise and the clutter. Most of his dissatisfaction and anger was directed against Andrew. Meanwhile, his mother seemed either to be looking after Liam or yelling at Gary. She also began to lose her patience more and more with her first son. Matters came to a head not long after Julie realised that she was pregnant for a third time. She said she could no longer cope with Andrew and could not be held responsible for what she might do to him: 'He drives me crazy. He was spoiled by his grandmother and ever since he's been a pain.' There were suspicions that he had been hit very hard on a number of occasions. The social workers who had been called in to investigate the case found a boy aged two years and three months who was fractious, unsmiling and dirty. After exploring various options, the decision was eventually made to place Andrew for adoption. He joined his new parents, Elaine and Ian Carey, a few months before his third birthday.

Elaine and Ian had two birth children, a boy aged eight years and a girl aged ten years at the time of Andrew's arrival. They had wanted a larger family but Elaine was advised against having another pregnancy on medical grounds. On first arrival, Andrew would sit and rock himself to and fro for hours. He seemed unable to control his eating. 'He would wolf everything down that was put in front of him, unable to stop it seemed.' He started to follow Elaine around wherever she went, not letting her out of his sight. 'I would sometimes sit with him on my knee in an old rocking chair we had for hours. That seemed to relax him.'

As he grew older, if Andrew got in a muddle over something, such as trying to button a shirt or build a car out of lego bricks, he would suddenly lose his temper and storm around the room. It was impossible to calm him down. He would blame his mother for giving him a shirt with button holes that were too small or his brother for causing the lego bricks not to lock together. But after a while, he would feel contrite and say that he was sorry. He loved the family being together. He would rush around the room at birthdays or Christmas in a very excited fashion, wanting everyone to be happy. Andrew was always generous with his presents, particularly those bought for his mother. As he got older, this became something of a problem. While his elder sister, and to some extent his brother managed to save some of their pocket money, Andrew 'no sooner had his than it was gone. On what, we never really knew but it seemed to slip through his fingers like water. No matter how much he had, it went. And so when it came to getting me a present, which he always saw as a vitally important occasion, he would get very troubled and upset until his dad bailed him out.'

When he was four years old, Elaine and Ian had to attend the funeral of a friend in Ireland requiring them to be away for three days. Andrew was left with Ian's mother. He was very subdued during the few days before they were due to go away and was clearly very anxious about them leaving him. He developed a high temperature while they were away and was very tearful and distraught. Elaine and Ian began to see a pattern whenever Andrew felt his life was about to change in some way. 'Whenever he had to move out of a familiar situation or thought he would have to be away from Elaine' said Ian, 'he would get very distressed and quickly fall to pieces. This has been an enduring feature throughout his life.' It took his mother a long time to get him used to staying at the local playgroup. He would cry and wail all the time she was away, but eventually he settled down.

When Andrew was five years old and just before he was due to start school the family decided to move to live in a new part of the country. They felt it would be hard for him to begin infant school and then change. So they planned to relocate over the summer. The story is picked up by Elaine and Ian:

'Life was beginning to go pretty well for Andrew. He had finally settled in his playgroup. We lived in a little cul-de-sac with lots of open spaces and other children and he liked that. But moving turned out to be a very poor experience for Andrew. He couldn't cope with it all. He was seriously distressed. The effects lasted years. He triggered the most difficult period of his childhood from the age of five till about nine. He just couldn't adjust to the new environment. Getting to school was a major problem. At least once a week he would get a stomach ache or a headache. He had this unconscious knack of getting himself a high temperature every time he got very anxious. I mean he really did get a high temperature. He got himself totally worked up.

He was always in the wrong, doing silly things that kept getting him into trouble. Like he poured ink into the school fish tank, which didn't please his teacher, or the fish. He said he thought the fish would like it better if the water was blue because that was the colour of the sea. At home he was totally unable to sit down and play. He would get so excited if friends were around. He went spiralling off. Me, his friends, we'd all get so exasperated with him because he'd get sillier and sillier ... We never got him to join the cubs or to go on school outings. We did once manage to get him to go on a short adventure holiday but he was so distraught by the time we arrived we gave up on the idea.'

Andrew began to bite his nails to the extent he disfigured his fingers. Throughout his childhood his eating was never quite under control. He would eat a box of chocolates the day it was given to him. He started to smoke when he was 15.

'We've tried every ploy to try and help him give up smoking, but nothing's ever worked. He drinks quite a lot now, but that's never got out of hand. Poor old Andrew is clearly susceptible to addictive behaviours, even still. But he's also cautious by nature. He tends to run away when he's anxious. He's not inclined to experiment when things look uncertain. His caution and addictive tendencies tend to balance themselves out.'

Intellectually he was about average but underperformed at school. His verbal skills were much better than his number skills. Many of his teachers thought he was idle, particularly at maths and the sciences. 'But we think he was just too frightened to try,' believed Elaine. 'You see, he was so anxious to please, really, that his gross inability at maths panicked him. He hated to be humiliated or appear a failure. He couldn't bear it and just couldn't handle it. If you pushed him too far and really exposed a weakness, say at doing a simple sum, he would explode and be beside himself. Then after a bit he'd cry.'

As he got older, his good sense of humour began to help him out socially. When he was younger he would hide in cupboards or under his bed rather than face people about a difficulty, a misbehaviour or a fear. But as he reached adolescence, he learned how to talk about his worries. He was always forgetting and losing things.

'Whenever a problem or the unknown faced Andrew – like at school, or getting a job, or having to do something difficult on his own – he'd try and escape. Or when the outside got too scary, stay put, avoid them. He'd lock himself in the bathroom or escape out of the window or climb an apple tree. He had perfected retreat ... And if things did go wrong, he'd endlessly blame other people. We'd made him late for school because we hadn't reminded him of the time; we'd made him leave his football boots at school because we had hassled him into getting home before it got dark.'

However, as Andrew progressed through his teenage years, his confidence grew. He became less anxious about whether his parents loved him or not. His sense of humour and generous character made him a more popular child. 'He's very kind and sensitive. He's always loved animals; loved things that are smaller than him.' Andrew left school, aged 17 years. He began an apprenticeship as a car mechanic, 'but was completely useless!' There followed two years in which he was in and out of work. When he was 20 he started work in a large hotel. He enjoyed working in the kitchens and restaurant. He is now 23 years old, still at home and working at the hotel where he is being trained. 'I think he likes the structure and routine of the hotel; I think he feels safe there.'

'Andrew's still growing up. We've taken the view that he needs time and so we aren't going to push the pace. He keeps talking about finding a flat, but so far nothing's materialised. He's a lovely lad; fun to be with but still a bit vulnerable. He now has girlfriends. They are always the first to end the relationship and it always devastates him. He showers them with presents and attention and it can all get a bit too much. But he's getting better. We love him dearly.'

Chapter 12
Angry Patterns

Children who experience their parents' care and interest as inconsistent and insensitive feel in a constant state of emotional arousal. Anxiety and distress, whether pitched high or low, trigger attachment behaviour. Thus, children who feel constantly anxious about their parents' emotional availability are likely find that their attachment behaviour is over-activated. Attachment behaviour causes children to approach their prime carer. However, if the responsiveness of the carer is experienced as irregular and unreliable, the approach is made using high levels of insistence, aggression and frustration that often leads to the child being described as fractious and whiney, demanding and difficult.

Heightened attachment behaviour

Two types of early care experience are associated with adopted children who show a pattern of heightened attachment behaviour and angry 'approach' responses: a small number of children adopted as babies, and a larger number of older-placed children who have experienced poor quality pre-placement care.

Baby adoptions

The children adopted as babies who follow the 'angry-hostile' pattern form a group that is not clearly understood. Most will have been placed within the first few weeks or months of life. There appears to be nothing unusual or out of the ordinary about the short period between their birth and placement. Similarly, the adoptive parents seem to be typical of those who adopt babies. There is a some evidence that the presence of biological children born to the adopters after placement is associated with problem behaviour in a number of baby adopted children (for example, Howe 1997). However, many adopters of these children say that they were difficult babies to parent almost from the day that they arrived. They seemed both insecure and irritable. 'Demanding and difficult' is a common description.

Various possible explanations have been given. One line of thought suggests that some children are deeply unsettled by their early moves from birth mother, to foster mother, to adoptive mother. Children who are sensitive and easily aroused may be emotionally overwhelmed by the anxiety generated by losing their carer at least once and possibly twice before they are finally settled. This might be consistent with the observation made by some parents that they find their children are often very creative and artistic. They appear unusually alert and extremely sensitive to what is happening around them. Even minor upsets and disturbances seem to unsettle them. Marjorie described her daughter Amy as very artistic, 'clever and responsive and yet so difficult ... Even as a baby Amy would have temper tantrums that would last for ages. It was very hard to comfort her and help her to settle.'

Some adoptive mothers say that they did not feel emotionally ready for the arrival of their baby. A 'pretty little baby girl' had been placed with Alice. She said that she invested 'a tremendous amount of love in her'. But four months later the birth mother decided not to go through with the adoption and reclaimed her. 'I was totally devastated; an emotional wreck.' In an attempt to help, the adoption worker arranged for another baby girl to be placed with Alice four months later. 'But I just wasn't ready for her. I was low and had little to give. I went through the motions with poor little Marianne. And she knew it. She was always cross with me. Even now I'm not sure she's really forgiven me.' Other mothers reported that they had waited so long for their baby that their eventual arrival felt an odd anti-climax. Feeling depressed and uninvolved, these mothers said that it took a long time before they felt fully engaged with their baby.

Theoretically, the quality of some adoptive parents' relationships with their children might be expected to produce ambivalent attachments. Although preparation and selection procedures are designed to identify competent and highly responsive parents, a small number might slip through who are not able to provide a secure base for their children. They may have experienced poor quality care themselves as children. They may not have adjusted to their own infertility. Or their marriage could be under stress. Whatever the reasons, their own emotional needs reduce their availability and sensitivity as far as the child is concerned.

Several of these elements may combine. For example, a temperamentally difficult baby who is placed with a couple who have not fully adjusted to their own infertility, partly as a result of their own adverse experiences in childhood, is likely to raise anxiety levels in her parents. The result could be an ambivalent attachment relationship in which the child becomes increasingly fractious and frustrated.

Poor start/late-placed children

These children could be placed any time after eight or nine months of age, but typically they would be adopted as toddlers or pre-school children. Their pre-placement experience is generally one of poor quality care and parenting. Neglect and sometime physical abuse often characterise their early years. The children may have been cared for by a variety of people in their short lives – placed with relatives or friends for a couple of weeks; short periods in respite foster care; different partners coming in and out of their mother's or father's life. The involvement of social workers and other child welfare agents is routine. Parents are either found to be caring for their children inadequately or they report that their children are beyond their control. After investigation, it is agreed by the authorities that the children are removed and looked after by foster parents or more rarely placed in residential care. If restoration to the family is not possible, many of the children will be placed for adoption.

Ambivalent attachment relationships

The baby-adopted and poor start/late-placed children in this pattern share a common early care history in which the quality of their relationship with their parents was experienced as erratic and uncertain. Attachment theorists have explored the dynamics of such relationships to try and understand the particular developmental pathways taken by these children.

When attachment figures fail to read their children's needs accurately or sensitively, infants have a psychological problem with which they have to deal. Parental care which is unpredictable, neglectful and unreliable does not help children to understand either·their own or other people's thoughts and feelings. In these cases, parenting behaviour lacks reciprocity. Misunderstandings abound. Communications between parent and child are inconsistent and poorly tuned. Children in such relationships can never quite trust their parents' continued availability or ability to respond appropriately or effectively. To this extent, these children experience a 'loss' of their parents, either totally or in part. Emotionally, the carer may not always be reliable or available. Sometimes the parent may be either physically or mentally 'lost' for periods of time – out all night with a sexual partner, 'unavailable' because she is high on drugs or alcohol, uninterested in the child's needs because he is too busy trying to satisfy his own.

Emotionally, it is very difficult for children to deal with attachment figures who are unresponsive and unavailable. When children are upset or hungry, hurt or confused, their level of anxiety rises. Anxiety normally activates attachment behaviour in which children seek out their selective attachment figure for comfort and security. The concern and interest of the attachment figure causes anxiety to drop. However, if the parent (attachment figure) is unreliable or unavailable, the anxiety which triggered the attachment behaviour remains. Furthermore, the emotional unresponsiveness of the parent itself adds to the anxiety resulting in an increase and exaggeration of attachment behaviour (crying, fretting, demanding, clinging, following, not letting go). The result is that children become quickly overwhelmed with a range of difficult emotions with which they find it hard to deal.

In attempts to keep the unreliable attachment figure in close proximity, the only strategy available to the children is to pursue the parent and protest when separation is threatened. The children's behaviour is anxious and fretful, insistent and angry. There is little time or energy for relaxed play and exploration. Most of the children's emotional efforts go into trying to prevent the parent either physically leaving or losing interest in them. The result is that children whine and are clingy. They need their parent's attention but are also angry that this person is also the cause of their frustration, hurt and anxiety. This is why such attachments are termed insecure and ambivalent. These children can never quite trust their parents or take them for granted. The fear of separation, or even abandonment is always present.

These fundamental doubts about one's capacity to influence other people coupled with their apparent inability to tune into and respond to one's needs, leads to feelings of low self-esteem, poor self-confidence and high anxiety. The individual's inner working model sees other people as uninterested and unresponsive and the self as uninteresting, ineffective and unworthy.

Such feelings often continue into adolescence and adulthood. The fear of losing the attention and interest of other people drives the anxious individual into close relationships that are formed quickly and often without discrimination. But the other person in the relationship is primarily there to meet the needs of the individual who is insecure. There is little reciprocity. So, although there is a constant urge to be in relationships, the continued availability or reliability of the other cannot be trusted or taken for granted. Thus, other people provoke feelings of ambivalence and anger. There is a need to be emotionally close, but to be dependent on someone who may hurt you by abandoning you is fraught with anxiety: 'I need you, but I can't trust you.' Such relationships are characterised by feelings of jealousy and possessiveness as well as constant conflict. And as people with an insecure, ambivalent history are often likely to form relationships with other people who are insecure, the result is a partnership that is full of upset, drama and argument. Mutual threats of leaving the relationship are mirrored by the mutual fear of being abandoned by the other. In such emotional cycles, feelings of anxiety and anger increase and often end in violence. There is a fear of 'letting go' of the other. And yet the emotional demands made on others by the insecure person can become so wearing that they soon exhaust parents, partners and friends. The 'ambivalent' individual conducts relationships in a very intense, demanding manner. They remain *preoccupied* with other people and the relationships they have with them. There is a need to be needed but an anxiety and anger that they remain exposed, vulnerable and fragile in relationships of such dependence.

The ambivalent personality is basically attention-seeking. There is a need to keep interactions alive and active – quietness and passivity are interpreted as a lack of interest, love and concern. The emotional demands and heightened quality of relationships is therefore designed to keep the fear of being rejected at bay. Threatening and violent behaviour is an attempt to control the other person and prevent him or her leaving the relationship.

Patterns of behaviour, personality and relationship style

The *internal working models* that form within children in ambivalent attachments see others' availability as unpredictable and unreliable. Their interest and responsiveness do not appear to correlate with the children's own needs and internal states. Rather, other people seem to behave mainly on the basis of their own emotional needs and anxieties. The self, therefore, is seen as lacking lovability and worth. Other people do not respond unless the children demand, insist and complain. In their attempts to cope with anxiety, ambivalently attached children have to *increase* their attachment behaviour in an effort to keep their parents' interest and attention. There is a constant worry that their attachment figures may leave or even abandon them. Parents, therefore, have to be kept in sight by any means possible. Mentally representing the self and other in these terms means that children's self-esteem, self-confidence and self-efficacy are unlikely to be very high. Whereas mildly insecure children blame other people for the collapse of their early relationships and retain a basically positive, albeit slightly insecure view of self, 'angry' children worry that they may not be very lovable or likeable and that is why their biological parents gave them up and why relationships with their adopters are difficult.

Poor start/late-placed children develop the basic structures of their internal working model prior to their placement. Once adopted, the models continue to influence the way children see others, view themselves and approach relationships. To this extent, ambivalently attached children generate social environments that are self-fulfilling. There is a *reactive* interaction between the children and their parents who begin to respond with increasing exasperation. Parents who feel under stress will find that their responses become increasingly determined by their own fraught feelings and anxieties. Emotionally, this makes them less available and less sensitive, thus confirming the children's mental representation of the self as unworthy and others as unavailable.

Ambivalently attached children's inner working models will only be revised towards a more secure, positive and less defended outlook if their adoptive parents are able to sustain high levels of responsive awareness of their children's needs. This can prove extremely difficult when children's models are firmly established or the stresses of looking after a demanding, hostile child go on for years and years. Children with easy temperaments might also find it easier to shift from insecure to secure attachment patterns. Not only will they react less negatively to the perceived demands of others, other people are likely to respond more positively to the children's more sociable and relaxed temperamental style. As we have seen, developmental recovery is possible and there is evidence that it is most strongly associated with warm, accepting and skilled parenting and children who arrive with the fewest behavioural and emotional problems.

There is one more ingredient that has a potent influence on these children's understanding of themselves and who they are. As they grow older, and particularly as they enter adolescence, the full implication of what it means to have been placed for adoption dawns. No matter how it is told or packaged, it appears that their parents could not or would not keep them. Given their interpersonal history and psychological make-up, this realisation confirms the main features of their inner working model of self and relationships with others: that they were not of sufficient value, lovability or interest to be kept by their biological parents. This is a deeply painful and disturbing thought. The need to be wanted is urgently present, but their insecurity means that other people cannot be trusted to remain available. As we have seen, this increases anxiety which leads to an over-production of attachment behaviour that is not easily switched off. The result is a preoccupation with relationships ('Do you really love me? I'm not sure you do') and an agitated concern with other people's availability ('Can I trust you to stay interested? Will you still be there?). The deep anxiety is one of losing close, protective relationships. The fear of loss and separation constantly disturbs these children's psychosocial functioning. A concern with the feelings and continued emotional availability of others leaves little time to concentrate on things like school work.

These children are easily tipped by setbacks and upsets, which, because of their anxieties, happen all too frequently. Changes of routine and upsets in the rhythm of daily life can quickly lead to fretful, querulous behaviour. 'Over the years,' said one mother:

'Katie could never cope with journeys and suitcases and any sort of suggestion of going anywhere. She was always tense and disturbed about going away. She'd be withdrawn and surly. She'd be thoroughly unpleasant. She just could not handle it. Once I had to go and visit my sister and went away for a couple of days. She was about eight or nine at the time. She was all right while I was away, but when I returned, all hell broke out. She was absolutely awful to me for days and days afterwards.'

The upshot of all these children's experiences is to make them demanding and difficult, restless and *angry*. Their anger at needing to be needed by people whose love and responsiveness is perceived not to be unconditionally available, and may be withdrawn or lost at any time, leads to conflict in all close relationships. The people who assume the most emotional significance and importance in their lives are therefore the ones who can hurt them most. Not surprising then that adoptive mothers and fathers are on the receiving end of most of their anger and hostility. The greatest preoccupation is with their relationship with their parents. This can also include the birth mother about whom these children feel profoundly ambivalent. Sack & Dale concluded their study of late-placed children who had suffered abuse during their first two years of life, speculating:

'As a result of past abuse, the child is torn between wanting an attachment and yet fearing retaliation ... Thus the provocative behavior would seem to carry both an attachment seeking element as a defence against the anxiety that too much closeness can lead to unpredictable painful consequences. For the parent, such behavior is usually interpreted simply as rejection and defiance.'

(Sack & Dale, 1982: p. 448)

As babies and young children they are hard to placate. They are people who are either in a state of crisis and drama or deep despair. Many children say that they do not feel that they 'fit' with their adoptive families. Jealousy and anger can also be directed towards other siblings, particularly if the adopters have younger born children. Ruth, for example, placed at 18 months after a history of neglect, abandonment and abuse by her drug abusing birth parents, seemed to spend every available opportunity in spiting and attacking her younger brother, Jonathon, who was born to Catherine and Peter a few months before Ruth's third birthday. She would place drawing pins in his bed, trip him whenever he passed by. Catherine continues the story:

'When I was pregnant with Jonathon and told Ruth that I would be going into hospital she asked 'Which mummy is going to get me up in the morning?' I think she felt her time was up with us. My mother looked after her and Ruth said to her 'When the baby's born, I'll have to leave won't I and go to another home.' I thought, my goodness, this is strong stuff ... When Jonathon was a baby, she was very edgy, very tense and very angry with him. She got particularly angry with him if he tried to reach for one of her toys. I remember seeing her once sitting on his head, grinding a sticklebrick into his head ... By the time he'd reach eight or nine, Jonathon was finding Ruth oppressive, to put it mildly. We found him weeping in corners and we found him taking out calendars and pencils and paper working out complicated sums about how many more months left until she would be 18 and might be leaving home.'

As the children get older, relationship problems can extend to friends. The desire for intimacy and the need to be liked mean that these children begin to place the same emotional demands on peers as they do on family members. As in all relationships, they wear other people out. The only way peers cope is by abandoning the relationship, the very thing that these insecure children fear. The children have friends but tend not to keep them.

In many cases, food looms large as an issue. Problems of over-eating are common. And as some children grow older, they begin to use food as a 'weapon'. It can be used to symbolise the giving and withholding of affection. Children might refuse to eat with the rest of the family, insisting that they have their food later or in their bedroom. Food prepared for a meal might be spoiled. 'Simon knew that I had spent a lot of time preparing things for my mother's dinner party the next day,' said Madeleine, 'and so I guess it was a very deliberate act. He mixed salt into the cherry and brandy dish that had taken me ages to prepare and which I had left overnight in the 'fridge. Totally ruined.'

Problems at school are common. Parents say that they 'dreaded' parents' evenings when they know they will be spending a long time with each teacher listening to a catalogue of concerns. Teachers describe the children as disruptive. An inability to concentrate runs through most accounts. Academically, the children underperform. Testing situations, such as reading aloud in class or exams, are avoided if at all possible. They are extra-sensitive to criticism and only try when they are taught by someone who senses and understands their anxieties. The more pressured and impersonal the school environment, the less these children seem able to cope. In the more extreme cases, children might be either suspended or excluded from school. Child psychologists and psychiatrists invariably become involved at some stage.

During adolescence, the level of anti-social behaviour reaches a peak. Lying and deceit become almost endemic. 'He seems to lie on principle,' said Kieron's mother. 'I never knew where I was with him or in fact where he was. A very stressful time.' In many cases, children begin to steal from home. Mothers in particular seem to be deliberately and pointedly targeted. Money might be stolen from purses; valuable possessions might go missing from bedrooms. Parents in the worst cases report developing a 'siege mentality' at home; locks are fitted to pantries, bedrooms and studies. A significant minority of children go on to commit criminal offences outside the home. Shoplifting is most common, but a few children graduate to house burglaries, fraud and more serious crime. Adoptive parents of these most troubled and troublesome children find themselves involved with police and probation officers, courts and even prisons.

These are extremely difficult and stressful times for parents. Relationships with their sons and daughters reach an all time low. Anger and conflict never seem far away. At their worst, the children refuse to take part in home life. They begin to stop out late at night and resist going away on family holidays. Children may say that their family is 'rubbish' and that they want nothing to do with them. The children are often at their most diagnostically revealing when they are most upset, confused and angry. The implications of what it means to have been 'given up' for adoption are often thrown into the heat of the quarrel. They say things that indicate their desperate insecurity and feelings of being unwanted and unloved. For example, Ruth said: 'I could understand my mother not coping on her own, but what I cannot see and what I shall never forgive is that when she did have a chance of settling down with this new man, she chose the man and not me.' And in tears after she had tried to attack her mother with a poker, 14 year old Anita, who was drunk on cider, broke down crying: 'Why did that bitch have me adopted? What was wrong with me. You don't love me. This family is total rubbish and I wish you were all dead.'

Their preoccupation with and anxiety over their adoptive parents' feelings for them leads to behaviour that is rude, nagging and unrelenting. If parents attempt to comfort their upset children they may be violently rebuffed. On the other hand, if they back off and try not to react they are accused of being unloving and not caring. 'Whatever we did,' recalled Sue, 'we just couldn't seem to win.' The conflict may put marriages under strain. It can spoil and distort the childhoods of other children in the family. 'Angry' children consume vast amounts of families' emotional energy without giving anything back in return. The end result in some cases can be the 'rejection' that the children always feared and predicted. Children may be packed off to boarding school. Some storm off to live with boyfriends or girlfriends. A few may even end up in prison. In many cases, these conclusions are presaged by episodes of stopping out all night and going 'missing' for a couple of days. These children rarely remain out of the picture for long. They return home but soon get into conflict with their parents. 'She crashed in and out of our lives for a good few years before we finally reached calmer waters,' said Shirley of her daughter.

However, not all angry children leave home in the heat of the moment. A few parents stagger on and try to 'stick with' with things until their sons or daughters eventually calm down, which, in most cases, they seem to do sometime in their late teens or early to midtwenties. Eventually, they seem able to accept the love of their parents without the feelings of ambivalence and anger that previously affected their ability to handle close relationships. The change – if it happens – in both those who stay at home and those who leave in anger can be quite sudden according to many parents. The children seem to have little memory of how bad their behaviour really was during their adolescent years.

These feelings of calmness and trust seem to be triggered by various experiences. Searching for and meeting a birth mother may help some children understand that the adoption was not their fault. Having a good relationship with a stable, secure partner can raise self-esteem and help people to like and value themselves. They are then able to accept their parents' love without feeling anxious, defensive and hostile. Producing a baby of their own clearly reassures some adopted people: they discover that they can love and be loved unconditionally. They then seem able to relate to their adoptive parents with greater confidence and security. In many cases, the dogged persistence of caring parents gradually establishes that their love is not going to be taken away; that they will always be there, no matter what happens. They finally experience their relationship with their parents as secure.

Indeed, many adopters report that just when you might normally expect children to separate and become more independent, their previously 'angry' children begin to increase interest, contact and concern. A daughter might decide to return to the neighbourhood and live in a flat just round the corner from her parents. A son might take to telephoning home several times a week where before his parents had been lucky to hear from him at all. Christmas and birthday presents, often of generous proportions might be bought for the first time since pre-adolescence.

Not all children are able finally to establish a close, more relaxed relationship with their parents. Sometimes, if adopters feel that too much pain and hurt has been suffered, they are not prepared to resume contact. Equally, a few children may have been so long out of touch with their parents that major re-involvement is unlikely. Parents may receive the odd postcard to say that all is well or be greeted with a fleeting visit from time to time, but there appear to be no immediate prospects of increased intimacy or contact.

Parents of this last group of 'angry' children report mixed feelings about the adoption. If a belated calm and a more secure relationship is established, the conclusion is that although it has been a difficult, stressful business 'it has been worth it in the end'. However, a few parents do express regrets. They feel that their children have either ruined a marriage, spoilt family life, or provided few feelings of pleasure or satisfaction. Table 12.1 summarises the major behavioural characteristics of insecure, angry children with ambivalent attachment histories.

Table 12.1 Angry and insecure children: behaviours, characteristics, achievements and personality.

General:	Demanding
	Difficult
	Resistant behaviour and ambivalent feelings in close relationships
	Prone to produce conflict in close relationships
	Externalising and oppositional problem behaviours
	At times of conflict parents feel: they cannot win exasperated/angry
	Not very good at giving and receiving comfort and affection
	Feel unloved/unwanted/rejected
	Low self-confidence and self-esteem
	Tendency to blame others when things go wrong
	Poor peer relationship skills
	Not very good at coping with change
School years:	Poor concentration
	Underachieve academically
	Can be disruptive in the classroom
	A significant minority of children:
	show physical aggression towards their parents
	show jealous/possessive/spiteful behaviour
	feel despair/depression
	are referred to a child psychiatrist/psychologist
	lie/deny extensively
	steal from their parents/home
	have an issue over food/an eating disorder
	A minority of children:
	self-abuse
	abuse/misuse alcohol/drugs
	commit criminal offences outside the home
	become involved with the police/courts/prison
	get pregnant before the age of 16 years
Late adolescence/early adulthood:	Leave home early but possibly with repeated 'aggressive hostile' returns
	Continued conflict in close relationships with friends and partners
	Initially poor employment record
	Possible problems with alcohol/drugs/criminal behaviour
	Increased likelihood of establishing more secure attachment with parents:
	less conflict
	more trust and willingness to be loved and accepted
Evaluation:	Mixed views by adopters:
	Qualified positive review if a belated recovery of good relationships has been established
	Negative review if relationships remain poor or severed.

Case example

Leisha

Leisha's birth mother was 16 years old when she was born. She left home and went to live with friends who were very involved with drugs. Leisha was often left with her mother's friends while she either disappeared for a few days or worked for a week or two. Social workers were called in on a number of occasions as neighbours, health visitors and relatives all expressed concern about Leisha's care. Neglect was diagnosed and minor physical abuse was suspected. Twice Leisha was looked after by foster parents for short periods while her mother tried to sort out some of the many financial and relationship problems she was suffering. When Leisha was 15 months old, her mother became depressed and lethargic. Leisha's care suffered. She cried a great deal and was said to be 'a picture of misery' by the social worker who found her standing forlorn in her cot while her mother was in a deep, drunken sleep downstairs. The little girl was once again looked after by foster parents. Leisha, with the consent of her mother, was finally placed for adoption aged 21 months with Stan and Elsie.

Within a couple of weeks they said that they found her to be a bright, alert child. However, as she grew older, her behaviour became more difficult. 'She was not an easy toddler,' said Elsie. 'There was a personality clash between Leisha and me. Leisha was the sort of child who always wanted to be centre stage – up front all the time. She was often naughty. We didn't have a very good relationship. As she got older she got worse. She always knew how to wind me up. Even as a young child, there would be days when she'd wake up and be awkward and she'd stay awkward all day. And when I put her to bed at night, I'd say "You haven't been a very nice girl today, have you?" And she said "No! No!" She knew.'

At primary school she never really applied herself. 'She never got switched on,' said Stan, 'unfulfilled potential.' When her parents visited the school, teachers always said the same thing: 'Nice girl, but could do better. She has no drive, motivation, effort or commitment.' Leisha did not cope well with changes of routine. Going on holiday was always a problem. Throughout the break she would be irritable, querulous and tearful. 'Once, when we were in Majorca,' said Stan, 'she got herself so agitated in the hotel lobby that she just sat down and screamed and yelled inconsolably. We'd no real idea what triggered it, but she just kept wailing how unhappy she was and that nobody cared. After that, we just went away for short holidays in England. It was no fun trying anything more adventurous. She could never handle it.'

It was when Leisha started secondary school that the real problems began. She fell behind with her French. When her father visited the school, the French teacher said to Stan that she hoped his wife was better. 'Leisha had maintained a fabrication over a year to the effect that Elsie had gone into hospital with a desperate condition and she was having to go to hospital to see her every day. She lied so much we never knew where we were with her.' It was during that year that Leisha began to truant.

Although she had friends, Stan did not think that she was a popular girl. He even thought she was a little bit of a bully. Leisha was 'intensely jealous' of her sister, Connie, born to Elsie and Stan 18 months after Leisha was first placed. Elsie and Stan said they dare not leave the two girls on their own as teenagers in case Leisha attacked Connie. It was also at this time that she began to steal from home.

Stan, in an attempt to understand his daughter, began to keep notes and a diary on his increasingly difficult daughter. He read the following extract:

'She has always seemed oddly unemotional. Rarely cried in child-hood. Didn't like being cuddled. Destructive of her toys. Never played with dolls. As a teenager, she seems troubled, lost; certainly troubled in some way about her adoption. She is very bitter towards her natural mother who she thinks rejected her. Uncommunicative in family. Only speaks to the dog – who doesn't answer back. Given to chronic lying and fabrication since early childhood. She's never to be believed, though on first meeting always plausible and convincing. Rarely owns up. Appears a Walter Mitty type living in a world of fantasy and make-believe. Conning us all the time. Once told someone her mother was dead ... She had recently conned her bank into increasing her overdraft saying I had died in the south of France and she had to sort out the return of my body.'

Leisha left school when she was 16. Her first job was as a hotel receptionist in another part of the country. She was keen to leave home and the job allowed her to live in the hotel. Unfortunately, Leisha stole money from her employers. She also started shoplifting. As well as losing her job, she had to go to court where she was fined. The family felt badly let down and very ashamed. Elsie and Stan felt under great strain. Leisha's grandmother paid the fine. 'But we realised it was a bottomless pit,' said Stan. She returned home for a while during which time she stole her father's cheque book.

Over the following months, Leisha, then aged 18, committed 'a whole string of money offences – stolen cheque books, credit cards, cash.' She accumulated several thousand pounds of debt by telling her bank lies designed to elicit sympathy. 'She was spending, spending all the time, non-stop. At one large department clothes shop she ran up a debt of over a thousand pounds. We kept bailing her out but it kept going on. We used to get bills from Harrods and the Savoy, where she stayed. She would walk away without paying. She led a very glamorous lifestyle. By 1980 she had total debts of £5600. And on top of this she had many other creditors chasing her. Deception was the main offence that she used to sustain this glamorous lifestyle.'

Somehow, Leisha managed to secure herself another job as a hotel receptionist, but again she stole money, credit cards and cheque books. The magistrate told her 'You have been a wicked, wicked girl and I shall defer sentence to Crown Court and you will be held in remand.' So at the age of eighteen and a half, Leisha went to prison. 'We were shattered,' said Elsie, 'but there was also a sense of relief. She was totally out of control. We needed a breather. At least she was out of harm's way.' After one month on remand she was given a probation order.

Leisha returned to her home town and again managed to gain a job as a receptionist. Although she committed one or two further minor offences, it seemed that she was beginning to 'steady down'. For a while she lived at home. She then found a boyfriend and went to live with him. 'He seemed to have a good influence on her. But she kept having rows with him and coming back home. This to-ing and fro-ing went on for a while. She's very untidy and lives in a tip. She was engaged to him, then she wasn't, then she was, then finally it was off.' From this point on, Leisha, aged 20, seemed to improve. She learned office skills and has been working successfully for her current employer for the last nine years. A year ago, she met her husband. 'She still spends like there is no tomorrow,' said Elsie.

Leisha's parents are of the opinion that during her difficult times, she had 'an identity crisis'. When she was in prison, Leisha wrote to her parents:

> 'Thankyou for coming to see me today. I have no idea why I keep doing all these things – the stealing, and the deception and the debts. I think it has something to do with the persistent feeling of not being wanted. I really do not like myself. I try to make myself more appealing by buying things, especially for my boyfriend James. When I started going out with him, I had this eternal fear of losing him. When he went for his job interview, I knew I would soon lose him. I spent money and bought things just to cheer myself up. I never regained James' love ... I did not do this to hurt anybody, least to you Mum and Dad. I never realised that Mums and Dads are the best friends you have ... I am, as you say, extremely jealous of Connie ... But I would like to make a fresh start.'

Aged 25, Leisha traced her birth mother but at first did not mention her plans either to Stan or Elsie. However, before making her first face-to-face contact with her birth mother, Leisha decided to discuss matters with her father but only on condition that he did not tell Elsie what was afoot, at least for the time being. 'She thought it best to keep her mum in the dark,' explained Stan, 'because she knew Elsie would become too emotional and upset and complicate the reunion.' The meeting between

Leisha and her birth mother went ahead. When Elsie was eventually told, she was extremely angry with both Leisha and Stan. 'It was a dreadful shock to me,' said Elsie. 'I'd like to have known about it. I could have taken it in my stride.'

Leisha's birth mother came to her wedding. 'They look very much alike,' Elsie noticed, 'and their mannerisms are the same.' They are in contact, but it is a fragile relationship. Leisha's birth mother, Maria, finds it difficult to cope with some of Leisha's occasional sleights. Leisha forgot Maria's birthday which upset her. Maria retaliated by allowing her dog to sleep on the duvet Leisha had bought her as a present. This led to a quarrel after which Leisha's birth mother said that she did not wish to see her daughter again. Stan intervened. He telephoned her, saying 'You can't reject Leisha again. Leisha is like this. For goodness sake, don't give her up for things as silly as that.'

Stan believed Leisha was 'looking for her roots'. Elsie recognises Leisha's insecurity. 'She now 'phones us every day. She even rang while she was on her honeymoon to ask if we were all right. She keeps telling me that she loves me and asks if I love her. I suppose I must confess that I have sometimes found it difficult to feel close to Leisha in the way that I have with Connie. However, Stan was unequivocal in his determination to 'stick by' Leisha:

> 'I am not sure that Leisha fully realises what we went through. She just expected me to clear up all her messes – deal with lawyers, psychiatrists, doctors. She'd left a trail of devastation behind her. There was no apparent contrition. We've tried to stick by her and we do love her. We didn't give up because we love her. And without us, she'd be living in a cardboard box by now. She's a very generous girl. She'll buy you anything! We love to see her. She can be fun to be with. She's a good cook. At the restaurant, she'll always choose the most expensive food and the most expensive bottle of wine! Other people kept telling us to give up on her. But we didn't.'
>
> I must say this about it all, it took me into spheres of life that I did not expect to experience. Police stations, courts, prisons, psychiatrists, lawyers. But experiences are part of life and perhaps my philosophy is that such experiences enlarge you in some sort of sense. We never got to the point of throwing her out.'

Chapter 13

Avoidant Patterns

Parents who find it hard to warm to their children cause them deep psychological distress. To feel emotionally rejected by one's attachment figure forces children to develop extreme defensive strategies. Parents who are hostile, intrusive and controlling offer little by way of comfort and understanding. The empathy that parents require if their responses are to be caring and accurate is missing. In these terse relationships, parents are more concerned about how their children are affecting them rather than how they are affecting their children. Mutuality and reciprocity are absent. Thus, parenting which is rejecting and controlling discourages children from displaying their own needs and feelings.

Anxiety and distress normally sponsor attachment behaviour. However, in these parent–child relationships, children know that their attachment figure is not a source of comfort, interest or understanding. Their parents feel distinctly uncomfortable with closeness and intimacy. The unspoken message to their children is 'keep your distance – physically and emotionally'. Therefore, children sense that approaching their parents not only fails to relieve distress, it heightens it. Children attempt to cope by trying to de-activate their attachment behaviour. This can involve denying emotional affect – after all there is little that you can do with anxiety if it is aroused, so better to try and shut down that side of your psychological make-up. Emotional proximity and involvement are best avoided. These appear to be emotionally constrained, self-contained children who lack warmth and reciprocity.

Although they appear to come from a variety of pre-placement backgrounds, there seems to be a common history of hostile, cold, critical parenting, sometimes coupled with multiple moves that often include a period in residential care. While under the care of their biological parents, physical and emotional abuse are common. The part that sexual abuse might play in avoidant attachments is less clearly understood, but it is certainly present in some cases. Social workers are usually called in to investigate when there are worries over neglect, abuse and parental rejection. Because these are often psychologically quite damaged children they are not always easy to foster. As a holding strategy, residential care is sometimes preferred. In adoption, nearly all of these children are late-placements, typically joining their adoptive families between 3 and 7 years of age.

Insecure, avoidant attachment relationships

Whereas insecure children who feel ambivalent about their attachment relationships find themselves in an inconsistent caring environment, insecure children who feel rejected in their attachment relationship face an environment that is uncaring and hostile. Parents, who themselves feel anxious and distressed when emotional demands are made on them, seek to control their social environment. This environment includes their children. They intrude on and attempt to control their children's experiences, perceptions and affective states. The children's own mental states are not read accurately; indeed parents prefer to define their children's experiences for them.

The only way to cope with an attachment figure who is emotionally ungiving, unresponsive and rejecting is to try and *avoid* closeness and intimacy. 'Avoidant' children learn that when they feel anxious, there is little point in approaching parents for comfort and concern. Being rejected simply increases the level of anxiety. These children, therefore, try to 'go it alone'; they attempt to become 'emotionally self-reliant' (Bowlby, 1988).

The defensive strategy is one of ignoring feelings that normally activate attachment behaviour. The significance of the attachment relationship is de-emphasised. To these children, the world of other people does not seem a rewarding place or an emotionally safe place. On the contrary, closeness and intimacy seem dangerous and potentially hurtful. They show little distress when separated from their parents. They rarely seek proximity with their carer, even when they are upset or frustrated. They are watchful and wary children who have a history of being rebuffed and emotionally rejected. Unlike ambivalently attached children who fear that they will not get what they want, 'avoidant' children fear what they want (Howe, 1995a). Emotionally, the conclusion must be that the self is certainly not likeable or lovable, and may well be bad in some way that it should be so loathed by significant others. These are deeply distressing and disturbing feelings. Although on the surface there appears to be a self-containment and a kind a strength, these are people with very low self-esteem and self-confidence.

Those who have experienced their primary caregiving relationships as avoidant attachments find it difficult to make close relationships. Emotional intimacy is avoided; it raises anxiety. Having failed to get close to others and learn about emotions within the interplay of close relationships, avoidant personalities develop poor levels of social understanding. Little or no interest is shown in other people's feelings, needs and beliefs. Displays of emotionality are not easily understood. In fact, they are likely to arouse anxiety, fear and ultimately aggression as they revive old pains and uncertainties. This makes such people potentially dangerous. As children and adults they can be bullies. A lack of emotional empathy means that they have little understanding of other people's feelings and they show little hesitation in causing hurt. And not having learned to understand other people, having been denied the experience of close, reciprocal relationships, they also fail to learn to understand their own thoughts and feelings in a full, connected and coherent way. In particular, these children seem cut off from their emotionality – they are emotionally illiterate.

Disconnection from affect can also mean that children are poor at processing and integrating feelings of their own, including an awareness of their own physical states. Control over bodily functions – including elimination, retention, eating and reactions to pain – can be poor. Children learn about their own states and feelings within reciprocal, sensitive, mutually attuned relationships. To be short-changed on such experiences denies children opportunities to understand and connect with their own sensations. Being obliged to go it alone, they learn to rely almost exclusively on their rational skills. They therefore may become particularly proficient at abstract, physical, mechanical skills that do not require social adroitness. But when interpersonal and emotional issues intrude, they may become highly distressed, angry and even aggressive.

In dealing with other people, the avoidant personality works on the principle that it is better to reject than be rejected. Those who do get into relationships with avoidant personalities will find little warmth or reciprocity. They dismiss shows of emotion as signs of weakness. Avoidant personalities need to be in control; they fear letting go. The boundaries of their fragile self are easily threatened when feelings begin to run high and relationships feel too close and intimate. As adults, this can include fear of intimacy with partners who may experience them as withholding, punishing, emotionally rigid and in cold control. But if the control and restraint is lost, impulsive anger or despair surface all too quickly and overwhelm the personality.

Patterns of behaviour, personality and relationship style

The *internal working models* formed by children who are avoidantly attached to their parents see other people as unavailable, controlling and rejecting. Children's internal states appear to be of no interest to other people. Parents seem not to respond in ways that attempt to acknowledge or understand their children's thoughts and feelings. In other words, children learn that their needs only serve to cause other people distress and upset that makes them hostile. The self is seen as unlovable and it is rebuffed. The self therefore must be 'bad'; the self is to blame. In the case of adopted children, they believe that this is why their biological parents could not or would not care for them; this is why they were placed for adoption.

In their attempts to cope with anxiety, avoidantly attached children *decrease* their attachment behaviour, which if it were to be activated would bring them into proximity with their unresponsive, rejecting attachment figure. Children begin to see feelings and their expression as emotionally dangerous. Their presence signals anxiety. The strategy is to keep them at bay, thus avoiding personal distress as well as hostile reactions.

As with the internal working models associated with other attachment patterns, the expectations of the self and others in relationship take on a self-fulfilling quality. Children who do not trust others and who appear emotionally self-reliant, ungiving and unresponsive prove hard going for parents, siblings and peers. In time, other people are likely to lose interest or feel cross and let-down. Emotionally, they retreat and stop giving. As far as the avoidant child is concerned this confirms that intimacy is distressing and hurtful. Their defensive strategy remains in place: it is better to avoid emotional involvement; it is much safer to avoid showing one's feelings, or indeed allowing oneself to have feelings.

Children whose inner working models are generated within avoidant attachments may be able to revise them if they subsequently find themselves in radically new social environments. Adoptive parents, for example, must be able to resist being drawn into the children's model in which other people are expected to be rejecting, even though the children's behaviour invites hostility and rebuff. Sustained experience of relationships that run counter to the 'avoidant' model may, in time, demand its revision. Warm, skilled, accepting parenting can act as a powerful change agent but it has to be sustained over very long periods of time. Children can then begin to trust other people, express feelings and explore closeness and intimacy. Once the model becomes more open and flexible, children can begin to learn about their own emotions, develop social understanding and so become more socially competent. However, modifying inner working models and shifting defensive strategies is a long haul business, requiring patience, consistency and commitment.

From the day they arrive, parents may feel that their children are 'hard to reach'. They are often described as not very 'cuddly' or tactile. They resist touch and closeness. Emotionally, these children have learned either to fend for themselves or to disconnect themselves from states of arousal of any kind. This makes them affectively flat and peculiarly matter-of-fact about all manner of things about which you might normally expect children to become excited.

One of the major corollaries of having a history of avoidant relationships is not to become socially involved. Parents describe children appearing 'to hover on the edge of family life'. The children themselves might well say that they feel they 'don't belong' – not necessarily in an accusatory way, more as a statement of fact. To this extent, many parents do find that they feel disappointed and hurt that they appear to get so little back from their children. Socially, they are loners and often not very popular with other children. A few may act as bullies.

Having a moral conscience or the ability to empathise is limited. The control of impulses and antisocial behaviour is therefore very poorly developed. Eating problems, often in the form of knowing when to stop when young, can be a problem. Some children, not fully in touch with their bodies and their feelings, are accident-prone. They rarely cry and get upset when they injure themselves. This can extend in some cases to having no sense of danger. 'In spite of my warnings, my shouting and my huge and obvious anxiety,' said Beth of her son, Alan, who was six years old at the time, 'I kept spotting him riding on his bike the wrong way on the busy road outside our house. And if you told him it was very, very dangerous, he would just shrug. It was this constant feeling that we were not making any connection with him. And when he did hurt himself, he never seemed to bother.'

Parents do get into rows and quarrels with their children, but the conflict tends to lack the drama and highly personalised and pointed quality that arguments with 'ambivalent' children have. Lying and stealing are not uncommon. Behaving in a hurtful way towards other people is not unusual. Initially at least, 'avoidant' personalities are unrewarding people with whom to get into relationships. They do not trust intimacy; they feel anxious when emotional demands are made of them. Their natural inclination is to 'move out and move away' when relationships threaten to revive old feelings of rejection, hurt and intrusive control. It is hardly surprising, then, that child psychologists and psychiatrists are frequently called in by parents and teachers to help this group of children.

Teachers find these difficult children to discipline. They are restless and underperform academically, although a few children do capitalise on their preference for handling matters cognitively and rationally, possibly showing prowess with computers or the more technical subjects. In adolescence, truancy can become a problem by day, while drifting off and not letting parents know their whereabouts can become a problem by night. Running away from home and going missing for several days causes some parents further upset and distress. The structure and routine of boarding schools seem to suit the need for control and order in many children. Once in the more organised setting, they behave in a more settled manner.

Many children leave home at relatively young and early ages, or contrive to be 'sent away' either to boarding school or some other form of care away from home. Children leave school at 16 or 17 and live on their own, in a hostel, a flat, or even sleep rough. Parents often describe their children as 'drifters' or 'wanderers'. Contact with families can be thin and infrequent. Some parents express relief when their children do leave. The stresses and frustrations of parenting such unresponsive,

unrewarding children can take a heavy toll. Casual employment
interspersed with long periods of unemployment are a common pattern. A few children with the more serious conduct disorders commit
criminal offences and may spend time in prison. 'Alan was caught for
silly offences, really,' said Beth. 'He did steal a car once. He even stole a
"walkie-talkie" from a policeman's car, would-you-believe! Prison for
Alan was like a womb. All the strain went from his face. He almost
blossomed. No decisions to make.'

As young adults, the same difficulty of forming and sustaining intimate relationship remains. Marriages break down. Episodes of angry
or violent behaviour are followed by abandonment of the relationship.
But interestingly, many children continue to maintain contact with
their adoptive parents either infrequently or indirectly. A neighbour
might see them walking past the house, stop briefly, and then walk on.
Or an older sister might be telephoned on some pretext, and a few
casual questions asked about 'Mum and Dad'. Children who may not
have been in touch for months or even years, suddenly visit 'out-of-the-
blue' and then disappear again for long periods. A few parents do lose
complete touch, and a small number of parents refuse to have any
dealings with children whose stealing, argumentativeness and even
violence prove too much in the end. But there is a pattern in some cases
of renewed, intermittent contact that suggests awkward, clumsy
attempts to get close. Parents see this as a vindication of their willingness to try and stay with what at first seems to be a very unpro-
mising, disappointing relationship. They recognise that these are
children who have had no early experience of mutually loving relationships. They never learned how to give and take love. These children
need very prolonged exposure to warm, attentive parenting and may
only begin to know how to get close when they are well into their
twenties.

Garth, for example, had been a very detached, uncommunicative
child. His parents felt that he cared little for them or the family. He
left home just before his 18th birthday and went to live in a town
some 20 miles away. They lost touch with him for over a year and
only heard through intermediaries how he was. After a period of not
doing very much, Garth, again without telling or informing his parents, began a catering course at the local college and in fact did very
well. His parents did not discover this until some four months later:
'This was Garth doing it all himself again, being independent, you
see.' For a while he worked successfully in hotels and restaurants
before deciding to take extra qualifications. When he was 23 he
managed to gain a place on a degree course studying economics. His
parents continue the story:

'He's now half way through the course. He's 24 years old. He has
met the most splendid girl who has helped him enormously, helped

him work things out. The last couple of years, I think he's thought a lot of things through. He's been to see our parents. He seems to be beginning to 'own' us and our family, I think. He comes home now with friends and actually introduces us for the first time as 'Mum and Dad'... We're just starting to get birthday cards and Christmas presents. He's even brought his girlfriend to meet us. We keep chalking up firsts even though he's twenty four!'

(Howe, 1996a: p. 126)

Table 13.1 summarises the major behavioural characteristics of insecure, 'avoidant' children.

Case example

Paul

Paul was the younger of two brothers. They were received into local authority care because of severe neglect. Paul had been left in his cot for 24 hours a day. After a short spell in hospital, the boys were placed in a children's home. Paul was aged 14 months. Various attempts were made to reunite him and his brother with their mother, but the efforts at rehabilitation were finally abandoned when the two boys were discovered once again on their own in their mother's flat. She had gone missing. Paul and his brother were underweight, very dirty and marked with old bruises. Paul was so badly undernourished, he was kept in hospital for three weeks before joining his brother in another children's home. He remained quiet and never smiled. He showed no interest in the adults who were caring for him. A decision was taken to place the brothers for adoption, but separately.

Wendy and Tim visited Paul in the home prior to his placement with them. 'Emotionally, he seemed to have switched off,' recalled Wendy. 'He had a particular look. He never came out from behind those eyes. Very defended. Quite a bit of rocking and a bit of headbanging for a few weeks but then that began to stop. But a beautiful child to look at.' After 13 months in the second children's home, Paul was finally placed with Wendy and Tim just before his third birthday.

The first thing his adoptive parents noticed was his eagerness for food. Paul ate everything that was put in front of him. Knowing when to stop eating remained something of a problem throughout his childhood. 'I think he gets frightened that he's never going to be fed again,' said Tim. 'He was always so desperately anxious about having food. Even after a huge meal, he'd crawl around on the floor picking up crumbs.' He was doubly incontinent until he was nearly six years old. 'He seemed to be unaware of what was happening. We eventually managed to train him. But he'd still have occasional accidents and soil himself even in his teens.'

Table 13.1 Avoidant and insecure children: behaviours, characteristics, achievements and personality.

General:	Not very cuddlesome as babies or toddlers Emotionally restrained and self-contained Emotionally distant and detached Uncomfortable with intimacy and affection Don't seem to 'belong' or fully commit themselves to family life Lack of reciprocity Lack of empathy Loners and wanderers, no close friends Often unpopular with peers Unrewarding and disappointing to parent Problems of over- or uncontrolled eating in many cases No sense of danger

School years:	Referral to a child psychologist/psychiatrist
	A significant minority of children:
	    have poor concentration
	    are disruptive in class
	    are suspended or excluded from school
	    leave school with a poor academic record
	    steal from home; a few go on to commit crimes outside the home
	    become aggressive and violent
	    run away from home

Late adolescence/early adulthood:	Leave home at a relatively young age
	Often an initially poor employment record
	Many parents describe their children as 'wanderers'
	Possible problems with alcohol/drugs/criminal behaviour
	In many cases slow improvement in parent–child relationships and increased contact/more secure attachment behaviour:
	    less conflict
	    more trust and ability to be emotionally close and open
	In a minority of cases parents lose all contact with their children

Evaluation:	Mixed views by adopters:
	    Qualified positive review if a belated recovery of good relationships has been established
	    Negative review if relationships remain poor, severed or lost.

Paul never seemed to smile or cry. As a toddler, he would quite happily go off with anyone who held out their hand. 'For about a year,' remembered Wendy:

'... he never said anything to me. But I would sing to him and rock him and finally get a kiss. When he first arrived I would take him to bed and we'd lie together and I'd have him very close to me. He seemed to like that. He would lie very still and quiet. But then after about a year, one night he refused to kiss me. And I felt ... I can't tell you the rage I felt. All I'd ever really got from him was that one nightly kiss and he even took that away from me. I went down stairs and I cried and cried. I felt dreadful. Upset. Guilty. Paul played with toys and things sort of OK. He was curious, but he would never relate. If we took him out somewhere, somehow the day would be sabotaged by him. It always went wrong and nobody had any fun. Whenever the family was having a good time, he got confused, it seemed. Like, he didn't know how to laugh and enjoy himself and got puzzled and bothered if we were all enjoying ourselves. You could see him wander to the edge of the room, or go and sit on the stairs and watch us and sometimes get quite angry. He'd circle around us, at a distance, keeping us in sight but not wanting to be near us. When he was older, we went on holiday on a plane. And in the airport, on the plane he'd sit maybe six seats behind us, watching us but refusing to join us. Desperately difficult and painful.'

Throughout his school years, Paul's teachers saw him as unco-operative and aggressive. When he was nine, he was caught stealing from other children. He lied routinely. On different occasions, he set fire to the contents of a waste paper bin, flooded a cloakroom, and smashed a large plate glass window with a stone. Fires and knives always seemed to fascinate Paul, and his parents had a constant fear that he might set fire to the house or injure another child. He never had any friends.

'When he was about ten or eleven, he began to steal from home, quite seriously. But not only that, he began to make up quite plausible stories, like how he had managed to come by £20. And for a while, I was believing him. He became increasingly horrid to his younger sister, who we'd adopted a couple of years after Paul joined us. All the time, we just felt this silent aggression. It was beginning to be hell to live with him. I'm sure we loved him, but we were certainly getting no love back.'

As he entered adolescence, his bullying of other boys increased. He organised gangs of his classmates to go shoplifting at lunchtime and after school. 'The psychiatrist who saw him at this time gave up in the end and simply said that he thought Paul was cold and calculating. A fat lot of help he turned out to be.' On a number of occasions he failed to return home at night. His parents contacted the police, but Paul would return sometime the next day, never explaining where he had spent the previous night. He began to steal money from home and on one occasion the school telephoned to say that they had found Paul selling a number of expensive items, including a watch and ring, that turned out to have been stolen from his parents.

The school eventually excluded Paul and his parents decided to send him away to board. For a while he seemed to settle well. He did very little school work and his teachers said that the best they could do was contain him until he was 16. This they just about managed to achieve. Paul returned home briefly, but kept disappearing for days at a time. Tim asked Paul what he wanted to do: 'And Paul replied "I want to be on my own. I want to be away on my own. I'd really rather live on my own." I said "Don't you like living with us?" "No, it's not that," he said, "it's just that I like to be on my own."'

Tim and his son explored various possibilities until Paul decided he wanted to live in a hostel in a nearby town. The day his parents took him to the hostel, Paul was very rude and angry, swearing a great deal. 'We had all sorts of funny feelings,' said Wendy. 'I felt just terrible. But I also felt relief.' Six week later, the police contacted Wendy and Tim to say that they had arrested Paul for shoplifting. They had to go to the police station where Paul was cautioned. Wendy said that Paul was very dirty and very subdued.

Tim was so upset by the experience that he really felt that he must make one last effort to help Paul. He had a friend who ran a small farm. It was agreed that Paul could work there for as many hours a day or a week that he felt like, but he would only be paid for the hours worked. Paul said he accepted the arrangement and also said that he would live at home again. When Tim was helping Paul to move out of the hostel, he said he came across a very strange note written by Paul.

'It was full of ... Well he'd written that he was worried that he was going to attack somebody. That he was frightened he might attack somebody. Very weird.' It was then that I went back to the adoption agency with Paul and we got some more background information. His father was a bit of an alcoholic we gather – and a wanderer! But he disappeared out of the picture while Paul was a baby. His mother had been brought up in a children's home and had the boys when she was very young. She sounded very pathetic, very sad really. We don't know what Paul made of all this. He had some counselling.'

Paul stuck the farm job for two weeks and then disappeared again for three months. This pattern was to repeat itself for the next few years. Paul drifted around the region, finding odd jobs that lasted a few weeks. He lived in hostels. His most successful period of employment was when he worked in a hotel kitchen and was given accommodation. This is where he met his wife-to-be.

Paul is now married. 'Of course, we didn't know anything about it at the time. He just turned up one day with this girl. Now that was a surprise – the visit and a girlfriend! She seems pleasant. Quiet. He seems to have settled down a lot,' said Wendy. 'He still wanders in and out of our lives. More out than in, but it's changing. He turns up out of the blue. I suppose we've got used to it. We try not to expect too much.' 'We may not have heard from him for say four months,' added Tim, 'and he'll arrive on the door step: "Hello Mum. Hello Dad." No explanation.' 'And the last time he called,' concluded Wendy, 'he brought his little baby daughter! We did know that Sharon had been pregnant, but were never told when she was born. And now we're grandparents! In a funny sort of way since Lisa was born, he seems more relaxed with us. Let's hope.'

Chapter 14

Non-attached Patterns

A few children may experience care that is so emotionally and inter-personally starved that they might actually find it difficult to form a selective attachment with any adult. There are good reasons to suspect that this is a rare experience. Children appear able to wring quite a lot out of even the thinnest relationship environments. However, three situations might arise in which babies find it very difficult to form an attachment relationship or affectional bond with other people.

The first affects babies raised in large residential nurseries. Although their physical care may be adequate, they lack opportunities to develop close relationships with the many carers with whom they have short-term, erratic contact – 'anonymous serial caregivers' in Lieberman & Pawl's (1988: p. 331) evocative phrase. The second group of children have mothers whose psychiatric condition is so severe that to all intents and purposes they are not available to their children. This category can shade into the third in which young children experience a bewildering array of poor quality carers. Their parents may neglect and abuse them. They are often left on their own for long periods before being farmed out to friends for a few days or weeks at which point social workers might intervene, remove the children and place them with foster parents or in a children's home followed by attempts to reunite them with their parents. And so on. The net effect of this welter of temporary, inadequate care arrangements is to deny the children the opportunity to establish a relationship with a permanent, responsive attachment figure. This also means that in such environments, children have an impaired ability to form close, meaningful and intimate personal relationships. These experiences have deep consequences for the formation of inner working models. As there is no regular pattern of relationships which to model, the self and others make very little sense.

Such patterns can go on for many years before children are finally removed, often to a children's home with a view to adoption. Placement with new parents offers a belated opportunity to form an attachment relationship. The type of attachments achieved will vary and again some children manage to establish surprisingly secure relationships with their adoptive parents. Perhaps with some echoes of their insecure and unstructured past, these children gradually adopt patterns that appear reasonably secure. These children provide further evidence that developmental recovery of a surprising order can often be seen in children who have suffered considerable adversity in early childhood. However, the more prolonged the neglect, the abuse and the lack of personalised care, the more likely it is that the children will become psychosocially disturbed. Good recoveries becomes increasingly difficult to achieve in these extreme cases, although even here parents report modest but often heartwarming progress.

Disorders of non-attachment

Children who have had no opportunities to develop selective attachment relationships show a number of profound developmental impairments. They have problems with social relationships. Their social dealings with other people are based on need. There is little preference for or interest in one person over another. People appear to be interchangeable so long as basic needs are met. Little distress is expressed at the departure of a caregiver. Non-attached children experience difficulties in controlling their impulses and feelings of aggression. There is some evidence that their cognitive development is impaired, although this is probably more to do with being reared in a grossly understimulating environment and most do seem to make good intellectual recovery when placed with adoptive families. Fraiberg (1977: p. 2) expresses her own strength of feelings on these matters when she writes: 'If we take the evidence seriously we must look upon a baby deprived of human partners as a baby in deadly peril. This is a baby being robbed of his humanity.'

For most social workers, then, there is an urgent need to provide children with permanent selective attachment figures. In terms of attachment, someone is generally better than no-one. As Fahlberg says:

> 'Although interrupted relationships are traumatic – and should be avoided whenever it is possible to meet the child's needs without a move – the long-term effects of a child without attachments for significant periods of his life are even more detrimental. Once a child has experienced a healthy attachment, it is more likely that with help, he can either extend this attachment to someone else or form additional attachments if necessary.'
>
> (Fahlberg, 1994: p. 18)

Non-attached children's ability to control aggressive impulses and feelings of frustration are very limited. When they are in their early school years they are prone to throw temper tantrums. They do not enjoy good peer relations and are somewhat quarrelsome. As a consequence they are often unpopular with their peers. They also have strikingly low levels of concentration. Many of these characteristics continue into adolescence and beyond.

Cadoret (1990) reported that adopted children who suffered social disruption during their first year or two of life before joining stable adoptive homes were at an increased risk of poorer mental health, such as depression, in adulthood. Having been removed from their birth mothers, these children typically would be looked after by a number of different caretakers over a considerable period of time before finally being placed with their adoptive parents. The absence of any opportunity to form close affectional bonds during early childhood frustrates children's chances of expressing attachment behaviour at later stages of the life cycle. Individuals who have not had attachment experiences handle social relationships in a superficial manner. They lack notions of reciprocity and mutuality. Other people are valued only insofar as they meet basic needs, including food, sex, money, and other material opportunities. Relationships with others are simply a means to an end and may be abandoned abruptly once the need has been met. Often, there is little long-term satisfaction for those who find themselves involved in relationships with people who have suffered such early emotional privation. For those who have not experienced a strong attachment relationship, there is no great sense of loss or anxiety when relationships disappear or breakdown. They are simply replaced. There is a lack of discrimination in the friendliness expressed towards others – anyone, it appears, will do. There is a tendency to be impulsive. There is frustration and conflict in relationships that deny access to what is wanted, leading to anger and aggression.

Patterns of behaviour, personality and relationship style

Not having experienced long-term relationships, of whatever quality, children with disorders of non-attachment will not have built up clear expectations of other people or learned to understand their own emotional states. In a sense, these children 'behave' rather than 'relate' with other people. There is no sensitivity to the subtleties and nuances of social life. Their social skills are seriously impaired. Not surprisingly, few children have friends as such although they have an enthusiasm to be where things are happening. Never having learned how to understand and conduct a social relationship, life is pursued in a headlong, 'thoughtless', unfocused fashion. This makes them extremely difficult children to parent. 'I found it difficult to get their feelings about things, even now when they're in their twenties,' said Annette of her two children. 'I think I managed them rather than mothered them! You just simply had to accept that for much of the time it was take and not give.' When a need is not met, anger, rage and frustration are the result.

The children do not get particularly upset by changes of carer, personnel or venue. They have not experienced interpersonal constancy or consistency in their lives and so the comings and goings of other people does not appear to bother them unduly. People are merely a potential source of interest and gratification.

Impulsive behaviour at home and school sees these children running around a great deal, often in a hectic, yet purposeless fashion. They are most steady in highly structured environments: families where there are clear rules and firm boundaries and schools in which there is order, regularity and routine. As their ability to concentrate is often limited, academic achievements are generally modest to poor.

Although children may wander off from family life once they have finished school, home acts as base to which to return when difficulties are met. The degree of adversity suffered by many of these children, often over many years, leaves them developmentally very damaged. The continued availability of parents allows further emotional growth and development to take place. Progress may seem very slow and unrewarding but these children need huge amounts of positive emotional experience to help them learn about themselves and others. Only then will they be able to 'do social life' in anything like a competent manner. Their impatience, anger and violent behaviour can make them frightening figures, but at heart they are probably more frightened than frightening.

Table 14.1 summarises the major behavioural characteristics of children who seemed to have lacked a selective attachment relationship for a large part of their early childhoods.

Case example

Rachel

Rachel was first removed from home when she was four months old. She was diagnosed as 'failing to thrive'. She was malnourished and weighed less than her birth weight. From hospital she went to a foster home. Three weeks into the placement the foster mother said that she was worried that Rachel needed more expert care than she could offer. The baby was returned to hospital where she stayed for ten days before being discharged to a children's home. At the age of nine months, Rachel was returned to her mother who had made a few, half-hearted visits to the children's home. By this stage, Rachel was proving to be a very difficult baby. Six weeks later she was admitted to hospital with a subdural haematoma, caused, it was suspected by a non-accidental injury. Rachel remained in hospital for another five weeks, returning to a short-term reception centre. She lived at the centre for four months where the decision was taken to transfer her to a long-stay children's home. Two unsuccessful attempts were made to place Rachel with long-term foster parents during her third year. She was finally placed, aged five years, with Shirley and Steve Oakland after a period of phased introductions.

Table 14.1 Children with a history of non-attachment disorders: behaviours, characteristics, achievements and personality.

General:	Demanding
	Friendly but indiscriminate behaviour
	Attention-seeking
	Impatient and easily frustrated – leading to anger, rage, temper
	Poor at delaying gratification
	Poor impulse control
	Poor staying power/concentration
	No close or sustained peer friendships
	Little upset at loss of relationships – move on to new relationships easily and quickly
	Unaffected by change
	Lack reciprocity
	Good, indiscriminate appetite
School years:	Difficult to control both at home and school
	Conflict, rows and arguments common
	Low on shame, guilt, empathy therefore can commit wrongdoings without apparent remorse
	Poor academic success
	Cope better with more structured environments
Late adolescence/early adulthood:	
	Many have alcohol problems
	Leave home early
	Many have a poor employment record
	Home used as a safe base at times of need, upset and problematic behaviour
	Adult relationships often conducted with some volatility
	Easily upset and frustrated
	Developmental recovery and maturation slow but still in evidence
Evaluation:	Most parents were under no illusions when they adopted children whose psychological development they knew to be very disturbed. Their reviews of outcomes are realistic along the lines that parenting the children had been hard work, progress was slow but the modest improvements are sufficient reward

They described her a 'hyperactive' child who ran everywhere in a 'harum-scarum' fashion. 'She seemed totally unfazed when she came. I'm not sure the long period of introductions made much difference, really,' thought Shirley. 'She arrived in the house and treated it immediately as home, jumping on the settee, running up and down the stairs and wanting to know what everything was and where things were. You know, very friendly, but in that way you know has little depth to it.' Shirley said that Rachel was never cuddlesome. 'If she hurt herself, she'd never cry and go running to someone.'

Not long after her arrival, Rachel began school. The teachers found her 'a bit wild, leaping and crashing about more than most of the other children.' She swore a great deal which did not bother her parents too much but did upset her class teacher. After a couple of years, she moved on to a local, private day school:

> 'She seemed to have no sense of the teachers being in some kind of authority and needing respect. She'd scribble on the other girls' books. She would get up and wander around the classroom when- ever she felt like it. She'd chat away to the headmistress, inappro- priately showing none of the distance that the other girls showed. But she did learn quite a bit, to everyone's surprise.'

Running about suited Rachel much more than sitting still. Shirley and Steve soon adopted the strategy of making sure that Rachel lead a very active life 'so as to tire her out! We took her swimming, to the park, long walks, built her a swing in the garden. It sort of worked. We were both very fit in those days!' She destroyed toys very quickly. 'When we first took her to the beach, we bought a bucket and spade to *make* sandcastles. But all Rachel did was run up and down the beach destroying other children's sandcastles. She couldn't make one of her own.' Shirley recognised that Rachel needed structure. 'I had to develop a rigid timetable with her for each day. Otherwise she just careered off out of control.'

Towards the end of her primary schooldays, Shirley remembers 'dreading' 3 o'clock: 'The phone would ring and the head teacher would say "Rachel has been particularly naughty today. You'll have to keep her off for a couple of days."' She found herself in trouble for scratching and punching other girls and pulling their hair. Teachers found her extremely difficult to manage in the classroom. Rachel did not have any close friends. If she did invite anyone home, she would end up fighting. Shirley could never leave Rachel on her own with a friend for fear of what would happen. 'And whenever we had visitors, she would constantly bother them. You could see them desperately smiling politely but thinking "Oh god. What a dreadful little girl. When will she go away?"'

When she was 12 years old she attended the local comprehensive school. She found the constant change of teacher for each subject dif- ficult. The school was permissive about discipline which did not suit Rachel. She became even more disruptive and was eventually sus- pended after two terms for 'bad behaviour'. Her parents then sent her to a boarding school. After one term, they said that they couldn't cope with her. The only thing that they discovered kept her still was when she was allowed to look after the school's animals – rabbit, chickens and a dog. For the next year she had a home tutor. Shirley and Steve were finding her more and more difficult to control. Aged 14 years, she was once returned by the police for 'disturbing the peace'. She stole small amounts of money from her mother's purse and her father's wallet. Whenever she felt frustrated or denied something, she would erupt into a violent temper, breaking things and hitting people. Psychological tests recommended that Rachel should be sent to a special boarding school for children with emotional and behavioural problems.

Shirley and Steve were impressed with the school and Rachel seemed to get on well with her teachers. But Shirley was reminded how emotionally uninvolved Rachel remained with them and the family:

'I went to visit the school once on an open-day. Rachel was serving behind a jam stall and she dashed up when she saw me arrive and said 'I need 50p! I need 50p!' I gave it to her, fully expecting she'd return and show me round and talk, but it clearly never entered her mind. I just left after a while with tears rolling down my face. I drove home and realised that all I could do was support Rachel, but that she really had no strong feelings for me more than she had for anyone else.'

She left the school when she 16 years old and began a youth training scheme. This involved going to the local college and working in local factories. However, Rachel was unable to get along with the other students. She was not able to share, take advice or mix socially. If anything went wrong, she would get in a temper and cause a scene. The trainers and the factory owners asked her to leave the course. Rachel always complained that she was being treated unfairly. It was at this time that she began to smoke heavily. She was keen to have money, but it slipped through her fingers as soon as she had any. Whatever casual jobs she managed to find, 'fizzled out after a few days or so'. After a year of drifting in and out of casual work, Rachel took a job as a kennel maid looking after cats and dogs. 'And that's where she's been for the last two and a half years,' said Shirley:

'She left home when she was 20. She's now 21 and shares a flat with another girl, who's also adopted ... If I was younger, yes, I think I would do it again. But Steve wouldn't, would you? You think she'd have been better off staying in the children's home, don't you? I'm just grateful we didn't have more problems. She was a very disturbed little girl when she arrived. We're still in touch with her. She comes around when she needs something. Money. If she's fallen out with her flat-mate. But in between times nothing except when I go over and visit her in the flat. I met her when she was five years old. And I thought that over the next five years with all our love, it would undo all the problems of her past. But of course, it doesn't quite work like that. I think we've done a lot for Rachel, but you can still see the effects of all those years of neglect.

Chapter 15

Patterns of Practice

Throughout the book, it has been acknowledged that children's psychological development is the product of complex interactions between nature and nurture, biology and environment. Adoption is a socially contrived practice that happens to provide social and behavioural scientists with opportunities to examine the nature of gene–environment interactions in human development. We can therefore ask: to what extent are we shaped by our biological inheritance on the one hand and our environmental experiences on the other?

Furthermore, modern developments in adoption practice have allowed theorists and investigators to tackle nature/nurture questions from two angles.

(1) The adoption of very young babies witnesses the growth and development of children in social environments to which they are genetically unrelated. For many behaviours and personality traits, the quality of the environment affects the way inherited characteristics express themselves, and particular hereditary traits influence the way the environment responds.

(2) The placement of older children with adoptive families provides a different kind of scientific opportunity. Here, it is possible to ask questions about the long-term impact of early life environmental experiences on later psychosocial development. It is hard to know in the case of children who remain with their biological parents whether it is the quality of past or present relationships that is having the greater impact on current behaviour. There is a continuity of experience. In the case of adopted children, there is a discontinuity of experience. It is therefore possible to explore the relative influences of children's early and later social environments on their development. So we might begin by asking, do children raised in adverse social environments suffer developmental impairment? If they do suffer impairment, are they able to recover developmentally if they are moved to new high-quality social environments such as adoption might offer? If full recovery is possible it speaks of the plasticity of children's psychosocial development and their ability to respond to new, positive experiences and reorganise their mental representations of the social world. If recovery is less than full, or is patchy (good in

some areas, poor in others), then we need to consider the importance of early life experiences in influencing subsequent psychosocial development. Such influences help in the formation of the major cognitive models used by children to make sense of and organise experience and expectations and that once formed in childhood, the models and cognitive structures prove difficult to revise. It could also be the case that it is not so much that the models themselves are hard to modify but that the social environment in which children find themselves tend to react to the behaviours sponsored by the mental models in such a way as to confirm the model's basic assumptions. In this last case, it is not gene-environment interactions that we are examining, but rather the interactions of the psychological products of early and late gene–environment interactions.

Clearly, although we can appreciate the pervasive presence of hereditary factors in adoption, it is the influence of the social environment that is of most interest to those who practise in the field of adoption. It is that element of the nature/nurture interaction that can be manipulated on behalf of children. These practices can take place at various stages in the adoption process:

(1) the initial transfer of children from one (often adverse) social environment to an approved new adoptive environment,
(2) subsequent efforts to support and sustain adopters in the care of their children,
(3) changes in policy and practice that affect adopted children's relationship with and access to their past and present social environments.

Fahlberg (1994: p. 6, 13) also feels strongly that attachment, separation and the quality of relationships are the threads that need to guide practice:

'Resurfacing ... are the significance of interpersonal relationships, the necessity of building alliances with children and adults by enhancing communication skills, increasing the individual's knowledge of self, and the importance of developing a plan for continuity of relationships throughout a lifetime.'

Adoption outcomes are therefore, in large part, the result of a series of complex psychological interactions between three major relationship experiences: (1) the quality of pre-placement biological parent–child relationships, (2) the quality of post-placement adoptive parent–child relationships, (3) the interpretation of what it means to be adopted by the adopted child (and possibly his or her parents).

As the quality of relationship experiences appears to be a major factor in influencing developmental outcomes, an attachment perspective has been used to model five adoption pathways. Each pathway is the product of children's attempts to handle their experiences of past and present relationships and the issue of being adopted itself. In the same way that we have used attachment theory and relationship-based perspectives to organise, analyse and map the findings of the adoption outcome studies, we can also use them to guide our understanding of the main types of adoption practice, particularly post-adoption practice.

The analysis and classification of the various developmental pathways into five patterns is underpinned by the formation of different inner working models within different quality parent–child relationships. We have also learned that close social relationships continue to have the capacity to help children revise their mental representations of the self and others. Such revisions then affect children's behaviour, personality traits and interpersonal skills. Thus, by continuing to understand the linkages between social experience, inner working models and psychosocial development, we can develop a simple classification of practice strategies.

Each intervention strategy is essentially designed to increase the flexibility and versatility of children's inner working models so that they can access and process more psychosocial information about themselves, others and their relationships. Healthy functioning requires children to learn how to understand the relationship between their emotional states and cognitive processing capacities. If they are successful in this, they are able to integrate and handle their feelings, thoughts and actions in a more conscious and socially competent manner. 'With such competence, individuals become capable of responding flexibly and adaptively to an increasingly wide range of situations and conditions' (Crittenden, 1992: p. 575).

In effect, the aim is to help all adopted children develop secure attachment relationships with their parents and others. Within such relationships they can learn how to relax, reduce high arousal states and integrate their affective and cognitive processing skills. A number of very helpful books now exist that provide detailed advice, guidance and help to both professionals and adoptive parents practising in this field (for example, see Fahlberg, 1994; van Gulden & Bartels-Rabb, 1995; Triseliotis *et al.*, 1997. Also see Phillips & McWilliam, 1996 for a useful review and guide to post-adoption services and support).

Using an attachment/relationship-based perspective, we might see that adoption practice has developed a range of policies, techniques and skills targeted at the three sites mainly responsible for generating adopted children's psychosocial experience:

(1) Adoptive parents.
(2) Parent–child relationships.
(3) Adopted children.

Adoptive parents

Adoption workers' interest in adoptive parents receives heightened attention at three points during the adoption cycle:

(1)   when would-be adopters apply to adopt a child;
(2)   when approved adopters are about to have a particular child placed with them;
(3)   when adopters request post-placement advice, help or support.

Relationship based theories add an extra layer of conceptual order to these tasks of assessment, preparation and support.

Assessment

Recent research in developmental psychology is recognising that the way parents have dealt with and continue to deal with their own childhood experiences affects the way they parent their own children (Main *et al.*, 1985; Fonagy *et al.*, 1991). If they developed secure, ambivalent or avoidant attachment relationships with their own parents and if the mental representations formed within those relationships are still governing their close relationship style, then we might expect the way parents relate to their adopted children will be influenced by their current inner working model of self and others. Because relationships with children have a high emotional content, then parents' own attachment behaviour, including any defensive strategies developed to deal with anxiety and distress, will affect the way they respond to their own children's emotional needs, demands and anxieties. Even though some parents will have successfully raised birth children, the extra emotional demands made by many late-placed adopted children can trigger less competent parenting styles that set adopter and child on a downward spiral.

This does not necessarily mean that a parent who experienced an insecure parent–child relationship herself will have a child who is insecurely and anxiously attached. If the mother is able to access the feelings that she had as a child and accurately remembers her experiences, then she is in a position to deal realistically with current emotional events. She is free to respond empathically to her child's emotional state rather than being governed by her own emotional anxieties and defensive patterns. Various experiences may have contributed to this form of resilience including having an easy temperament, good cognitive skills, and a stable relationship with a responsive, secure partner.

The skills to assess such intergenerational patterns require considerable expertise for which extensive training is necessary. At the moment such skills remain confined to the world of developmental research and have not been explored, adapted or tested as a possible tool for adoption workers to help them assess would-be adopters.

Preparation

Adoption workers have become extremely good at preparing adopters for the job of parenting adopted children. With the large number of older children now being placed, many of whom have various 'special needs', it is important for parents to understand their children's background, needs and behaviour. Preparation work is now conducted with considerable imagination. Would-be adopters may see videos of children with behavioural disturbances, meet experienced adopters of late-placed children, be asked to reflect on their own childhoods, participate in exercises that provide insights into children's experiences of being cared for, and share thoughts and feelings in a group with other applicants (for a good review of preparation and selective procedures for adopters see Triseliotis *et al.*, 1997, Chapter 7).

Adding an attachment/relationship perspective helps parents to understand that children's emotional needs and behavioural styles will vary according to the character of their pre-placement care. Not all late-placed children will have experienced similar kinds of socio-emotional adversity. The emotions and behaviours of children who have been disliked and rejected will be different from those who have been neglected and parented unskilfully. Theoretical preparation helps adopters develop more subtle appreciations of the emotionally varied character of late-placed children, vital if they are to make sense of what is taking place in their parent–child interactions.

Support, counselling and guidance

Post-adoption workers recognise the need to support, help and advise adopters throughout their children's placements. Again, this is particularly true for parents who adopt older and special needs children. Many, of course, will not need the services of post-adoption agencies but given the developmentally poor condition of the majority of children at the time of placement, the provision of post-placement support appears both prudent and moral. We know from the research evidence that the skills and emotional resources of adopters are a key factor affecting outcomes. It is therefore sensible as well as just to support and foster adopters in their task of raising children whenever they feel the need for help and guidance.

If a secure attachment is taken to be the most developmentally healthy pathway that any child can take, then it behoves all those involved to ensure that parents and other prime carers remain emotionally available, responsive, sensitive, attentive and generally interested in their children. No-one is looking for perfection; simply 'good-enough' parenting. All of which is to say that the help given to adopters is basically designed to increase the level of emotional security that children experience in their relationships with their parents and other family members. We need to remember that adopted children, particularly late-placed children, have to handle two extra, potentially problematic relationship experiences: adverse pre-placement care, and the psychological interpretation of what it means to be adopted. Adopted children, then, remain particularly sensitive to the quality of relationships with their parents.

Parents who have not successfully adjusted to their own *infertility* may find that it interferes with the way they relate to the needs of their adopted children. Many commentators have observed that if parents have not been able to resolve their feelings about a major loss, then this is likely to affect the way they feel about and react to their children's experiences of loss and separation (Brebner *et al.*, 1985; Brodzinsky, 1987). At their worst, unresolved feelings about loss distort parent–child relationships. Parents who fail to adjust remain affected by their own feelings of pain, hurt and anger. They are not fully open or available to respond to their children's emotional needs. The feedback loops that become generated in such parent–child relationships are likely to amplify feelings of anxiety and insecurity in both parent and child. Skilled grief counselling can help in such cases.

Support is one of social life's most important components and a major source of psychosocial protection. When other people show interest, concern, sympathy and understanding we feel connected, worthwhile and understood. Such feelings are likely to affect our self-esteem. Good relationships with others not only produce emotional satisfaction but also advice, expertise and resources. Therefore, we feel effective as well as valued. This positive psychosocial circle is completed when our feelings of self-worth and social potency allow us to respond more fully to other people. If those other people happen to be our children, they will experience their relationships with us as more secure.

Research suggests that stable, reciprocal marriages and partnerships amongst parents are associated with successful adoption outcomes. Supportive relationships with friends and extended family members are also reported as positive experiences. Post-adoption workers have recognised the support that parents can receive from other adopters. *Support groups* and *adoptive parent networks* prove to be an invaluable source of advice and reassurance, comfort and understanding, expertise and practical help. In Britain, Parent to Parent Information on Adoption Services (PPIAS) is an example of a highly successful and valued support service operating at both a national and local level, producing not only personal contacts and friendships but workshops and practically-minded literature.

Acknowledgement of the many stressors present in adoption has also lead to an increasing recognition of the value of practical and material support. The provision of adoption allowances and subsidies has meant that as well as recruiting more families from a variety of economic backgrounds, families caring for a child who may need expensive and specialised provisions can receive financial support (Hill *et al.*, 1989; Meezan & Shireman, 1985; McWilliam, 1996).

More specialist support may be given by professionals able to offer counselling, marital therapy, guidance and advice. An expert knowledge of the psychology of adoption is essential if a sensitive and effective service is to be delivered. Parents dealt with by counsellors and therapists whose knowledge of adoption is limited report high levels of dissatisfaction (Howe, 1996a). But whatever the nature of the support, the message that emotional understanding, practical help and shared acceptance help parents remain available for and responsive to their children is an important one if children are to feel psychologically secure and become socially competent.

Parent–child relationships

Once children join their adoptive families, the dynamics of the new relationships begin to form. The quality of the parent–child relationship is most important. However, it is the one most likely to run into difficulty, particularly when children have experienced very poor pre-placement care. Again, all intervention strategies are basically designed to reduce anxiety and increase the security of the attachment. Older placed children arrive with an inner working model of how relationships between the self and others work. The task of adoptive parents and their families is to supply responses that are warm and steady, sensitive and consistent. The positive information contained in these responses is necessary if children are to revise the way they mentally represent themselves and others.

The aim is to help children (1) who 'over-respond' (ambivalent attachment experiences) to shift their defensive manoeuvres away from an enmeshed, aggressive preoccupation with others; and (2) who 'under-respond' (avoidant attachment experiences) to shift their defensive manoeuvres away from being uninterested in and disconnected from their own and other people's feelings and perspectives. In order to achieve this, a variety of techniques are used to alter the quality and character of parent–child relationships. These include psychosocial insight, understanding and support; behaviour modification and skills training (for parents) and cognitive techniques.

The deep purpose of all the techniques is to decrease anxiety in order to help revise inner working models so that children learn to see other people as available and the self as loved. To the extent the interventions are successful, children become less defended. Parents are helped to understand the psychosocial dynamics set up by children with severely deprived histories. They are supported in their attempts not to feel so overwhelmed by their children or drawn into the negative outlook of their mental representations of themselves and others. These strategies enable parents to become more skilled, empathic, available and responsive. In turn, such parenting allows children to connect more effectively with their own strong but confused feelings. Emotions can then be accessed, understood and articulated rather than let loose, feared and acted-out. Children learn to process information about their own feelings and relationships in a more positive, resourceful way.

However, in the most demanding cases, everything conspires to frustrate the delivery of positive relationship experiences. It might take children with very disturbed behaviours many years to feel less insecure, even though they experience continuous good parenting. The prolonged disjuncture between what parents do and what children perceive them to be doing, can lead to the breakdown of effective parenting. The 'social environment' begins to *react* to the children's behaviour in a self-fulfilling way. When parents feel exhausted, anxious, angry and guilty, they have less emotional strength to resist and disconfirm the assumptions made by their children's 'inner working model' of relationships. The children continue to see themselves as unwanted and unlovable and other people as unavailable, unreliable, hostile and rejecting in spite of the initial evidence to the contrary. The negative interpretations given to the meaning of being adopted only serve to compound matters.

Help for improving parent–child relationships can be pitched at different levels and in various ways. We might classify them into two broad categories:

(1) Help designed to change the way parents respond to their children: behavioural procedures and skills training.
(2) Help designed to change the way parents analyse and understand their children's behaviour, development and manner of relating: teaching in theories of parent–child relationships and children's development, and changing the way the self, others and interpersonal relationships are semantically modelled.

Behavioural procedures and parenting skills

The emotional demands and behavioural difficulties that some adopted children present require parenting skills of a high order. Many experienced and not-so experienced adopters have these skills in good measure or they find ways of working with their children that suit them and their family. But some children place great demands on even the most experienced of parents. In these cases, adopters may need more formal advice and training to deal with their children's difficult behaviour. Training courses in parenting skills in which a range of skills and behavioural procedures are taught may prove helpful. The skills and techniques offered are a recognisable distillate of what researchers have found to be effective in parenting all children, including difficult and disturbed children. They are directed at ensuring that parents feel strong and positive about themselves and that their children experience a regime that is firm but fair, consistent but caring, loving but with limits.

Parents are encouraged to develop clear rules and expectations; to be pro-active rather than reactive; to concentrate on prevention rather than intervention; to think of solutions rather than to identify problems. The use of praise for and reinforcement of desired behaviours should occur whenever and wherever possible. An atmosphere of warmth, humour and mutuality help. Reflective listening, helping children to put their feelings into words, and operating consistently are all advised. Children's feelings need to be accepted and validated. Parents should be in control. They are authoritative but not authoritarian. And finally, parents are told to look after themselves – to eat and sleep well; to seek out and value support; to feel good about success.

A variety of specialist programmes and therapies aimed at adopted parents experiencing difficulties with their adopted children have been developed. A broad diagnostic category of 'reactive attachment disorder' is sometimes used to describe and explain children whose behaviour is proving difficult. The behaviours that inform the diagnosis vary depending on who is using the term. In some cases, the behaviours described are very similar to those characteristic of children who are showing the angry patterns of ambivalent attachment behaviour. These children appear angry and confused. Anger is one of the most difficult emotions with which parents have to deal (van Gulden & Bartels-Rabb, 1995: p. 199). These children experience problems in their relationships with other people, the cause of which lies in the very poor quality care experienced in their early years. In other cases, the behaviours seem more characteristic of either children with avoidant attachment patterns or even those with disorders of non-attachment. Here, children appear either reluctant to initiate or respond to social interaction, or they show indiscriminate sociability.

Cline (1992: p. 43) lists a number of signs that point to a 'lack of attachment', including:

- lack of ability to give and receive affection;
- self-destructive behaviour; cruelty to others;
- phoniness;
- severe problems with stealing, hoarding and gorging on food;
- speech pathology;
- marked control problems;
- lack of long-term friends;
- abnormalities in eye contact;
- parents appear angry and hostile;
- preoccupation with fire, blood and gore;
- superficial attractiveness and friendliness with strangers;

- various types of learning disorders;
- a particular pathological type of lying.

Adopted children who have been moved around are said to become increasingly unavailable emotionally. They begin to 'show non-directed anger, defiance and are extremely difficult to control. They become more and more difficult to love!' (Cline, 1992: p. 55). Unresolved feelings of loss and unprocessed feelings of grief witness adopted children getting stuck at the stage of rage and anger. Children remain angry at the loss of a loved person and their departure.

The therapy recommended by many of those who diagnose 'reactive attachment disorder' is based on a variety of *intrusive* and *confrontive* techniques (Cline, 1992). This approach is premised on the belief that children need parents to be in control. But children with an attachment disorder can only develop close relationships 'when they realize that it is safe to let other people exercise some control over them; when they realize that others can be trusted. For this reason it is not in the child's best interests for them to be in control: their interests are served when the parents are in control, i.e. when they allow their parents to be parents' (PPIAS, undated: p. 4).

However, children with attachment problems do not like being held, contained and confined by adults whom they feel that they cannot entirely trust. They have problems with touch and intimacy. They have very strong emotional defences. 'They have survived by standing alone, protecting themselves and trusting no-one,' says Archer (1996: p. 62). 'People who lack basic trust,' writes Cline (1992: p. 34), 'have great problems allowing others to control their behaviour. They do not feel good putting themselves "in the hands of others".' Having made this observation, Cline says that he 'learned of the amazing response that occurs when a *non-trusting* individual is *forced* into a situation that allows others to have *complete control* and the situation *turns out well*. When treated in a loving and accepting manner, and, when everything works out well, the person will completely reverse a previous attitude!' (Cline, 1992: p. 34–35 emphases original). Thinking along these lines leads to the use of intrusive therapies with adopted children who are said to have a reactive attachment disorder. There is a need to 'break through' and this is achieved by a combination of intrusive techniques and paradoxical injunctions.

Intrusive therapies are designed to provoke children to express their feelings of loss and pain, anger and rage, helplessness and hopelessness in a safe, loving and accepting environment. Using verbal and physical techniques that force children to react and relate (rather than their usual withdrawal or controlling responses) to their carers, the aim is to help children resolve their feelings. Holding therapies are perhaps one of the best known intrusive therapies (Welch, 1988). Holding therapy sees a tight connection between: 'the safe expression of rage and working through anger; a relinquishment of control; a development of trust; working through of loss and separation; and the building of attachment and bonding.'

(Cline, 1992: p. 75–76).

The technique forces attention, interaction, compliance and responsiveness out of children as they are literally held by their parent or therapist. The need to be held, loved and feel wanted by one's adoptive parents is initially fiercely resisted, but after a time of 'forced' holding, children relax, become calm and more trusting, they feel contained and under control. The previously 'out of control' children are actively and forcibly held. They feel helpless and tense. Anger and rage follow before the exhausted child finally capitulates, becomes calm and snuggles. 'The intrusive techniques ... do not assume the presence of basic trust, but form it in various ways by purposefully recapitulating the first-year-of-life experiences' (Cline, 1992: p. 75). The end result is said to be bonding and attachment.

In general, the behaviour of adopted children with an attachment disorder is said to be *oppositional*. The children do not respond to reason; indeed they exploit other people's reasonableness to manipulate and increase their own control. The need to feel in control is an attempt to ward off deep fears and anxieties in order to feel safe. If the children's behaviour manages to make their parents angry, then there are feelings of having won, remaining in the driving seat, and being in control. Children have to learn to trust and feel that bad things do not necessarily occur when someone else is in control. This realisation sponsors another wave of therapeutic techniques, based on paradoxes, to be used by parents when they decide to intrude on their children's way of controlling events:

'Instead parents gain control when they do not behave in the way the child expects, when they act unpredictably and illogically. This works because it forces the child into thinking about her behaviour ... Do not enter into control battles you cannot win. Remember these children's whole life centres around control. They feel that the best way to be in control is to enter into battles with you and win. They win if they refuse to do as you ask and you have no way of enforcing it, and they win if they make you angry.'

(PPIAS, undated: p. 5)

Archer (1996) recommends that parents take one step at a time. 'If a parent can take on one issue they feel they can challenge with their child in one week, and succeed in breaking the child's stranglehold on the family, they will gain in confidence and dynamism for further battles. We explain that parents must only take on a control issue if they believe that it is in their power to win, since a win for the parent is a win for the child' (Archer, 1996: p. 59). Such is the emotional drain on parents of an 'attachment disordered' child that in extreme cases respite care is recommended. This can give parents a needed break which helps them to keep going rather than give up on the child. Respite care is increasingly being seen as a valuable resource and support for many parents of late-placed children (du Porto & Phillips, 1996).

Paradoxes involve setting up a tension and degree of self-consciousness between what a child has been told to do and what he or she would normally expect to do. Parents, for example, might encourage a child to shout even louder and be even more angry, saying to them 'I'm sure it will do you good.' This out-manoeuvres the child and subtly puts the parent back in control. It also has the effect of inhibiting the undesired behaviour. In effect, like most effective parenting skills, the message is: 'No matter what you do, I want to be close and caring with you' (Fahlberg, 1994: p. 281). The poor impulse control shown by these children requires parents to be in a position to provide the necessary external controls. The use of humour and 'Over The Top' reactions to surprise and discommode an angry child are also suggested. Likewise, encouraging and accepting regressive behaviour is supported; children with an attachment disorder have missed out on nurturing experiences.

The notion of reactive attachment disorders to be dealt with by intrusive and paradoxical techniques remains controversial. However, they continue to be popular with and enthusiastically supported by many parents who have experienced extreme problems with their adopted children. The techniques are strong meat for a number of parents and therapists, but their heady qualities help some adopters feel more confident and in control. Systematic and scientific evaluations of the treatments are currently thin on the ground. However, there is no denying the importance given to the approach by those parents who have been helped to live with a child previously described as 'impossible' and 'rage-filled.'

Understanding children's psychosocial development and patterns of adoption

If parents appreciate the factors involved in children's psychosocial development, they can revise the way they understand their own children's emotional states and behaviour. The more parents are able to make sense of their children, the more likely it is that they will be able to free up their own emotional availability for their children. Cognitive skills allow people to increase their control and understanding of emotional events. Children who are difficult and demanding easily pull parents into behaving the way the inner working models of the children expect them to respond. If parents can learn to think about what is going on rather than become overwhelmed by their own feelings of distress, they can remain steady and attentive in the face of strong emotions and desperate behaviour. To be intellectually detached gives parents the strength to be emotionally available.

The ability to make sense of some of the developmental complexities involved in adoption helps parents feel more in control. In turn this increases competence which improves self-esteem, thus making for more relaxed and effective parenting. Providing parents with conceptual frameworks to discern some order and regularity in their children's development contributes to their protection. Improving parents cognitive understanding therefore strengthens a major protective process in adopted children's psychosocial development.

Adopted children

The developmental principles implied in attachment and relationship-based theories appear to lend support to a range of modern practices with adopted children (see Fahlberg, 1994 for a comprehensive and wise treatment of this field of practice). If the information about oneself and others carried in relationships helps form people's inner working models, then it becomes of great concern to both adoption workers and adoptive parents what information is available to adopted children. Inner working models formed within insecure attachment relationships in which the supply of positive, reciprocal and coherent information was either restricted or distorted, generate defensive strategies that were adaptive at the time, but become maladaptive when used to handle potentially positive relationships. The aim is to introduce information that reduces anxiety, improves self-esteem and allows less defended explorations of close relationships.

Much of this information is biographical. We all need to know who we are, where we have come from, where we are going, and to whom we belong (biologically as well as socially). The *provision of detailed background information* at appropriate times and in an appropriate form throughout childhood allows children to connect with their past and dispel confusion. New as well as old information bears repeated discussion at various stages of childhood. Children's cognitive and processing skills change as they get older and they will need fresh opportunities to rework both facts and feelings. *Life story work and books*, perhaps sometimes used too mechanically, provide children with a personal narrative (for example, see Fahlberg, 1994: pp. 353–367; Triseliotis *et al.*, 1997: pp. 125–128). The life story book allows children to locate themselves in time and place; it tells them who is who and how they connect with all the people with whom they have been involved over the years. It may provide a chronological framework that allows children to reflect on and possibly talk about the losses, separations and traumas they have experienced. The information in the book must remain sensitively true to the actual story and not distort, disguise or avoid what adults feel might be too painful for the child.

Minimising the trauma of moves and *the use of bridge pla*
now established as good practice objectives. Between rem
their biological family and placement with their adoptive pare
children are looked after by foster parents. It is now underst
foster parents can help form an attachment *bridge* that enables
to cross over to their adoptive family with less trauma and more
security. Fahlberg (1994: pp. 167–223) is particularly helpful in
explaining the importance of such transitions and ensuring that they
are handled well. She points out that abrupt moves that break caring
relationships with attachment figures are psychologically injurious.
The trauma of losses and separations can be lessened if children are
carefully prepared for transitions. Honesty, openness and sensitivity
are recommended. Emotions have to supported and explanations given
to children about all that is happening and is planned to happen to
them. A sense of maintaining as much security, trust and understanding
must govern each step. Insecurity, wariness and confusion cause
anxiety levels to soar and deny children the opportunity to process new
experiences in a constructive, manageable fashion.

The use of pre-placement visits is strongly recommended. They help
diminish fear and can be used to transfer attachments. They allow the
grieving process to take place at a psychologically healthy pace. Considerable contact between foster carers and adopters, particularly in
the case of transferring pre-verbal children, is required. 'Unresolved
separations may interfere with the development of new attachments.
New attachments are not meant to replace old ones. They are meant
to stand side-by-side with existing relationships' (Fahlberg, 1994:
p. 160).

The use of transition objects (favourite cuddly toys that go with them
wherever the child goes; new toys brought by the adoptive parents
when they visit the foster home but which they take back with them so
that the child will find familiar objects when they transfer) needs careful
thought and sensitive management. Post-placement contacts with previous carers are also advised. Children do not suddenly lose contact
with people that have been and continue to be very important to them.
This helps prevent denial and avoidance, develops a sense of continuity
and trust in others, decreases loyalty issues, and facilitates the transfer
of attachment relationships from the old carers to the new ones. 'Post-
placement contacts decrease the child's feelings of diminished self-
worth ... Regular visits and mutual sharing of information between all
adults involved are the two most potent tools for aiding the resolution
of separation issues' (Fahlberg, 1994: p. 171). The continued involvement of foster parents gives children permission to move on and
emotionally commit themselves to their new family. An attachment
perspective demands that adults give much thought to what is likely to
decrease children's feelings of anxiety and distress on the one hand and
increase their feelings security and being understood on the other,
particularly during periods of major transition.

The argument for increased openness in adoption on the face of it seems to receive theoretical support from a developmental perspective. *Adoption with contact* keeps the biological parents clearly in the child's psychological frame. It dispels fantasy and counters misleading information. Children are able to access and process concrete experiences rather than feelings that free-float. Contact may help remove much of the preoccupation that many angry children have with their birth parents. With steady support they can learn to see that their adoption was the result of their parents failings or difficulties and not because they are unlovable children with a flawed make-up that no-one really wants to parent. This experience can have a profound impact on the schemata being used by children and their inner working models. They can see themselves as more worthwhile and others as more responsive. The clearer children are about the way they understand and feel about their own adoption, the less likely they are to distort relationships with their adoptive parents.

However, this analysis ignores the feelings of adoptive parents. Although children, particularly late-placed children, may be able to handle 'dual-parenting' fairly comfortably, it is less clear whether all adoptive parents feel positive about sharing their role. And if adopters are the main suppliers of the protective experiences that adopted children need to achieve positive developmental outcomes, it will probably matter how adopters feel about open contact, whether the contact is an exchange of information, letters, telephone calls or personal meetings. Many adopters wish to become 'normal' parents and normal parents do not share the experience of being a parent. The ideal would be to approve only those adopters able to cope with contact in a relaxed, positive manner. The research evidence that will help resolve this issue is still some way off. Meanwhile, cautious moves in the direction of more open contact seem advisable. The negative interpretation that many adopted children give to what it means to be adopted needs information that counters their poor self-image. The selective use of adoption with some form of contact looks a promising line of new policy and practice development.

The formation and re-formation of the self in social relationships

The practice of adoption has allowed social scientists to gain a glimpse of how nature on the one hand and nurture on the other might influence children's psychosocial development. What at first sight might appear peculiar to adoption in fact throws much light on the universal picture of human growth and development. Although the adoption story is one born of loss, it so often ends on a note of triumph. The willingness of parents to raise other people's babies; to care for children who have been physically abused, sexually assaulted and emotionally neglected; and to make life long commitments to infants with learning difficulties and physical disabilities speaks highly of the human spirit. The personal success of so many adopted people is testimony to their resilience and responsiveness.

It is accepted that inherited characteristics play a significant role in psychosocial development, and it is important that they be recognised and understood. But, the major theme to emerge in the present analysis is the power of close social relationships to disturb as well as to mend. The quality and character of intimate relationships has a deep impact on children's development at all stages of the young life cycle. Of particular importance and of long-lasting influence are children's experiences of close relationships during their early years. Later relationships can propel children along new developmental trajectories, for better or worse, but the influence of early attachment experiences remains strong. Children who form secure attachments during infancy show resilience in the face of later adversity. Children who experience insecure, anxious attachments in their early years, may not find social relationships easy even when they find themselves in benign environments. The children often lack resilience. The degree of developmental recovery achieved by late-placed adopted children raised in high quality social environments will vary depending on a host of factors. We conclude, therefore, that the quality of children's early life experiences can have long term consequences, but that in the case of disadvantaged children placed for adoption, degrees of developmental recovery, ranging from high to low, are possible.

The self forms and re-forms in the close relationships experienced throughout life. An intricate dance takes place as nature and nurture interact to form the self, and that self in turn ceaselessly engages with the shifting, changing social world in which it finds itself. Each pathway traced is unique but there are deeper rhythms and regularities that define many of the broader movements. In recognising that there are patterns of adoption, we are acknowledging the common ground that all children tread on their way from infancy to adulthood and that personal relationships heal as well as hurt.

References

Ainsworth, M., Blehar, M., Waters, E. & Wall, S. (1978) *Patterns of Attachment*. Erlbaum, Hillsdale, NJ.

Archer, C. (1996) Attachment disordered children. In: *After Adoption: Working with Adoptive Families*, (eds R. Phillips & E. McWilliam). BAAF, London.

Bagley, C. (1993) *International and Transracial Adoptions*. Avebury, Aldershot.

Barker, D. (1991) The intrauterine environment and adult cardiovascular disease. In: *The Childhood Environment and Adult Disease*, (eds G. Block & J. Whelan). Ciba Foundation Symposium No. 156. Wiley, Chichester.

Barth, R. & Berry, M. (1988) *Adoption and Disruption: Rates, Risks and Responses*. Aldine de Gruyter, New York.

Belsky, J. & Cassidy, J. (1994) Attachment: theory and evidence. In: *Development Through Life: A Handbook for Clinicians* (eds M. Rutter & D. Hay). Blackwell Science, Oxford.

Benet, M.K. (1976) *The Character of Adoption*. Jonathan Cape, London.

Berry, M. (1992) Contributors to adjustment problems of adoptees: a review of the longitudinal research. *Child and Adolescent Social Work Journal*, 9, 525–540.

Berry, M. & Barth, R. (1990) A study of disrupted adoptive placements of adolescents. *Child Welfare*, **LXIX**(3), 209–225.

Bohman, M. (1970) *Adopted Children and Their Families*. Proprius Press, Stockholm.

Bohman, M. (1978) Some genetic aspects of alcoholism and criminality. *Archives of General Psychiatry*, 35, 269–76.

Bohman, M. (1996) Predisposition to criminality: Swedish adoption studies in retrospect. In: Ciba Foundation Symposium. *Genetics of Criminal and Antisocial Behaviour*. Wiley, Chichester.

Bohman, M. & Sigvarsson, S. (1990) Outcome in adoption: lessons from longitudinal studies. In: *The Psychology of Adoption* (eds D. Brodzinsky & M. Schechter. Oxford University Press, New York.

Boneh, C. (1979) *Disruptions in Adoptive Placements: A Research Study*. Department of Public Welfare, Office of Research Evaluation, Boston.

Borland, M., O'Hara, G. and Triseliotis, J. (1991) Placement outcomes for children with special needs. *Adoption and Fostering*, 15(2), 18–28.

Bouchard, T., Lykken, D., McGue, M., Segal, N. & Tellegen, A. (1990) Sources of human psychological differences: the Minnesota Study of Twins reared apart. *Science*, 250, 225–28.

Bowlby, J. (1952) *Maternal Care and Mental Health*. World Health Organisation, Geneva.

Bowlby, J. (1979) *The Making and Breaking of Affectional Bonds*. Tavistock, London.

Bowlby, J. (1988) *A Secure Base*. Routledge, London.

Brebner, C., Sharp, J. & Stone, F. (1985) *The Role of Infertility in Adoption*. BAAF, London.

Brennan, P. & Mednick, S. (1993) Genetic perspectives on crime. *Acta Psychiatrica Scandinavica* Suppl., 370, 19–26.

Brennan, P., Mednick, S. & Jacobsen, B. (1996) Assessing the role of genetics in crime using adoption cohorts. In: CIBA Foundation Symposium. *Genetics of Criminal and Antisocial Behaviour*. Wiley, Chichester.

Brinich, P. (1980) Some potential effects of adoption on self and object representations. *Psychoanalytic Study of the Child*, 35, 107–133.

Brinich, P. (1990) Adoption, ambivalence and mourning: clinical and theoretical interrelationships. *Adoption and Fostering*, 14, 6–15.

Brodzinsky, D. M. (1987) Adjustment to adoption: a psychosocial perspective. *Clinical Psychological Review*, 7, 25–47.

Brodzinsky, D. (1990) A stress and coping model of adoption adjustment. In: *The Psychology of Adoption* (eds D. Brodzinsky & M. Schechter). Oxford University Press, New York.

Brodzinsky, D. (1993) Long-term outcomes in adoption. *The Future of Children*, 3, 153–166.

Bronfenbrenner, U. (1986) Ecology of the family as a context for human development. *Developmental Psychology*, 22, 723–42.

Brown, C. (1959). The adjustment of adopted children. *Child Adoption*, 31, 6–19.

Brown, G., Harris, T. & Bifulco, A. (1986) Long term effects of early loss of parent. In: *Depression in Young People* (eds M. Rutter, P. Izard & P. Read). Guilford Press, New York.

Buss, A. & Plomin, R. (1984) *Temperament: Early Developing Personality Traits*. Erlbaum, Hillsdale, NJ.

Cadoret, R. (1990) Biologic perspectives of adoptee adjustment. In: *The Psychology of Adoption* (eds D. Brodzinsky & M. Schechter). Oxford University Press, New York.

Cadoret, R., O'Gorman, T. & Heywood, E. (1985) Genetic and environmental factors in major depression. *Journal of Affective Disorders*, 9, 155–64.

Capron, C. & Duyme, M. (1989) Assessment of effects of socio-economic status on IQ in a full cross-fostering study. *Nature*, 340, 552–4.

Cardon, L., Fulker, D., DeFries, J. & Plomin, R. (1992) Multivariate genetic analysis of specific cognitive abilities in the Colarado Adoption Program at age 7. *Intelligence*, 16, 383–400.

Caspi, A., Elder, G. & Herbener, E. (1990) Childhood personality and the prediction of life course patterns. In: *Straight and Devious Pathways from Childhood to Adulthood* (eds L. Robin and M. Rutter), pp. 13–35. Cambridge University Press, Cambridge.

Charles, M., Rashid, S. & Thoburn, J. (1992) The placement of black children with permanent new families. *Adoption and Fostering*, 16(3), 13–19.

Ciba Foundation Symposium (1996) *Genetics of Criminal and Antisocial Behaviour*. Wiley, Chichester.

Clarke, A. & Clarke, A. (eds) (1976) *Early Experience: Myth and Evidence*. Open Books, London.

Cline, F. W. (1992) Hope for High Risk and Rage Filled Children: Reactive Attachment Disorder. E. C. Publications, Evergreen, CO.

Clonginger, C. & Gottesman, I. (1987) Genetic and environmental factors in antisocial behaviour disorders. In: *The Causes of Crime: New Biological Approaches* (eds S. Mednick, T. Moffit & S. Stack), Cambridge University Press, Cambridge.

Cloninger, C., Sigvardsson, S. & Bohman, M. (1988) Childhood personality predicts alcohol abuse in young adults. *Alcohol Clinical Research*, 12, 494–504.

Cohen, J. (1984) Adoption breakdown with older children in adoption. In: *Adoption: Current Issues and Trends* (ed. P. Sachdev). Butterworth, Toronto.

Cohen, N., Coyne, J. & Duvall, J. (1993) Adopted and biological children in the clinic: family, parental and child characteristics. *Journal of Child Psychology and Psychiatry*, 34, 545–562.

Crittenden, P. (1992) Treatment of anxious attachment in infancy and early childhood. *Development and Psychopathology*, 4, 575–602.

Crowe, R. (1974) An adoption study of antisocial personality. *Archives of General Psychiatry*, 40, 1065–69.

du Porto, S. & Phillips, R. (1996) A family based respite care scheme. *After Adoption: Working with Adoptive Families* (eds R. Phillips & E. McWilliam). BAAF, London.

Dumaret, A. (1985) IQ, scholastic performance and behaviour of sibs raised in contrasting environments. *Journal of Child Psychology and Psychiatry*, 26, 553–80.

Dunn, J. (1993) *Young Children's Close Relationships: Beyond Attachment*. Sage, Newbury Park, CA.

Dunn, J. & Plomin, R. (1986) Determinants of maternal behavior toward three year old siblings. *British Journal of Developmental Psychology*, 4, 127–37.

Dunn, J. & Plomin, R. (1990) *Separate Lives: Why Siblings Are so Different*. Basic Books, New York.

Dunn, J. Stocker, C. & Plomin, R. (1990) Assessing the relationship between young siblings. *Journal of Child Psychology and Psychiatry*, 31, 983–91.

Eaves, L., Eysenck, H. & Martin, N. (1989) *Genes, Culture and Personality*. Academic Press, London.

Eldred, C., Rosenthal, D., Wonder, P., Kety, S., Schulsinger, F., Welner, J. & Jacobsen, B. (1976) Some aspects of adoption in selected samples of adult adoptees. *American Journal of Orthopsychiatry*, 46, 279–290.

Elonen, A. & Schwartz, E. (1969) A longitudinal study of emotional, social and academic functioning of adopted children. *Child Welfare*, 48, 72–8.

Erikson, E. H. (1963) *Childhood and Society*, 2nd edn. Norton, New York.

Fahlberg, V. (1994) (UK ed) *A Child's Journey Through Placement*. BAAF, London.

Farrington, D. (1995) The Twelfth Jack Tizard Memorial Lecture. The development of offending and antisocial behaviour from childhood. *Journal of Child Psychology & Psychiatry*, 36, 929–64.

Fergusson, D.M., Linskey, M. & Horwood, L.J. (1995) The adolescent outcomes of adoption: a 16 year longitudinal study. *Journal of Child Psychology and Psychiatry*, 36(4), 597–616.

Festinger, T. (1986) *Necessary Risk: A Study of Adoptions and Disrupted Adoptive Placements*. Child Welfare League of America, Washington D.C.

Fonagy, P., Steele, M. & Steele, H. (1991) Intergenerational patterns of attachment. *Child Development*, 62, 891–905.

Fonagy, P., Steele, M., Steele, H., Higgitt, A. & Mayer, L. (1994) The theory and practice of resilience. *Journal of Child Psychology and Psychiatry*, 35, 231–258.

Fraiberg, S. (1977) *Every Child's Birthright: in Defense of Mothering*. Basic Books, New York.

Fratter, J. (1996) *Adoption with Contact: Implications for Policy and Practice*. BAAF, London.

Fratter, J., Rowe, J., Sapsford, D. & Thoburn, J. (1991) *Permanent Family Placement: A Decade of Experience*. BAAF, London.

Frith, U. (1989) *Autism: Explaining the Enigma*. Blackwell, Oxford.

Gill, O. & Jackson, B. (1983) *Adoption and Race: Black, Asian and Mixed Race Children in White Families*. Batsford, London.

Goldstein, J., Freud, A. & Solnit, A. (1973) *Beyond the Best Interests of the Child*. Free Press, New York.

Goldstein, J., Freud, A. & Solnit, A. (1980) *Before the Best Interests of the Child*. Burnett Books, New York.

Hersov, L. (1990) The Seventh Jack Tizard Memorial Lecture: aspects of adoption. *Journal of Child Psychology and Psychiatry*, 31(4), 493–510.

Heston, L. (1966) Psychiatric disorders in foster home-reared children of schizophrenic mothers. *British Journal of Psychiatry*, 112, 819–25.

Hetherington, E. (1989) Coping with family transition: winners, losers and survivors. *Child Development*, 60, 1–14.

Hill, M., Lambert, L. & Triseliotis, J. (1989) *Achieving Adoption with Love and Money*. National Children's Bureau, London.

Hodges, J. & Tizard, B. (1989a) IQ and behavioural adjustment of ex-institutional adolescents. *Journal of Child Psychology and Psychiatry*, 30, 53–76.

Hodges, J. & Tizard, B. (1989b) Social and family relationships of ex-institutional adolescents. *Journal of Child Psychology and Psychiatry*, 30, 77–98.

Hoopes, J. (1982) *Prediction in Child Development: A Longitudinal Study of Adoptive and Nonadoptive Families*. Child Welfare League of America, New York.

Hoopes, J., Sherman, E., Lawder, E., Andrews, R. & Lower, K. (1970) *A Followup Study of Adoptions (Vol. II): Post-placement Functioning of Adopted Children*. Child Welfare League of America, New York.

Howe, D. (1995a) *Attachment Theory for Social Work Practice*. Macmillan, Basingstoke.

Howe, D. (1995b) Adoption and Attachment. *Adoption and Fostering*, 19, 7–15.

Howe, D. (1996a) *Adopters on Adoption*. BAAF, London.

Howe, D. (1996b) Adopters' relationships with their adopted children from adolescence to early adulthood. *Adoption and Fostering*, 20, 35–43.

Howe, D. (1997) Parent reported problems in 211 adopted children: some risk and protective factors. *Journal of Child Psychology and Psychiatry*, 37, 401–412.

Howe, D. & Hinings, D. (1987) Adopted children referred to a child and family centre. *Adoption and Fostering*, 11(3), 44–7.

Humphrey, M. & Ounsted, C. (1963) Adoptive families referred for psychiatric advice: I the children. *British Journal of Psychiatry*, 109, 599–608.

Jacka, A. (1973) *Adoption in Brief*. NFER, Windsor.

Jaffee, B. & Fanshel, D. (1970) *How They Fared in Adoption: A Follow-up Study*. Columbia University Press, New York.

Jerome, L. (1993) A comparison of the demography, clinical profile and treatment of adopted and non adopted children at a children's mental health centre. *Canadian Journal of Psychiatry*, 38(4), 290–4.

Kadushin, A. (1970) *Adopting Older Children*. Columbia University Press, New York.

Kadushin, A. & Seidl, F. (1971) Adoption failure. *Social Work*, 6, 32–37.

Kagan, M. & Reid, J. (1986) Critical factors in the adoption of emotionally disturbed youths. *Child Welfare*, XLV, 63–73.

Kaye, K. (1990) Acknowledgement or rejection of differences? In: *The Psychology of Adoption* (eds D. Brodzinsky & M. Schechter). Oxford University Press, New York.

Kety, S., Rosenthal, D., Wender, P., Schulsinger, F. & Jacobson, B. (1978) The biologic and adoptive families of adopted individuals who became schizophrenic: prevalence of mental illness and other characteristics. In: *The Nature of Schizophrenia* (eds L. C. Wynne, R. Cromveel & S. Mathysse). Wiley, New York.

Kirk, H.D. (1964) *Shared Fate: A Theory of Adoption and Mental Health*. Free Press, New York.

Kirk, H.D. (1981) *Adoptive Kinship*. Butterworth, Toronto.

Kornitzer, M. (1968) Adopted Children and Family Life. Putman, London.

Kotszopoulos, M.D., Walker, S.W., Copping, W., Cote, A. & Chryssoula, S. (1993) A Psychiatric follow-up study of adoptees. *Canadian Journal of Psychiatry*, 38(6), August 391–6.

Lambert, L. & Streather, J. (1980) *Children in Changing Families: A Study of Adoption and Illegitimacy*. Macmillan, London.

Leff, J. & Vaughn, C. (1985) *Expressed Emotion in Families: Its Significance for Mental Illness*. Guilford Press, New York.

Lieberman, A. & Pawl, J. (1988) Clinical applications of attachment theory. In: *Clinical Implications of Attachment* (eds J. Belsky & T. Nezworski). Lawrence Erlbaum, Hillsdale, NJ.

Lindholm, B.W. & Touliatos, J. (1980) Psychological adjustment of adopted and non-adopted children. *Psychological Reports*, 46, 307–10.

Lipman, E.L., Offord, D.R., Boyle, M.H. & Racine, Y.A. (1993) Follow-up of psychiatric and educational morbidity among adopted children. *Journal of the American Academy and Child and Adolescent Psychiatry*, 32(5), 1007–12.

Locke, J. (1690) *Essay Concerning Human Understanding*

Lohlin, J. 1992 Genes and Environment in Personality Development. Sage, Newbury Park, CA.

Loehlin, J.C., Horn, J. & Willerman, L. (1989) Modelling IQ changes. *Child Development*, 60, 993–1004.

Loehlin, J.C., Willerman, L. & Horn, J. (1985) Personality resemblances in adoptive families when the children are late-adolescent or adult. *Journal of Personality and Social Psychology*, 48, 376–92.

Loehlin, J.C., Horn, J.M. & Willerman, L. (1990) Heredity, environment and personality change: evidence from the Texas Adoption Project. *Journal of Personality*, 58(1), 221–43.

Lowing, P., Mirsky, A. & Pereira, R. (1983) The inheritanace of schizophrenia disorder: a reanalysis of the Danish adoption study data. *American Journal of Psychiatry*, **1400**, 1167–1171.

Macaskill, C. (1984) *Against the Odds*. Batsford, London.

Main, M., Kaplan, N. & Cassidy, J. (1985) Security in infancy, childhood and adulthood. In: *Growing Points of Attachment Theory and Research* (eds J. Bretherton & E. Waters). Monograph of the Society for Research in Child Development, 50 (1–2 Serial No. 209), London.

Main, M. & Solomon, J. (1986) Discovery of an insecure disorganized/disoriented attachment pattern. In: *Affective Development in Infancy* (eds M. Yogman & T. Brazleton). Ablex, Norwood, NJ.

Main, M. (1994) A move to the level of representation in the study of attachment organisation: implications for psychoanalysis. Annual lecture given to the British Psycho-Analytical Society, London, 6 July.

Mandell, B. (1973) *Where are the Children? A Class Analysis of Foster Care and Adoption*. D.C. Heath, Lexington, MA.

Martin, N.G. *et al.* (1986) *Proc. Nat. Acad. Sci. USA*, 83, 4364.

Maurer, R., Cadoret, R. & Colleen, C. (1980) Cluster analysis of childhood temperament data on adoptees. *American Journal of Orthopsychiatry*, 50, 522–34.

McCrae, R. & Costa, P. (1990) *Personality in Adulthood*. Guilford Press, New York.

McRoy, R., Zurcher, L., Lauderdale, M. & Anderson, R. (1982) Self esteem and racial identity in transracial and inracial adoptees. *Social Work*, 27(6), 522–526.

McWhinnie, A.M. (1967) *Adopted Children: How They Grow Up*. Routledge & Kegan Paul, London.

McWilliam, E. (1996) The use of adoption allowances to sustain adoption placements. In: *After Adoption: Working with Adoptive Families* (eds R. Phillips & E. McWilliam). BAAF, London.

Maughan, B. & Pickles, A. (1990) Adopted and illegitimate children growing up. In: *Straight and Devious Pathways from Childhood to Adulthood* (eds L. Robins & M. Rutter). Cambridge University Press, Cambridge.

Mednick, S., Gabrielli, W. & Hutchings, B. (1987) Genetic factors in the etiology of criminal behaviour. In: *The Causes of Crime: New Biological Approaches* (eds S. Mednick, T. Moffat & S. Stack). Cambridge University Press, Cambridge.

Meezan, W. & Shireman, J. (1985) *Care and Commitment: Foster-parent Adoption Decisions*. State University of New York Press, Albany, NY.

Mendlewicz, J. & Rainer, J. (1977) Adoption study supporting genetic transmission in manic-depressive illness. *Nature*, 268, 327–29.

Menlove, F. (1965) Aggressive symptoms in emotionally disturbed adoptive children. *Child Development*, 36, 519–532.

Moffitt, T. (1987) Parental mental disorder and offspring criminal behaviour: an adoption study. *Psychiatry*, 50, 346–60.

Nelson, K. (1985) *On the Frontiers of Adoption*. Child Welfare League of America, New York.

Nemovicher, J. (1959) A comparative study of adoptive boys and non-adopted boys in respect of specific personality characteristics. D. Phil. thesis, School of Education. New York University (mimeograph).

Norvell, M. & Guy, R. (1977) A comparison of self-concept in adopted and non-adopted adolescents. *Adolescence*, 12, 443–8.

Offord, D., Aponte, J. & Cross, L. (1969) Presenting symptomatology of adopted children. *Archives of General Psychiatry*, 20, 110–6.

Ounsted, C. (1970) The dark side of adoption. *Child Adoption*, 63, 23–36.

Parents to Parents Information on Adoption Services (undated) *A Handbook of Strategems for Parents of Children with an Attachment Disorder: Parent Assertiveness Using Consequences with Empathy*. PPIAS, Daventry.

Parker, R. (1966) *Decision in Child Care*. Allen & Unwin, London.

Parkes, C.M. (1986) *Bereavement: Studies of Grief in Adult Life*. 2nd edn. Penguin, Harmondsworth.

Parkes, C.M. & Weis, R. (1983) *Recovery from Bereavement*. Basic Books, New York.

Phillips, R. & McWilliam, E. (eds) (1996) *After Adoption: Working with Adoptive Families*. BAAF, London.

Plomin, R. (1996) General discussion III. In: Ciba Foundation Symposium. *Genetics of Criminal and Antisocial Behaviour*. Wiley, Chichester.

Plomin, R. (1994) *Genetics and Experience: The Interplay Between Nature and Nurture*. Sage, Newbury Park, CA.

Plomin, R., Chipuer, H. and Loehlin, J. (1990)) Behavioral genetics and personality. In: *Handbook of Personality: Theory and Research* (ed. L. Previn), pp. 225–243. Guilford Press, New York.

Plomin, R. & Bergeman, C. (1991) The nature of nurture: genetic influence on environmental measures, *Behavioral and Brain Sciences*, 14, 373–428.

Plomin, R. & DeFries, J. (1985) *Origins of Individual Differences in Infancy: The Colorado Adoption Project*. New York, Academic Press.

Plomin, R., Defries, J. & Loehlin, J. (1977) Genotype-environment interaction and correlation in the analysis of human behavior. *Psychological Bulletin*, 84, 309–22.

Plomin, R., Scheier, M., Bergeman, C., et al (1992) Optimism, pessimism and mental health: a twin/adoption analysis. *Personality Individual Differences*, 13, 921–930.

Quinton, D., Rushton, A., Dance, C. & Mayes, D. (in press) *Establishing Permanent Placements in Middle Childhood*. Wiley, Chichester.

Raynor, L. (1980) *The Adopted Child Comes of Age*. Allen & Unwin, London.

Rende, R. & Plomin, R. (1994) Genetic influences on behavioural development. In: *Development Through Life* (eds M. Rutter & D. Hay), pp. 26–48. Blackwell Science, Oxford.

Rosenthal, J. & Groze, V. (1994) A longitudinal study of special-needs adoptive families. *Child Welfare*, LXXIII, 689–706.

Rowe, J. & Lambert, L. (1973) *Children Who Wait*. National Children's Bureau, London.

Rushton, A. & Mayes, D. (1997) Forming fresh attachments in childhood: a research update. *Child and Family Social Work*, 2, 121–27.

Rushton, A. & Minnis, H. (1997). Annotation: transracial family placements. *Journal of Child Psychology and Psychiatry*, 38, 1–13.

Rushton, A., Treseder, J. & Quinton, D. (1933) New parents for older children: support services during eight years of placement. *Adoption and Fostering* 17, 39–45.

Rushton, A., Treseder, J. & Quinton, D. (1995) An eight-year prospective study of older boys placed in permanent substitute families: a research note. *Journal of Child Psychology and Psychiatry*, 36, 687–696.

Rutter, M. (1990) Psychosocial resilience and protective mechanisms. In: *Risk and Protective Factors in the Development of Psychopathology* (eds J. Rolf, A. Masten, D. Cicchetti, A. Nuechterlein & S. Weintraub). Cambridge University Press, Cambridge.

Rutter, M. (1991) A fresh look at maternal deprivation. In: *The Development and Integration of Behaviour* (ed. P. Bateson). Cambridge University Press, Cambridge.

Rutter, M. (1995a) Psychosocial adversity: risk, resilience and recovery. *Southern African Journal of Child and Adolescent Psychiatry*, 7, 75–88

Rutter, M. (1995b) Causal concepts and their testing. In: *Psychosocial Disorders in Young People: Time Trends and Their Causes* (eds M. Rutter & D. Smith). Wiley, Chichester.

Rutter, M. (1996) Introduction: concepts of antisocial behaviour, of cause, and of genetic influences. In: Ciba Foundation Symposium. *Genetics of Criminal and Antisocial Behaviour*. Wiley, Chichester.

Rutter, M. & Rutter, M. (1993) *Developing Minds: Challenge and Continuity Across the Life Span*. Penguin, Harmondsworth.

Ryburn, M. (1994) *Open Adoption: Research, Theory and Practice*. Avebury, Aldershot.

Sack, W. & Dale, D. (1982). Abuse and deprivation in failing adoptions. *Child Abuse and Neglect*, 6, 443–451.

Sameroff, A., Seifer, R., Baldwin, A. & Baldwin, C. (1993) Stability of intelligence from preschool to adolescence: the influence of social and family risk factors. *Child Development*, 64, 80–97.

Sants, H. (1964) Genealogical bewilderment in children with substitute parents. *British Journal of Medical Psychology*, 37, 133–141.

Scarr, S. & McCartney, K. (1983) How people make their own environment. *Child Development*, 54, 425–35.

Scarr, S., Webber, P.L., Weinberg, R. & Wittig, M. (1981) Personality resemblances among adolescents and their parents in biologically related and adoptive families. *Journal of Personality and Social Psychology*, 40, 885–98.

Seglow, J., Pringle, M.K., & Wedge, P. (1972) *Growing Up Adopted*. NFER, Windsor.

Sigvardsson, S., Bohman, M. & Cloninger, C. (1987) Structure and stability of childhood personality: prediction of later social adjustment. *Journal of Child Psychology and Psychiatry*, 28, 929–46.

Silverman, A. & Feigelman, W. (1981) The adjustment of black children adopted by white families. *Social Casework*, 62, 529–536.

Silverman, A. & Feigelman, W. (1990) Adjustment in interracial adoptees: an overview. *The Psychology of Adoption* (eds D. Brodzinsky & M. Schechter). Oxford University Press, New York.

Simon, R. & Alstein, H. (1977) *Transracial Adoption*. John Wiley, New York.

Simon, R. & Alstein, H. (1987) *Transracial Adoptees and Their Families: A Study of Identity and Commitment*. Praegar, New York.

Skeels, H. (1965) Effects of adoption on children from institutions. *Children*, 12, 33–4.

Skeels, H. & Harms, I. (1948) Children with inferior social histories: their mental development in adoptive homes. *Journal of Genetic Psychology*, 72, 283–294.

Skodak, M. & Skeels, H. (1949) A final follow up study of 100 adopted children. *Journal of Genetic Psychology*, 75, 85–125.

Smith, D. (1995) Youth crime and conduct disorders: trends, patterns and causal explanations. *Psychosocial Disorders in Young People: Time Trends and Their Causes* (eds M. Rutter & D. Smith). Wiley, Chichester.

Sorich, C. & Siebert, T. (1982) Towards humanizing adoption. *Child Welfare*, 61, 207–216.

Sweeny, D.S., Gasbarro, M.S.W. & Gluck, M.R. (1963) A descriptive study of adopted children seen in a child guidance center. *Child Welfare*, July, 345–52.

Teasdale, T.W. (1979) Social class correlations among adoptees and their biological and adoptive parents. *Behaviour Genetics*, 9, 103–14.

Thoburn, J. (1990) *Success and Failure in Permanent Family Placement*. Avebury, Aldershot.

Thoburn, J. (1996) Psychological parenting and child placement. In: *Attachment and Loss in Child and Family Social Work* (ed. D. Howe). Avebury, Aldershot.

Thoburn, J., Murdoch, A. & O'Brien, A. (1986) *Permanence in Child Care*. Blackwell, Oxford.

Thoburn, J., Norford, L. & Rashid, S. (1997) *Ten Years On: The Placement of Black Children With Permanent New Families*. School of Social Work, University of East Anglia, Norwich.

Thoburn, J. & Rowe, J. (1988) A snapshot of permanent family placement. *Adoption and Fostering*, 12(3), 29–34.

Thoburn, J. & Sellick, C. (1996) *What Works in Family Placement?* University of East Anglia/Barnados, Norwich.

Thompson, A. (1986) Adam – a severely-deprived Columbian orphan: a case report. *Journal of Child Psychology and Psychiatry*, 32, 743–56.

Tienari, P., Lahti, I., Sorri, A., Naarala, M., Moring, J., Kaleva, M., Wahlberg, K. & Wynne, L. (1990) Adopted-away offspring of schizophrenics and controls. In: *Straight and Devious Pathways from Childhood to Adulthood* (eds L. Robins & M. Rutter). Cambridge University Press, Cambridge.

Tienari, P., Sorri, A., Lahti, I., Naarala, M., Wahlberg., Ronkiko, J., Pohjila, J. & Moring, J. (1985) The Finnish adoptive family study of schizophrenia. *Yale Journal of Biology and Medicine*, 58, 227–327.

Tizard, B. (1977) *Adoption: A Second Chance*. Open Books, London.

Trasler, G. (1960. *In Place of Parents*. Routledge & Kegan Paul, London.

Triseliotis, J. (1973) *In Search of Origins*. Routledge & Kegan Paul, London.

Triseliotis, J. & Russell, J. (1984) *Hard to Place: The Outcome of Adoption and Residential Care*. Heinemann, London.

Triseliotis, J., Shireman, J. & Hundleby, M. (1997) *Adoption: Theory, Policy and Practice*. Cassell, London.

van Gulden, H. & Bartels-Rabb, L. (1995) *Real Parents, Real Children: Parenting the Adopted Child*. Crossroad, New York.

Versluis-den Bieman, H. & Verhulst, F. (1995) Self-report and parent reported problems in adolescent and international adoptees. *Journal of Child Psychology and Psychiatry*, 36, 1411–1428.

Von Knorring, A., Bohman, M. & Sigvardsson, S. (1982) Early life experiences and psychiatric disorders: an adoptee study. *Acta Psychiatric Scandinavia*, **65**, 283–291.

Wachs, T.D. (1992) *The Nature of Nurture*. Sage, Newbury Park, CA.

Warren, S. (1992) Lower threshold for referral for psychiatric treatment for adopted adolescents. *Journal of the American Academy of Child and Adolescent Psychiatry*, **31**, 512–7.

Wedge, P. & Mantle, G. (1990) *Sibling Groups in Social Work*. Gower, Aldershot.

Welch, M. (1988) *Holding Time*. Simon and Schuster, New York.

Werner, E. & Smith, R. (1982) *Vulnerable but Invincible*. McGraw-Hill, New York.

Westen, D. (1996) *Psychology: Mind, Brain and Culture*. Wiley, New York.

Westhues, A. & Cohen, J. (1990) Preventing disruption of special needs children. *Child Welfare*, **LXIX**, 141–155.

Willerman, L. (1979) The effects of family on intellectual development. *American Psychologist*, **34**, 923–9.

Winnick, M., Meyer, K. & Harris, R. (1975) Malnutrition and environmental enrichment by early adoption. *Science*, **190**, 1173–1175.

Witmer, H.L., Herzog, E., Weinstein, E. & Sullivan, M. (1963) *Independent Adoptions*. Russell Sage Foundation, New York.

Wolkind, S. & Kozaruk, A. (1986) Hard to Place? Children with medical and developmental problems. In: *Finding Families for 'Hard-to-Place' Children* (eds P. Wedge & J. Thoburn). BAAF, London.

Zwimpfer, D. (1983) Indicators of adoption breakdown. *Social Casework*, **64**, 169–177.

Index